ROUGH GUIDES

POCKET **ROUGH GUIDE**
NEW YORK CITY

Written and researched by
STEPHEN KEELING AND ANDREW ROSENBERG

CONTENTS

NEW YORK CITY

No superlative, no cliché does New York City justice. It may not serve as the official capital of the US or even of New York State, but it's the undisputed capital of the world in many regards. High finance, media, art, architecture, food, fashion, popular culture, urban style, street life...it's all here, in plenitude and peak form. Best of all for visitors (and residents), you don't have to look too hard for any of it. Often the sights, both big and small, are just staring you right in the face: the money fortresses of Wall Street; the raised torch of the Statue of Liberty; the iconic Empire State Building; the hype and hustle of Times Square; Fifth Avenue's foot traffic; the proud lions of the Public Library. For energy and dynamism, cultural impact and sheer diversity, New York cannot be beaten.

View over Manhattan with the Empire State Building at its centre

You could spend weeks here and still barely scratch the surface, but there are some key attractions and pleasures you won't want to miss. The city is packed with vibrant neighbourhoods of historic cultural importance, like Chinatown and Harlem, and the artsy enclaves of Chelsea, Tribeca and Greenwich Village. Of course, you will find the celebrated modern architecture of corporate Manhattan in Midtown and the Financial District, complemented by row upon row of elegant brownstones in landmarked areas like Brooklyn Heights. Then there are the city's renowned museums, not just the Metropolitan Museum of Art or the Museum of Modern Art, but countless smaller collections – the Old Masters at the Frick, the prints and manuscripts of the Morgan Library – that afford days of happy wandering.

In between sights, you can (and should) eat just about anything, cooked in any style: silky Korean pork buns to pressed sea urchin sandwiches, Jewish deli to Jamaican food cart. You can drink in virtually any company at any time in any type of watering hole imaginable: unmarked cocktail dens that mix up the latest artisanal concoctions or joints where folks will look at you sideways if you order anything but a bottle of beer. You can see comedy or cabaret, hear jazz combos or jug bands, and attend obscure movies. The more

Graffiti

established arts – dance, theatre, opera and classical music – are superbly catered for; and New York's clubs are varied and exciting.

For the avid consumer, the choice of shops is vast, almost numbingly exhaustive, in this heartland of the great capitalist dream. You can spend your dollars at big names like Bloomingdale's or contemporary designers like Marc Jacobs, and visit boutiques full of vintage garments or thrift stores with clothes priced by the pound.

What's new

In Downtown Manhattan the former Ground Zero site continues to develop, with the incredible Oculus (see page 29) housing a fancy shopping mall while new digs for the 9/11 Tribute Museum which opened in 2018 (see page 29). On the Lower East Side, the massive Essex Crossing development (see page 56) is set to transform the area, with new premises for the Essex Street Market and the International Center of Photography Museum. Midtown's MoMA is finishing a huge expansion (see page 108) while up in Harlem, a major redevelopment of the Studio Museum (see page 147) should be complete in 2020.

When to visit

Pretty much any time is a good time to visit New York. Winter can be bitingly cold but the city can be delightful during the run-up to Christmas, when the trees are lit up, the windows decorated and shops open extra-late. It's coldest in January and February, coinciding with one of the few times to find bargains on flights and hotels, and in any case New York has some wonderful crisp and clear sunny days even then. Spring, early summer, and the fall are the most appealing times to visit, when temperatures can be comfortably warm. It's wise to avoid visiting between mid-July and August: the temperatures tend be sweltering and the humidity worse. On the other hand, locals tend to leave town then, so weekends are less crowded.

New York City comprises the central island of Manhattan along with four outer boroughs – Brooklyn, Queens, the Bronx and Staten Island. To many, Manhattan is New York, and you're likely to spend a bulk of your time here – though Brooklyn and, increasingly, Queens demand plenty of visitor attention. The former has the ragged glory of Coney Island and the hip nightlife of Williamsburg and Greenpoint; the latter a number of cool art spaces, including the uplifting Noguchi Museum in Long Island City. Don't overlook the Bronx either, for baseball at Yankee Stadium and a stunning botanical garden a bit further north. These are just a few of the attractions that make worthy detours, and you'll find great neighbourhood restaurants and bars along the way. The subway and bus system can take you everywhere, but New York is great to explore on foot too.

Momofuku Noodle Bar

Where to...

SHOP

For big-ticket retail, look no further than Midtown, specifically Fifth Avenue, where Saks, Bergdorf Goodman and many others congregate. Madison Avenue on the Upper East Side also has its share of famous brands. Somewhat edgier fashion can be found in Soho and Nolita: Prince and Spring streets are crammed with designer boutiques and hip jewellery and shoe shops. Those looking for vintage duds or the avant-garde might find the Lower East Side and Williamsburg more suitable.
OUR FAVOURITES: Beacon's Closet (Williamsburg), see page 160. Academy Records (Flatiron), see page 96. Strand (East Village), see page 67. Bergdorf Goodman (Midtown), see page 110.

EAT

From street food to haute cuisine, it's here, it's excellent and it's in abundance. Chinatown is most accessible for ethnic eats. The Lower East Side, traditional home to Jewish-American food, now teems with fashionable restaurants, while the East Village is the locus for great late-night eats. Continue up to Midtown for powerhouse names like Aquavit and Oyster Bar. Further north, Harlem has fabulous soul food, barbecue and African restaurants. Queens' Astoria has great international spots, and Brooklyn's Williamsburg and Carroll Gardens are packed with voguish options.
OUR FAVOURITES: Hometown Bar-B-Que (Red Hook), see page 162. Oyster Bar (Midtown), see page 112. Nom Wah Tea Parlor (Chinatown), see page 52. Ivan Ramen (Lower East Side), see page 59. Momofuku Noodle Bar (East Village), see page 71.

DRINK

Bars are everywhere and come in every stripe: pubs, dives, beer gardens, hidden speakeasies, exclusive hotel lounges. Drinkers descend on the Lower East Side and East Village, especially streets like Ludlow and Avenue A, which can seem like a carnival – but are good destinations nonetheless. Rocker hangouts and swanky wine bars also hover around Union Square, and Ninth Avenue, starting in Chelsea and moving up to Hell's Kitchen. The most exciting and charuserful places are in the outer boroughs, specifically Long Island City and Williamsburg.
OUR FAVOURITES: Dear Irving (Union Square), see page 99. Bohemian Hall and Beer Garden (Astoria), see page 163. Angel's Share (East Village), see page 72.

GO OUT

Clubbing hotspots jump around but the East and West Villages always offer a few standbys, and the Meatpacking District can be good if you're looking to put on your dancing shoes. Keep your ears open, get current listings magazines and aim downtown. Music venues are more established: the West Village and Harlem have historic venues for jazz; Lincoln Center holds top spots for classical music, dance and opera, with Carnegie Hall just a few blocks away; and the coolest rock clubs are mostly in Williamsburg and on the Lower East Side.
OUR FAVOURITES: Village Vanguard (West Village), see page 83. Mercury Lounge (Lower East Side), see page 61. Shrine Bar (Harlem), see page 151. Terra Blues (West Village), see page 83.

New York City at a glance

Chelsea and the Meatpacking District p.84.
Excellent galleries and energetic clubs.

Union Square, Gramercy Park and the Flatiron District p.92.
Genteel east-side neighbourhoods.

The East Village p.62.
This still vibrant neighbourhood was once the hangout of rebels, artists and the beats.

The West Village p.74.
Bohemian area fondly known as "the Village".

Soho and Tribeca p.36.
Fashion chic, urbane shopping and fine art.

The Lower East Side p.54.
Dynamic shopping, drinking dancing and food.

Financial District and the Harbor Islands p.24.
Lady Liberty and the historic heart of the city.

Chinatown, Little Italy and Nolita p.46.
The city's boisterous Chinese quarter and reminders of its Italian past.

The outer boroughs p.152.
Hit Brooklyn, Queens and the Bronx for must-see sights, Staten Island for the ferry ride.

Harlem and north Manhattan p.146.
The bedrock of twentieth-century black culture.

he Upper West Side p.138.
ffluent residential area, home
Lincoln Center and Columbia
niversity

Central Park p.124.
The first landscaped
public park in the US.

The Upper East Side p.128.
New York's wealthiest
neighbourhood boasts
the Frick, the Met and
the Guggenheim.

**Times Square and the
Theater District** p.114.
Prepare for sensory
assault on Broadway.

Midtown p.100.
High-rise commercial zone home to
MoMA, Grand Central and the
Rockefeller Center.

15

Things not to miss

It's not possible to see everything that New York City has to offer in one trip – and we don't suggest you try. What follows is a selective taste of the city's highlights, from its world famous skyscrapers to its world-class culinary scene.

> **EMPIRE STATE BUILDING**
See page 95
Still the most original and elegant
skyscraper of them all.

< **STATUE OF LIBERTY**
See page 31
There's no greater symbol of
the American dream than the
magnificent statue that graces
New York Harbor.

∨ **METROPOLITAN MUSEUM
OF ART**
See page 129
You could easily spend a whole
day (or week or month) at
the Met, exploring everything
from Egyptian artefacts to
modern masters.

< BASEBALL
See page 159

A summertime treat: enjoy a hot dog, a cold beer and America's pastime in the Yankees' or Mets' homes – or for a more intimate experience, see a Cyclones game in Coney Island.

∨ BROOKLYN BRIDGE
See page 34

Take the less-than-a-mile walk across the bridge to see beautiful views of the downtown skyline and Harbor Islands.

< **9/11 MEMORIAL & MUSEUM**
See page 28
The pools in the buildings' footprints and museum artefacts including the "Last Column" can't help but stir emotion.

∨ **MUSEUM OF MODERN ART**
See page 108
Simply put, MoMA holds the most comprehensive collection of modern art in the world, curated in a breathtaking setting of glass atriums and statuary.

∧ THE HIGH LINE
See page 84
This plant-lined Chelsea walkway offers a unique perspective on the city below and on the power of progressive urban renewal.

< CENTRAL PARK
See page 124
The city's most beloved swathe of green: take a boat ride, watch Shakespeare in the Park or enjoy a picnic after a morning spent museum-hopping.

∧ **STATEN ISLAND FERRY**
See page 31
Savour Manhattan's skyline
and the Statue of Liberty from a
boat's-eye view – absolutely free.

∨ **CONEY ISLAND**
See page 155
Ride on classics like the Wonder
Wheel or Cyclone, or on the newer
Thunderbolt coaster, high above
the boardwalk, for a seaside thrill.

∧ WHITNEY MUSEUM OF AMERICAN ART

See page 84
As the anchor of the High Line, this Meatpacking District museum shows off modern American art, with a healthy dose of terrace views.

< TENEMENT MUSEUM

See page 55
A Lower East Side apartment dwelling turned museum, this local treasure brilliantly captures the lives of three generations of immigrants.

< **LIVE JAZZ**
See page 151
New York's jazz scene is vibrant, but Harlem is first choice for characterful venues and late-night jam sessions.

∨ **PIZZA**
See pages 81 and 163
The city calls many dishes its own, but none takes centre stage like pizza. Try a slice or a pie at one of the many old-school (John's) or more nouveau (Roberta's) joints in town.

THINGS NOT TO MISS

Day One in New York City

Battery Park. See page 30. Ferries set out from here to the Harbor Islands; leave early and plan on a full morning.

Statue of Liberty. See page 31. One of the city's most potent symbols is just as exciting up close as from a distance, especially if you climb the steps to the crown.

Ellis Island. See page 32. The sensitive and moving museum drives home New York's immigrant roots.

Back on shore, stop for lunch at **Adrienne's Pizzabar** on pedestrianized Stone Street (see page 35).

Stroll along **Wall Street** to see the buildings at the heart of world finance, then head up Trinity Place (Church Street) to the 1766 St Paul's Chapel, with its 9/11 exhibit (page 25). The National September 11 Memorial is across the street (page 28).

The High Line. See page 84. If you've got the time on your way uptown, take a stroll along this elevated promenade on the West Side.

For a pre-theatre meal, choose from traditional dining spots such as **Chez Napoleon** and **Joe Allen** (see page 120).

Taking in a **Broadway** play or musical is a must for theatre-lovers; any venue will suffice, as long as the show is up to standard.

Atmospheric **Jimmy's Corner** (see page 122) is full of crusty barflies and boxing memorabilia; a drink at the bar provides a fitting end to a full day.

Immigration Museum, Ellis Island

Broadway

Jimmy's Corner

Day Two in New York City

Zabar's. See page 143. Pick up some provisions at Zabar's and enjoy them in the attached café or head for a picnic in Central Park.

Central Park. See page 124. Wander across the park, starting at Strawberry Fields in the west, then walking along the Lake and across the Ramble or Great Lawn, emerging on the east side.

Metropolitan Museum of Art. See page 129. Goya, Vermeer, the Hudson River School and the Temple of Dendur are among the highlights at this colossal museum.

Grand Central. See page 101. Lunchtime tours (Wed and Fri) of Grand Central Terminal help illuminate the magnificent Main Concourse and other features of this architectural marvel.

Oyster Bar. See page 112. Enjoy a late lunch in the bowels of Grand Central at this timeless Midtown hangout.

Empire State Building. See page 95. The obligatory trip to the 320m-high viewing platform provides just what you'd expect: a great vantage point of the city.

Soho shopping. See page 40. Prada and the Apple Store are destination shops, but there's plenty more to browse along Spring, Prince, Broadway and the smaller side streets.

Soho and Tribeca are full of excellent high-end restaurants; if you can foot the bill, Aquagrill, Bouley or Blue Ribbon Sushi will certainly fit the bill (see page 41).

Central Park

Inside Grand Central

Apple Store

Budget New York

New York can be an expensive place to visit, but there are a surprising number of inspiring sights and activities that are cheap or completely free.

Staten Island Ferry. See page 31. The free boat ride across New York harbour offers mesmerizing views of the city and the Statue of Liberty.

Governors Island. See page 32. Explore the historic houses, parks and galleries of this tranquil island – bikes are free weekdays 10am–noon.

Pizza slices at Artichoke. See page 68. The iconic NYC budget snack is done to perfection at this tiny, low-key East Village pizza joint.

Chelsea art galleries. See page 88. Wander a neighbourhood packed with cutting-edge contemporary art galleries (all free).

Free Fridays MoMA (see page 108), the Morgan Library (see page 100), Neue Galerie (see page 131), the Whitney Museum of American Art (see page 84) and the Asia Society (see page 134) are free or donation only on Friday evenings.

Dinner in Chinatown. See page 52. Best-value meals in Manhattan – eat like an emperor for less than $20 at Great N.Y. Noodletown.

Governors Island

Matthew Marks Gallery

Ping's Seafood

Kids' New York

Most sights are perfectly appropriate for kids, but beyond the expected – such as the Statue of Liberty – you can easily tailor a day or two to their interests.

Good Enough to Eat. See page 144. Load up with pancakes, French toast or corned beef hash at this relaxed restaurant.

American Museum of Natural History. See page 139. Go early to miss the crowds for the innovative special exhibits.

Carousel in Central Park. See page 125. If the kids are too old for this, check out the skaters and performance artists at the nearby Mall or Sheep Meadow.

Flatiron and Chrysler buildings. See pages 93 and 101. Their supporting roles in Spiderman and other action movies should compensate for any initial reticence about chec out architecture.

Madison Square Park. See page 94. Besides places to run and play, Madison Square boasts the Shake Shack, perfect for lunch or a midday snack.

Books of Wonder. See page 96. If it's a weekend, you might hear a reading at this kids' bookstore; regardless, there are plenty of volumes to browse.

The Museum of the Moving Image. See page 157. Swing a trip to Queens for interactive film fun, movie memorabilia and quirky screenings.

Zenon Taverna. See page 163. Astoria is filled with cheerful, family-friendly Greek restaurants along the lines of this affordable spot.

Carousel in Central Park

Flatiron Building

Zenon Taverna

PLACES

New York Harbor

Financial District and the Harbor Islands

New York was born on the southern tip of Manhattan in the 1620s. Today, the heart of the world's financial markets is also home to some of the city's most historic streets, sights and One World Trade Center, scene of the nation's biggest tragedy and now its most ambitious development. In recent years the neighbourhood has become increasingly residential, as former bank buildings are converted to luxury condos. To the north, City Hall Park remains the seat of New York's government, while the Brooklyn Bridge zooms eastward from here over the river. Take to the water to visit some of the city's offshore highlights and experience unbeatable views of Manhattan's celebrated skyline; just to the south of the Financial District, in New York Harbor, lies historic Ellis Island, the Statue of Liberty and the bucolic charms of Governors Island.

Wall Street

MAP P.26, POCKET MAP D23
Subway #4, #5, #2, #3 to Wall St.
Wall Street was named after the wooden stockade built by the Dutch at the edge of New Amsterdam in 1653, to protect themselves from the British colonies further north. The street has been associated with money for hundreds of years, and remains the apex of the global financial system

New York Stock Exchange

thanks to the Stock Exchange. Yet Wall Street has gained a new leisurely air since much of it has been closed to traffic, and fitness studios have opened up in empty office spaces. The old Bank of Manhattan Trust at no. 40 was briefly the world's tallest building in 1930 (927ft) – today it's known as the Trump Building after the flamboyant tycoon who bought it in 1995.

Trinity Church

MAP P.26, POCKET MAP C23
79 Broadway, at Wall St. Subway #4, #5 to Wall St. ☎ 212 602 0800, ⊕ www. trinitywallstreet.org. Daily 8am–6pm. Free.
Trinity Church held its first service at the western end of Wall Street in 1698, but this striking neo-Gothic version – the third model – only went up in 1846, and for fifty years was the city's tallest building. Trinity has the air of an English church (Richard Upjohn, its architect, was English), especially the sheltered graveyard, resting place of the first Secretary of the Treasury, Alexander Hamilton, and steamboat king Robert Fulton.

New York Stock Exchange

MAP P.26, POCKET MAP D23
11 Wall St. ⊕ www.nyse.com. Subway #4, #5, #2, #3 to Wall St. Closed to the public.
Behind the imposing Neoclassical facade of the **New York Stock Exchange** (on Broad St and usually draped with a giant US flag), the purse strings of the capitalist world are pulled. First established in 1817, two to three billion shares are now traded and $50 billion changes hands on an average day. Owing to security concerns, the public can no longer view the frenzied trading floor.

Federal Hall National Memorial

MAP P.26, POCKET MAP D23
26 Wall St. Subway #4, #5, #2, #3 to Wall St. ☎ 212 825 6888, ⊕ www.nps.gov/feha. Mon–Fri 9am–5pm. Free.

One of New York's finest examples of Greek Revival architecture, **Federal Hall** was completed in 1842 on the site of the old city hall, and is best known for the monumental statue of George Washington on its steps. Exhibits inside cover the heady days of 1789 when Washington was sworn in as America's first president here, as well as the later incarnations of the hall as US Customs House and Treasury. Washington's inaugural Bible is displayed, and there are special exhibits on Alexander Hamilton.

The Museum of American Finance

MAP P.26, POCKET MAP D23
48 Wall St. Subway #4, #5, #2, #3 to Wall St. ☎ 212 908 4110, ⊕ www.moaf.org. Tues–Sat 10am–4pm. $8.
Housed in the opulent banking hall of the former headquarters of the Bank of New York, the **Museum of American Finance** is the best place to gain an understanding of what's going on in the streets outside. Stocks, bonds and futures trading are demystified through multimedia presentations and a stack of rare artefacts, including a bond signed by Washington, and a stretch of ticker tape from the opening moments of 1929's Great Crash. Despite the inclusion of a detailed timeline of the 2008–2009 financial crisis, the overall message is unequivocally positive; that financial markets are a crucial factor in the development of modern society.

St Paul's Chapel

MAP P.26, POCKET MAP C22
209 Broadway, at Fulton St. Subway E to World Trade Center; A, C, #4, #5 to Fulton St. ☎ 212 233 4164, ⊕ www. trinitywallstreet.org/about/stpaulschapel. Mon–Sat 10am–6pm, Sun 7am–6pm. Free.
St Paul's Chapel dates from 1766, making it almost prehistoric by New York standards. Inside, the "St. Paul's: Community of Faith, Faith in Community" exhibit

Financial District and the Harbor Islands

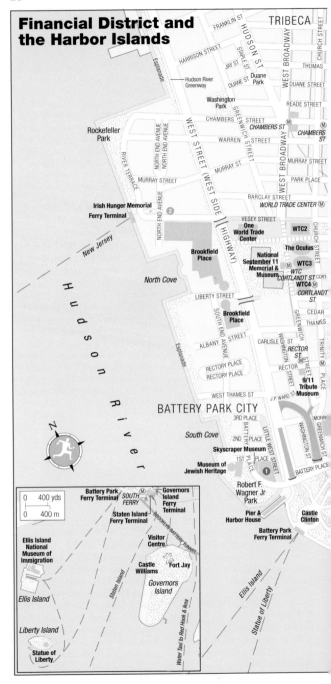

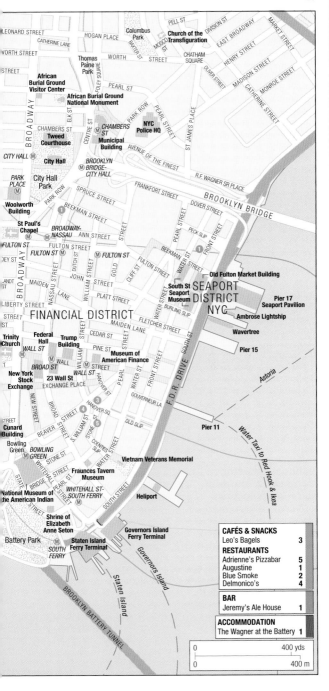

CAFÉS & SNACKS	
Leo's Bagels	3
RESTAURANTS	
Adrienne's Pizzabar	5
Augustine	1
Blue Smoke	2
Delmonico's	4

BAR	
Jeremy's Ale House	1

ACCOMMODATION	
The Wagner at the Battery	1

0	400 yds
0	400 m

Trinity Church

charts the history of the church from its humble beginnings to the attacks of 9/11, commemorated in more detail inside the 9/11 Chapel of Remembrance. For eight months after September 11, the chapel served as a sanctuary for rescue workers, and the exhibit chronicles this period, with a moving ensemble of photos, artefacts and testimonies. Even George Washington's pew, preserved shrine-like from 1789, served as a foot treatment chair for firefighters.

National September 11 Memorial & Museum

MAP P.26, POCKET MAP C22–23
180 Greenwich St, between Fulton and Liberty sts. Subway: R, W to Cortlandt St; #1 to Rector St or WTC Cortlandt, #4, #5 to Fulton St. ☎ 212 266 5211, Ⓦ www.911memorial.org. Memorial daily 7.30am–9pm; museum Sun–Thurs 9am–8pm, last entry 6pm, Fri & Sat 9am–9pm, last entry 7pm. Free (memorial); $24, children 7–12 $15, 13–17 $20 (museum).

The incredibly moving **National September 11 Memorial & Museum** was dedicated on 11 September 2011 to commemorate the ten-year anniversary of the 9/11 attacks. The two memorial pools, representing the footprints of the original towers, are each around one acre in size, with 30ft waterfalls tumbling down their sides. The names of the 9/11 victims are inscribed on bronze parapets surrounding the pools, while the contemplative eight-acre Memorial Plaza is filled with nearly four hundred oak trees. The underground **9/11 Memorial Museum** (which you have to pay to enter, and go through airport-like security) lies in between the two memorial pools. Ramps lead down to the **Foundation Hall**, containing remnants of the original Twin Towers, a half-crushed FDNY fire truck and the heavily inscribed "Last Column", the last piece of steel to be removed from Ground Zero in 2002. The heart of the museum is the **September 11, 2001 Historical Exhibition**, a poignant blend of images, recordings and videos covering the 9/11 attacks minute by minute.

One World Trade Center

MAP P.26, POCKET MAP C22–23
285 Fulton St (enter on West St, at Vesey St). Subway: A, C, #2, #3, #4, #5 to Fulton St; E to World Trade Center; R, W to Cortlandt St; #1 to Rector St or WTC Cortlandt. ☎ 844 696 1776, Ⓦ www. oneworldobservatory.com. Daily: early May–early Sept 9am–10pm (last entry 9.15pm); early Sept–early May 9am–8pm (last entry 7.15pm). $34, children 6–12 $28 (reserve tickets online).

The tallest skyscraper in the US (if the spire is included), **One World Trade Center** (1776ft) finally opened to the public in 2015, with visits to the **observatory** on floors 100, 101 and 102 (1250ft) – five high-speed elevators called Sky Pods will whisk you to the top in just sixty seconds, where sensational views of the city await. There are also dining options up here, but you must have an Observatory ticket to visit them.

The Oculus

MAP P.26, POCKET MAP C22–23

185 Greenwich St (also 50 Church St). Subway: A, C, #2, #3, #4, #5 to Fulton St; E to World Trade Center; R, W to Cortlandt St; #1 to Rector St or WTC Cortlandt. Mall open Mon–Sat 10am–9pm, Sun 11am–7pm.

A striking, bone-white 160-foot-tall edifice by Santiago Calatrava, **The Oculus** opened next to 3 World Trade Center in 2016, its two spiky steel ribs resembling a giant porcupine. Below it lies the World Trade Center Transportation Hub and a posh Westfield shopping mall. It's worth admiring the futuristic interior, with its soaring curves and arching skylight evoking the spirit of a great Gothic cathedral.

9/11 Tribute Museum

MAP P.26, POCKET MAP C23

92 Greenwich St. Subway R, W to Cortlandt St; #1 to Rector St or WTC Cortlandt; #4, #5 to Fulton St. ☎ 866 737 1184, ⓦ 911tributemuseum.org. Mon–Sat 10am–6pm, Sun 10am–5pm. $15 (with tours of 9/11 site $35).

A short walk from the World Trade Center site, the **9/11 Tribute Museum** commemorates the 9/11 attacks with a touching exhibit about the day itself, embellished with video and taped accounts of survivors. Items from the site make heart-rending symbols of the tragedy.

Irish Hunger Memorial

MAP P.26, POCKET MAP B22

290 Vesey St, at North End Ave. Subway E to World Trade Center; #1, #2, #3 to Chambers St. Daily 8am–6.30pm. Free.

This sobering monument to the more than one million Irish people who starved to death during the Great Famine of 1845–52 was designed by artist Brian Tolle in 2002. He transported an authentic famine-era stone cottage from County Mayo, and set it on a 25ft embankment overlooking the Hudson River. The passageway underneath echoes with haunting Irish folk songs, and there is a meandering path through the grassy garden.

Museum of Jewish Heritage

MAP P.26, POCKET MAP C24

36 Battery Place. Subway R, W to Whitehall St; #4, #5 to Bowling Green. ☎ 646 437 4200, ⓦ www.mjhnyc.org. Sun–Tues 10am–6pm, Wed & Thurs 10am–8pm, Fri

Museum of Jewish Heritage

10am–5pm; Nov to mid-March museum closes at 3pm on Fri. $12, free Wed 4–8pm. This moving and informative museum begins with everyday Eastern European Jewish life, before moving on to the horrors of the Holocaust. It ends with the establishment of Israel and subsequent Jewish achievements, even covering the successes of entertainers and artists like Samuel Goldwyn and Allen Ginsberg. The Zen-like "Garden of Stones" is on the second-floor terrace.

The National Museum of the American Indian

MAP P.26, POCKET MAP D24
1 Bowling Green, the US Customs House. Subway R to Whitehall St; #4, #5 to Bowling Green. ☎ 212 514 3700, ⊚ www. nmai.si.edu. Daily 10am–5pm, Thurs 10am–8pm. Free.

Cass Gilbert's US Customs House is now home to the Smithsonian's **National Museum of the American Indian**, a thoughtful collection of artefacts from almost every tribe native to the Americas. The permanent collection includes intricate basketry and woodcarvings, quilled hides, feathered bonnets and objects of ceremonial significance. Completed in 1907 and in use till 1973, the

National Museum of the American Indian

Beaux Arts **Customs House** is itself part of the attraction. The facade is adorned with elaborate statuary representing the major continents (carved by Daniel Chester French) and the world's great commercial centres, while the spectacular marble-clad Great Hall and Rotunda are beautifully decorated; the sixteen murals covering the 135ft dome were painted by Reginald Marsh in 1937.

The Fraunces Tavern Museum

MAP P.26, POCKET MAP D24
54 Pearl St, at Broad St. Subway #1 to South Ferry; #4, #5 to Bowling Green; R, W to Whitehall St. ☎ 212 425 1778, ⊚ www. frauncestavernmuseum.org. Mon–Fri noon–5pm, Sat & Sun 11am–5pm. $7.

Having survived extensive modification, several fires and nineteenth-century use as a hotel, the three-storey, ochre-and-red-brick **Fraunces Tavern** was almost totally reconstructed in 1907 to mimic its appearance on December 4, 1783, when, after hammering the Brits, a weeping George Washington took leave of his assembled officers, intent on returning to rural life in Virginia. The **Long Room** where his speech was made has been decked out in the style of the time, while the adjacent Federal-style **Clinton Room** is smothered in florid French wallpaper from 1838. The tavern's upper floors contain exhibits tracing the site's history, two hundred flags and a collection of Revolutionary War artefacts; look out for the lock of Washington's hair.

Battery Park

MAP P.26, POCKET MAP C24
Subway #1 to South Ferry; #4, #5 to Bowling Green; R, W to Whitehall St.

Lower Manhattan lets out its breath in **Battery Park**, a bright and breezy landscaped area in which memorials and souvenir vendors lead up to a sweeping view

Visiting the Harbor Islands

The only way to get to any of the Harbor Islands is by ferry. Take the #1 train to South Ferry or the #4 or #5 trains to Bowling Green, then walk to the boat pier in Battery Park. From the pier, Statue Cruises go to Liberty Island, then on to Ellis Island (daily, every 30–45min: Oct–May 9am–3.30pm; June–Aug 8.30am–5pm; Sept 8.30am–4pm; last ferry departs Liberty Island at 5pm (Oct–May), 6.45pm (June–Aug) and 5.45pm (Sept); round-trip $18.50, audio guide included); last ferry from Ellis Island 5.15pm (Oct–May), 7pm (June–Aug) and 6pm (Sept). Note that you must be at security 30 minutes before departure. You can buy tickets at Castle Clinton (in the park), or buy them in advance (recommended) at ☎ 877 523 9849 or ⊚ www.statuecruises. com. Queues can be extremely long at any time of year (45min or more), but they're especially bad in the summer; you must queue to buy tickets, and then join another queue to clear security before boarding the ferry. Start out early: keep in mind that if you take the last ferry of the day to Liberty Island, you won't be able to see Ellis. Ferries to Governors Island (May–Oct; hourly: Mon–Fri 10am–4.15pm; last ferry back 6pm; Sat & Sun every 30min 10am–5.30pm; last ferry back 7pm; $3 return; free Sat & Sun before noon) depart from the Battery Maritime Building just northeast of the Staten Island Ferry Terminal and Battery Park.

To simply get a closer view of the islands, catch the Staten Island Ferry (every 30min; free; ☎ 212 639 9675; ⊚ www.siferry. com), which departs from the terminal north of Battery Park. The twenty-five-minute ride across to Staten Island provides a beautiful panorama of the harbour and downtown skyline.

of America's largest harbour. The squat 1811 **Castle Clinton** (daily 8am–5pm; free), on the west side of the park, is the place to buy tickets for and board ferries to the Statue of Liberty and Ellis Island, visible in the distance. Jutting into the harbour on the western side of Battery Park, **Pier A Harbor House** is a lavish nineteenth-century relic dating from 1886, originally the headquarters of the New York Harbor Police. A mammoth renovation has filled the old wooden structure with a mix of shops, oyster bar and restaurants, plus plenty of outdoor seating.

The Statue of Liberty

MAP P.26, POCKET MAP A16
Liberty Island. ☎ 212 363 3200, ⊚ www.
nps.gov/stli. Daily: Oct–May 9am–3.30pm;
June–Aug 9am–5pm; Sept 9am–4pm. Free

(with ferry ticket).
Standing tall and proud in the middle of New York Harbor, the **Statue of Liberty** has served as a symbol of the American Dream since its dedication in 1886. The monument was the creation of the French sculptor Frédéric Auguste Bartholdi, a gift from France in recognition of the fraternity between the French and American people. The 151ft statue (305ft with pedestal), which consists of thin copper sheets bolted together and supported by an iron framework designed by Gustave Eiffel (of Eiffel Tower fame), was built in Paris between 1874 and 1884.

The basic ferry ticket (see page 31) allows entry to Liberty Island grounds only. To access the interior of the statue, the museum inside and the pedestal observation

Castle Williams

deck (168 steps up), you must buy a special ticket in advance (no extra charge). To enjoy the spectacular views from the crown of the statue, you'll need to book a Crown Ticket ($21.50; includes ferry) and climb 354 steps. You must pass another security screening at the statue.

Ellis Island

MAP P.26, POCKET MAP A15
ⓘ 212 363 3200, ⓦ www.nps.gov/elis or ⓦ www.libertyellisfoundation.org. Museum open daily: Oct–May 9am–3.30pm; June–Aug 9am–5pm; Sept 9am–4pm. Free.
Just across the water from Liberty Island, **Ellis Island** became an immigration station in 1892. It was the first stop for more than twelve million immigrants, all steerage-class passengers, and today some one hundred million Americans can trace their roots here. Closed in 1954, it reopened in 1990 as a **Museum of Immigration**, an ambitious project that eloquently recaptures the spirit of the place with artefacts, photographs, maps, and personal testimonies of the immigrants who passed through. On the first floor, the excellent permanent exhibit, "Peopling of America", chronicles four centuries of immigration, while the huge, vaulted Registry Room upstairs has been left imposingly bare.

Governors Island

MAP P.26, POCKET MAP B15–16
Ferry from 10 South St, Slip 7. ⓘ 212 825 3045, ⓦ www.nps.gov/gois or ⓦ www.govisland.com. Late May to Oct Mon–Fri 10am–6pm, Sat & Sun 10am–7pm. Free.
Until the mid-1990s, **Governors Island** was the largest and most expensively run Coast Guard installation in the world, but today it's being developed into a leafy historical park, the island's bucolic village greens and colonial architecture reminiscent of a New England college campus. Many of the buildings are being restored as art galleries and craft stores, and the **Historic Landmark District** at the northern end is managed by the National Park Service.

Ferries arrive at Soissons Dock, where you'll find the small visitors' centre. From here it's a short stroll up to the solid walls of **Fort Jay**, completed in 1794, and the nearby shady lanes of **Nolan Park**, home to some beautifully preserved

Neoclassical and Federal-style mansions. Other highlights include **Castle Williams**, a circular fort completed in 1811, but there are also plenty of green spaces in which to lounge in the sun – you can stroll or cycle right down to the southern tip, dubbed **Picnic Point**, via **The Hills**, four man-made humps, rising 80ft above the harbour. On route, **Hammock Grove** is an enticing space just south of Liggett Terrace, studded with comfy red hammocks (first come, first served).

Seaport District NYC

MAP P.26, POCKET MAP E22
Fulton St, at Water St. Subway: A, C, J, Z, #2, #3, #4, #5 to Fulton St. ☏ 212 748 8600, ⓦ www.southstreetseaportmuseum. org. Museum Wed–Sun 11am–5pm. $12.
The cobbled streets and busy promenade of **Seaport District NYC** were devastated by Hurricane Sandy in 2012, prompting a massive redevelopment of the site. The **old Fulton Market Building** now contains several ritzy boutiques and a branch of posh cinema chain **iPic Theaters** (daily 10am–2am; ⓦ ipictheaters.com), while the new **Pier 17**, designed by lauded SHoP Architects, contains stores, restaurants and a panoramic roof deck. The **South Street Seaport Museum**, lodged in a series of painstakingly restored 1830s warehouses showing maritime art and trade exhibits, reopened in 2016, with access to moored ships like the *Ambrose Lightship* (1908) and the *Wavertree* (1855).

City Hall

MAP P.26, POCKET MAP D22
Subway J, Z to Chambers St; R, W to City Hall; #2, #3 to Park Place; #4, #5, #6 to Brooklyn Bridge-City Hall.
At the north end of City Hall Park sits graceful **City Hall**, completed in 1812. It's the oldest city hall in the US to retain its original government function; inside is the mayor's office and city council. The

sumptuous interior can be seen on free prearranged tours via the Art Commission (Thurs 10am; 1hr; ☏ 212 788 2656, ⓦ www.nyc.gov) or by just signing up for the public tours (Wed noon) at the tourist kiosk opposite the Woolworth Building. Tours include the sensational, white coffered Rotunda.

The Woolworth Building

MAP P.26, POCKET MAP C22
233 Broadway, between Barclay St and Park Place. Subway R to City Hall; #2, #3 to Park Place; #4, #5, #6 to Brooklyn Bridge-City Hall. ☏ 203 966 9663, ⓦ www. woolworthtours.com. 30min tours Fri & Sat 1pm ($20); 1hr tours , Tues, Thurs & Fri 2pm, Sat 11.30am ($30); 1hr 30min tours Tues, Wed, Sat & Sun 2pm ($45).
The world's tallest skyscraper until 1930, the **Woolworth Building** (792ft) exudes money, ornament and prestige. The soaring, graceful lines of Cass Gilbert's 1913 "Cathedral of Commerce" are fringed with Gothic-style gargoyles and elaborate decorations. Guided tours must be booked online in advance.

African Burial Ground National Monument

MAP P.26, POCKET MAP D21
Monument, at Duane St and Elk St; visitor centre at 290 Broadway. Subway J, Z to

Woolworth Building

Chambers St; R to City Hall. ☎ 212 637 2019, ⓦ www.nps.gov/afbg. Tues–Sat 10am–4pm (monument closed Nov–March). Free.

In 1991 construction workers uncovered the remains of 419 skeletons near Broadway, a tiny portion of an African burial ground that covered five blocks during the 1700s. After being examined, the skeletons were re-interred at this site in 2003, marked by seven grassy mounds and a highly polished black granite monument, a symbolic counterpoint to the infamous "gate of no return" on Gorée Island in Senegal. To learn more, walk around the corner to the visitor centre (look for the dedicated entrance). Videos, displays and replicas of the artefacts found here are used to recount the history of the site, and shed light on the brutal life of the city's often forgotten enslaved population.

The Brooklyn Bridge

MAP P.26, POCKET MAP D22–F22
Subway (Manhattan) J, Z to Chambers St;

Brooklyn Bridge at sunset

#4, #5, #6 to Brooklyn Bridge–City Hall; (Brooklyn) A, C to High St.

Completed in 1883, the **Brooklyn Bridge** was the first to connect what were the then two separate cities of New York and Brooklyn across the East River, and for twenty years after it was the world's longest suspension bridge. Indeed, the bridge's meeting of art and function, of romantic Gothic and daring practicality, became a sort of spiritual model for the next generation's skyscrapers. But the bridge didn't go up without difficulties: John Augustus Roebling, its architect and engineer, crushed his foot taking measurements and died of tetanus, and twenty workers perished during construction. The entrance to the boardwalk that carries walkers above the traffic is opposite City Hall Park. It's best not to look back till you're midway: the Financial District's giants cluster shoulder to shoulder through the spidery latticework of the cables, a mesmerizing glimpse of the twenty-first-century metropolis.

Cafés and snacks

Leo's Bagels

MAP P.26, POCKET MAP D23
3 Hanover Sq, at Stone St. Subway #2, #3
to Wall St. Mon–Fri 6am–5pm, Sat & Sun
7am–5pm.

Get your bagel fix at this popular
local joint, with the hand-rolled,
chewy main event going for $1.25
or $2.95–5.95 with huge dollops of
cream cheese and various *schmears*.

Restaurants

Adrienne's Pizzabar

MAP P.26, POCKET MAP D23
54 Stone St. Subway #2, #3 to Wall St.
🕿 212 248 3838. Mon–Wed 11.30am–11pm,
Thurs–Sat 11.30am–midnight, Sun
11am–10pm.

One of the better Italian restaurants
downtown, with alfresco seating
in the summer. Serves nonna-style
square pizzas with a crispy crust;
the crumbled sausage topping is
especially tasty (from $25).

Augustine

MAP P.26, POCKET MAP D22
5 Beekman St, at Nassau St. Subway A,
C, J, Z, #2, #3, #4, #5 to Fulton St. 🕿 212
375 0010. Mon–Thurs 7.30am–11pm, Fri
7.30am–midnight, Sat 10am–midnight, Sun
10am–10pm.

Famed NY restaurateur Keith
McNally's Beekman Hotel
outpost is one of his best so far,
a fittingly elegant space with an
enticing brasserie-type menu,
blending French and American
flavours; think posh burgers with
Comté cheese and frites ($27),
duck a'l'orange ($33) and porc
calvados ($27).

Blue Smoke

MAP P.26, POCKET MAP B22
255 Vesey St, between West St and North
End Ave. Subway J, Z to Broad St, #2, #3
to Wall St. 🕿 212 889 2005. Mon–Thurs
11.30am–10pm, Fri 11.30am–11pm, Sat
11am–11pm, Sun 11am–10pm.

Blue Smoke

Authentic Southern barbecue
comes to FiDi courtesy of pitmaster
Kenny Callaghan and the Danny
Meyer empire, with a perfect
chopped barbecue sandwich ($16)
and classics such as baby back ribs
($19–34) and pepper beef brisket
($18–33).

Delmonico's

MAP P.26, POCKET MAP D23
56 Beaver St, at S William St. Subway #2,
#3 to Wall St. 🕿 212 509 1144. Mon–Fri
11.30am–10pm, Sat 5–10pm.

Many a million-dollar deal has
been made at this 1837 landmark
restaurant that features pillars from
Pompeii and classics like lobster
Newburg (market price) and
succulent steaks (from $49); finish
with a baked Alaska ($13), created
here in 1867.

Bar

Jeremy's Ale House

MAP P.26, POCKET MAP E22
228 Front St, at Peck Slip. Subway A, C, J, Z,
#2, #3, #4, #5 to Fulton St. Mon–Fri 8am–
midnight, Sat 10am–midnight,
Sun noon–midnight.

This local bar, with bras and ties
hanging from the rafters (donated
by happy patrons), serves pints of
draft beer from $6.50 (in plastic
cups) and excellent burgers ($6.95)
– happy hour Mon–Fri 4–6pm.

Soho and Tribeca

North of the Financial District, Tribeca, the "Triangle Below Canal Street", is a former wholesale garment district that has been transformed into a gentrified community that mixes commercial establishments with loft residences, galleries, celebrity hangouts and chic restaurants. To the northeast, the historic district between Houston and Canal known as Soho (short for "South of Houston") owes its distinction to the cast-iron architecture used by nineteenth-century manufacturers and wholesalers. Decades after toiling immigrant women had left the premises, artists reclaimed the abandoned lofty factory floors as living spaces and studios in the 1960s. Since then, Soho has come to signify fashion chic, urbane shopping and art, and its high-end chains attract celebrities and hordes of tourists; it's a grand place for brunch and browsing, and there are still a few good galleries to speak of.

Duane Park

MAP P.38, POCKET MAP C21
Subway #1, #2, #3 to Chambers St.
Duane Park, at the confluence of Duane, Hudson and Greenwich streets, was the first open space acquired by the city specifically to be a public park. Once part of a 62-acre farm, the city bought the park in 1797 for $5, scaled it down and watched it go through various stages of beauty and neglect. From

Rockefeller Park

the 1940s, trees and flowers were replaced with patches of concrete, until the park became a scar of what it once was. The most recent restoration was completed in 1999, harking back to its genteel days of 1887 and the design of Samuel Parsons, Jr and Calvert Vaux, famous for their work on Central Park. Wrought-iron fences are back, as are the World's Fair-style benches, historic-looking streetlights and cobblestones.

Rockefeller Park and Hudson River Park

MAP P.38, POCKET MAP B21
Subway #1, #2, #3 to Chambers St.
At the far western end of Chambers Street is **Rockefeller Park**, a charming parcel of lawn and gardens jutting into the Hudson River with fabulous views of New Jersey. In the summer, expect to see the wide lawn filled with sunbathers and the large playground jumping with children. From here you can stroll along **Hudson River Park** north towards Chelsea and Midtown, and south along the shady Battery Park City Esplanade, or cycle the parallel **Hudson River Greenway** all the way to Harlem.

West Broadway

MAP P.38, POCKET MAP C21
Subway #1, #2, #3 to Chambers St.
West Broadway is one of Tribeca's main thoroughfares, with several of the neighbourhood's best boutiques and restaurants, old and new. Across **West Broadway**, at 14 North Moore at the intersection of Varick, stands the New York Fire Department's **Hook and Ladder Company #8**, a nineteenth-century brick-and-stone firehouse that starred in the *Ghostbusters* movies (note the mural on the sidewalk outside), and played a crucial role in the rescue efforts of September 11. As it is a working firehouse, you can't do more than admire it externally.

E. V. Haughwout Building

The Haughwout Building

MAP P.38, POCKET MAP D20
488–492 Broadway. Subway R, N, W to Prince St; #6 to Spring St.
The magnificent 1857 **Haughwout Building** is perhaps the ultimate in the cast-iron architectural genre. Rhythmically repeated motifs of colonnaded arches are framed behind taller columns in this thin sliver of a Venetian-style palace – the first building ever to boast a steam-powered Otis elevator. The first two floors opened as a cosmetics store designed by Zaha Hadid in 2018 (it's otherwise closed to the public).

Spring Street

MAP P.38, POCKET MAP C19–D19
Subway R, N, W to Prince St; #6 to Spring St.
Cutting across the heart of Soho, **Spring Street** east of Sixth Avenue is lined with old buildings, plush restaurants and boutiques; mostly high-end brands such as Chanel and John Varvatos, as well as trendy labels like Ben Sherman, especially as you get closer to

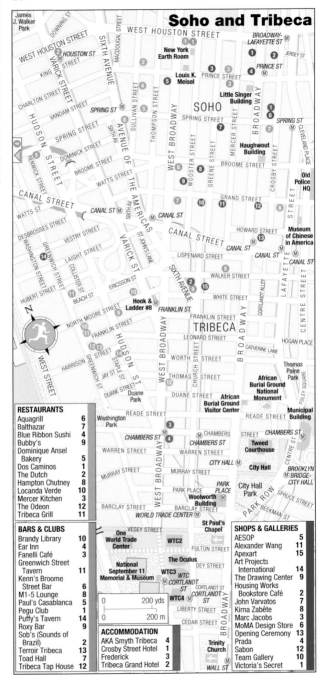

Soho and Tribeca

RESTAURANTS

Aquagrill	6
Balthazar	7
Blue Ribbon Sushi	4
Bubby's	9
Dominique Ansel Bakery	5
Dos Caminos	1
The Dutch	2
Hampton Chutney	8
Locanda Verde	10
Mercer Kitchen	3
The Odeon	12
Tribeca Grill	11

BARS & CLUBS

Brandy Library	10
Ear Inn	4
Fanelli Café	3
Greenwich Street Tavern	11
Kenn's Broome Street Bar	6
M1-5 Lounge	8
Paul's Casablanca	5
Pegu Club	1
Puffy's Tavern	14
Roxy Bar	9
Sob's (Sounds of Brazil)	
Terroir Tribeca	13
Toad Hall	7
Tribeca Tap House	12

ACCOMMODATION

AKA Smyth Tribeca	1
Crosby Street Hotel	4
Frederick	3
Tribeca Grand Hotel	2

SHOPS & GALLERIES

AESOP	5
Alexander Wang	11
Apexart	15
Art Projects International	14
The Drawing Center	9
Housing Works Bookstore Café	2
John Varvatos	7
Kirna Zabête	8
Marc Jacobs	3
MoMA Design Store	6
Opening Ceremony	13
Prada	4
Sabon	12
Team Gallery	10
Victoria's Secret	1

Cast-iron architecture

Soho contains one of the largest collections of cast-iron buildings in the world, erected between 1869 and 1895. **Cast-iron architecture** was designed so that buildings could be assembled quickly and cheaply, with iron beams rather than heavy walls carrying the weight of the floors. The result was greater space for windows and remarkably decorative facades. Glorifying Soho's sweatshops, architects indulged themselves in Baroque balustrades, forests of Renaissance columns, and all the effusion of the French Second Empire. Many fine examples of cast-iron architecture can be glimpsed along **Broadway** and **Greene Street**.

Broadway. You'll find a few French bistros and cafés towards Sixth Avenue, while there's a small craft market on the corner of Wooster Street.

The Little Singer Building

MAP P.38, POCKET MAP D19
561 Broadway. Subway R, N, W to Prince St; #6 to Spring St.

In 1904, Ernest Flagg took the possibilities of cast iron to their conclusion in this office and warehouse for the sewing machine company, a twelve-storey terracotta design whose use of wide window frames pointed the way to the glass curtain wall of the 1950s. The first floor is a Mango fashion store, but you won't get much sense of the building inside (the rest is off limits).

Prince Street

MAP P.38, POCKET MAP C19–D19
Subway R, N, W to Prince St.

The pulse beats here between Sixth Avenue and The Bowery, where the streets are always packed with shoppers looking to max-out their credit cards at the Apple Store, Camper and Michael Kors. In between the shops are small cafés and art galleries, such as **Louis K. Meisel** (where *Sex and the City* character Charlotte worked). On clear days, artists peddle original artwork and handmade jewellery from the sidewalks, though the crowds can get stifling at the

weekends. The Belgian-block pavements of nearby Mercer and Greene streets retain the neighbourhood's historical charm. Just north of Prince Street at 141 Wooster Street, the **New York Earth Room** (Ⓦwww.diaart. org; Wed–Sun noon–3pm and 3.30–6pm; free) is a permanent installation by land artist Walter de Maria; a second-floor loft completely covered in two feet of moist brown earth. The installation is closed from mid-June to mid-September.

Clothing store on Prince Street

Shops and galleries

AESOP

MAP P.38, POCKET MAP C19
438 W Broadway, at Prince St. Subway C
to Spring St, R, N, W to Prince St. Daily
11am–8pm.

The current darling of the skincare industry, Aussie-born Aesop crafts lush, all-natural products such as bergamot face wash and geranium leaf body scrub. The store is spare but inviting.

Alexander Wang

MAP P.38, POCKET MAP C20
103 Grand St, between Greene and Mercer
sts. Subway N, Q, R, W to Canal St, #6
to Spring St. Mon–Sat 11am–7pm, Sun
noon–6pm.

This avant-garde Taiwanese-American designer is a bona fide international brand. Wang is the brains behind a number of very successful fashion collaborations with houses both high (Balenciaga) and fast (H&M).

Apexart

MAP P.38, POCKET MAP C20
291 Church St, between Walker and White
sts. Subway N, Q, R, W to Canal St; #1 to
Franklin St. Tues–Sat 11am–6pm.

Founded in 1994, the thematic multimedia exhibits here are known for their intellectual diversity. Seven group exhibitions are presented each year, with a focus on contextualizing contemporary world art and culture.

Art Projects International

MAP P.38, POCKET MAP B20
434 Greenwich St, at Vestry St. Subway #1
to Canal St. Tues–Sat 11am–6pm.

Highly respected for showing leading contemporary artists from Asia, this gallery's engaging exhibits are mostly in print and have featured artists like Zheng Xuewu, Gwenn Thomas and Richard Tsao. No sign – just walk in.

The Drawing Center

MAP P.38, POCKET MAP C20
35 Wooster St, between Grand and Broome
sts. Subway A, C, E, N, R, Q, W to Canal St.
Wed, Fri–Sun noon–6pm, Thurs noon–8pm.

Masters like Marcel Duchamp and Richard Tuttle, as well as emerging and unknown artists, are shown together at this committed nonprofit organization.

Housing Works Bookstore Café

MAP P.38, POCKET MAP D19
126 Crosby St, between Houston and Prince
sts. Subway B, D, F, M to Broadway-
Lafayette, N, R, W to Prince St, #6 to
Bleecker St. Mon–Fri 9am–9pm, Sat & Sun
10am–5pm.

Extra-cheap and secondhand books in a spacious and comfy environment, with a café at the back. Proceeds benefit AIDS charities.

John Varvatos

MAP P.38, POCKET MAP C19
122 Spring St, at Greene St. Subway N, R,
W to Prince St, #6 to Spring St. Mon–Sat
11am–7pm, Sun noon–6pm.

Boxy though flattering casual wear and suits, plus the New York-based American designer's highly successful line of leather Converse trainers.

Kirna Zabête

MAP P.38, POCKET MAP C20
477 Broome St, between Greene and
Wooster sts. Subway N, R, W to Prince St.
Mon–Sat 11am–7pm, Sun noon–6pm.

Fashion-forward store that stocks hand-picked highlights from hot designers such as Jason Wu, Rick Owens and Proenza Schouler.

Marc Jacobs

MAP P.38, POCKET MAP C19
113 Prince St. Subway N, R, W to Prince St.
Mon–Sat 11am–8pm, Sun noon–6pm.

Doyen of the New York fashion world, Jacobs sells his women's ready-to-wear lines, accessories, shoes and men's clothes at this minimalist store.

Apexart

MoMA Design Store

MAP P.38, POCKET MAP D19
81 Spring St, between Broadway and Crosby
St. Subway N, R, W to Prince St, #6 to Spring
St. Mon–Sat 10am–8pm, Sun 11am–7pm.
A trove of creatively designed
goods that range from cheap
to astronomical.

Opening Ceremony

MAP P.38, POCKET MAP D20
35 Howard St, between Broadway and
Cosby St. Subway J, N, Q, R, W Z, #6
to Canal St. Mon–Sat 11am–8pm, Sun
noon–7pm.
Wildly popular boutique that has
expanded to manufacture its own
line. The shop is four vibrantly
decorated storeys, and filled to the
rafters with colourful, edgy designs.

Prada

MAP P.38, POCKET MAP D19
575 Broadway, at Prince St. Subway N, R,
W to Prince St. Mon–Sat 11am–7pm, Sun
11am–6pm.
This jaw-dropping flagship store
designed by Rem Koolhaas is as
much of a sight as the famous
clothes inside.

Sabon

MAP P.38, POCKET MAP D20
458 Broadway, at Grand St. Subway J, N, Q,
R, W, Z, #6 to Canal St. Mon–Sat 10am–8pm

& Sun 11am–8.30pm.
Luxury body and bath fragrances,
soaps and aromatic oils from Israel;
friendly assistants help you try the
products at the old-fashioned sink
in the middle of the store.

Team Gallery

MAP P.38, POCKET MAP C20
83 Grand St, at Greene St. Subway N, Q, R to
Canal St. Tues–Sat 10am–6pm.
Beautiful, voyeuristic and cutting-
edge work by artists such as Tracey
Emin and Genesis P-Orridge,
and web artist Cory Arcangel, is
shown here.

Victoria's Secret

MAP P.38, POCKET MAP D19
591 Broadway, at Houston St. Subway N, R,
W to Prince St. Mon–Sat 10am–9pm, Sun
11am–8pm.
The enduring appeal of the "world's
most glamorous lingerie" is about
quality, comfort and design, as
much as their celebrity models.

Restaurants

Aquagrill

MAP P.38, POCKET MAP C19
210 Spring St, at Sixth Ave. Subway C, E
to Spring St. ☏ 212 274 0505. Mon–Thurs
11.30am–2.30pm & 5.30–10pm, Fri

11.30am–2.30pm & 5.30pm–11pm, Sat 11am–3.30pm & 5.30pm–11pm, Sun 11am–3.30pm & 5.30–10pm.

At this enticing Soho spot, you'll find seafood so fresh it's still flapping. Russian Osetra Caviar chimes in at $185 per ounce, or try the grilled yellowfin tuna for $33. The excellent raw bar and Sunday brunch dishes are not prohibitively expensive, between $16 and $20. Reservations recommended.

Balthazar

MAP P.38, POCKET MAP D19
80 Spring St, between Crosby St and Broadway. Subway #6 to Spring St. ☎ 212 965 1414. Mon–Thurs 7.30am–midnight, Fri 7.30am–1am, Sat 8am–1am, Sun 8am–midnight.

Still one of the hottest reservations in town, *Balthazar*'s tastefully ornate Parisian decor and stylish clientele keep your eyes busy until the food arrives. Then you can savour highlights such as the fresh oysters ($24/dozen) or exquisite pastries. Entrées $22–47.

Blue Ribbon Sushi

MAP P.38, POCKET MAP C19
119 Sullivan St, between Prince and Spring sts. Subway C, E to Spring St. ☎ 212 343 0404. Daily noon–2am.

Widely considered one of the best and freshest sushi restaurants in New York, with fish flown in daily from Japan. Have some cold sake and dine at the sushi bar or in the cosy back room. Special rolls from $8, platters from $20.

Bubby's

MAP P.38, POCKET MAP C21
120 Hudson St, between Franklin and N Moore sts. Subway #1 to Franklin St. ☎ 212 219 0666. Sun–Thurs 8am–11pm, Fri & Sat 8am–midnight.

A relaxed place serving comfort food like matzo-ball soup ($12) and fried chicken and pancakes ($24). The pies really pull in the crowds though – try the peanut butter chocolate ($7).

Dominique Ansel Bakery

MAP P.38, POCKET MAP C19
189 Spring St, between Thompson and Sullivan sts. Subway C, E to Spring St. ☎ 212 219 2773. Mon–Thurs 8am–7pm, Fri & Sat 8am–8pm, Sun 9am–7pm.

The bakery responsible for the "Cronut" craze that swept NYC in 2013; fans still line up an hour before opening to get their hands on the fried, flaky (and trademarked) delight that's a cross between a donut and a croissant ($6).

Dos Caminos

Dos Caminos

MAP P.38, POCKET MAP C19
475 W Broadway, at Houston St. Subway #1
to Houston St. ☎ 212 277 4300. Sun–Tues
11.30am–10pm, Wed & Thurs 11.30am–
11pm, Fri & Sat 11.30am–midnight.
Thoughtful, real-deal Mexican
served with style – try the table-side
guacamole ($15). Brunch should
set you back $20–25 per person,
while dinner entrées range between
$19 and $33.

The Dutch

MAP P.38, POCKET MAP C19
131 Sullivan St, at Prince St. Subway C,
E to Spring St. ☎ 212 677 6200. Mon–Fri
11.30am–11pm, Fri 11.30am–11.30pm, Sat
10am–11.30pm, Sun 10am–11pm.
Andrew Carmellini's popular American
bistro has become a staple of the Soho
scene, offering locally sourced produce
and seasonal dishes including shellfish,
sandwiches, tasty chillis, delicious fried
chicken and freshly baked fruit pies
(dinner mains $25–36).

Hampton Chutney

MAP P.38, POCKET MAP D20
143 Grand St, between Lafayette and
Crosby sts. Subway J, N, Q, R, W, Z, #6
to Canal St. ☎ 212 226 9996. Mon–Sat
11am–8pm, Sun 11am–7pm.
This place is all about dosas (from
$9.45), uttapas and naan breads,
traditional south Indian fare,
albeit with plenty of American
ingredients. Orders are spiced up
with a choice of fresh, home-made
chutneys: cilantro, curry, mango,
tomato or peanut.

Locanda Verde

MAP P.38, POCKET MAP C21
377 Greenwich St, at N Moore St. Subway
#1 to Franklin St. ☎ 212 925 3797.
Mon–Thurs 7am–3pm & 5.30–11pm; Fri
7am–3pm & 5.30–11.30pm, Sat 8am–3pm &
5.30–11.30pm, Sun 8am–3pm & 5.30–11pm.
This casual Italian taverna is a
showcase for star chef Andrew
Carmellini's exceptional creations;
try the *porchetta* sandwich ($24),
grilled black bass ($36) or his
fabulous pastas ($27–28).

Mercer Kitchen

MAP P.38, POCKET MAP C19
99 Prince St, at Mercer St in Mercer Hotel.
Subway R, N, W to Prince St. ☎ 212 966
5454. Mon–Thurs 7am–midnight, Fri & Sat
7am–1am, Sun 7am–11pm.
This hip basement hangout and
restaurant for hotel guests and
scenesters entices with the casual
culinary creations of star chef
Jean Georges Vongerichten, who
makes ample use of his raw bar and
wood-burning oven. Brunch items
between $15 and $25 and dinner
plates from $25.

The Odeon

MAP P.38, POCKET MAP C21
145 West Broadway, at Thomas St. Subway #1,
#2, #3 to Chambers St. ☎ 212 233 0507. Mon
& Tues 8am–11pm, Wed–Fri 8am–midnight,
Sat 10am–midnight, Sun 10am–11pm.
Keith McNally's original
restaurant was a 1980s icon – it
featured in Jay McInerney's Bright
Lights, Big City. It's having a
renaissance mainly thanks to
the Condé Nast crowd (who
work nearby), but its French and
American standards (moules frites
to steaks; $23–40) and Art Deco
bar are definitely worth savouring.

Tribeca Grill

MAP P.38, POCKET MAP C21
375 Greenwich St, at Franklin St. Subway #1
to Franklin St. ☎ 212 941 3900. Mon–Thurs
11.30am–10pm, Fri 11.30am–11.30pm, Sat
5.30–11.30pm, Sun 11am–10pm.
The Grill is part-owned by Robert
De Niro, but it's really the food
– fine American cooking with
Asian and Italian accents – that
takes centre stage. The setting is
attractive, too: an airy, brick-
walled eating area in a 1905
warehouse, around a central
Tiffany bar. Main dishes range $23
to $45 (for the steak).

Bars and clubs

Brandy Library

MAP P.38, POCKET MAP C20

26 N Moore St, at Varick St. Subway #1 to Franklin St. Sun–Wed 5pm–1am, Thurs 4pm–2am, Fri & Sat 4pm–4am.

Stylish lounge bar, with rows of bottles lining the "bookshelves" and a menu of over 100 cocktails, rare single malt whiskeys and the signature cognacs.

Ear Inn

MAP P.38, POCKET MAP B20

326 Spring St, between Washington and Greenwich sts. Subway C, E to Spring St, #1 to Houston St. Daily 11.30am–4am.

"Ear" as in "Bar" with half the neon "B" chipped off. This historic pub near the Hudson opened in 1890 (the building dates from 1817). Its creaky interior is as cosy as a Cornish inn, with a good mix of beers on tap and basic, reasonably priced American food.

Fanelli Café

MAP P.38, POCKET MAP D19

94 Prince St at Mercer St. Subway R, N, W to Prince St. Sun–Thurs 9.30am–12.30am, Fri & Sat 9.30am–1.30am.

Established in 1922 (the building dates from 1853), *Fanelli* is one of the city's oldest pubs, relaxed and informal and a favourite of the not-too-hip after-work crowd.

Greenwich Street Tavern

MAP P.38, POCKET MAP B20

399 Greenwich St, at Beach St. Subway #1 to Franklin St. Sun & Mon 11am–10pm, Tues & Wed 11am–11pm, Thurs–Sat 11am–1am.

Friendly neighbourhood bar, refreshingly unpretentious for this part of town, with a solid menu of snack food, easy-going (generally male) clientele and beers for $3 in happy hour (Mon–Fri 5–8pm).

Kenn's Broome Street Bar

MAP P.38, POCKET MAP C20

363 W Broadway, at Broome St. Subway #1 to Franklin St. Sun–Thurs 11am–1.30am, Fri & Sat 11am–2.30am.

Open since 1972 but set in an ageing 1825 Federal-style house, this comfortable bar offers 15 beers

(eight draughts), from Brooklyn Lager to Dogfish IPA (they also have Stella on tap), and serves food, including decent burgers from $12.

M1-5 Lounge

MAP P.38, POCKET MAP C20

52 Walker St, between Church St and Broadway. Subway N, Q, R, W to Canal St. Mon–Fri 4pm–4am, Sat 1pm–4am.

Ultra-hip lounge bar, with a decent range of beers, wines and cocktails to accompany the sleek design and good food. Live music and DJs set the scene.

Paul's Casablanca

MAP P.38, POCKET MAP B20

305 Spring St, between Hudson and Greenwich sts. Subway C, E to Spring St. Thurs–Sun 10pm–4am.

Super hip cocktail bar with Moroccan decor, especially packed during Fashion Week (it was opened by Paul Sevigny, actress Chloë's brother). DJs focus on a different genre every night, from rock to hip hop (The Smiths are featured on Sunday nights). Look for the "McGovern's Bar" sign.

Pegu Club

MAP P.38, POCKET MAP C19

77 W Houston St, at West Broadway. Subway B, D, F, M to Broadway-Lafayette St, N, R, W to Prince St. Sun–Thurs 5pm–2am, Fri & Sat 5pm–4am.

One of NYC's most celebrated cocktail lounges, an elegant pioneer that perfected the gin-gin mule (ginger beer with Tanqueray gin, fresh mint and lime juice).

Puffy's Tavern

MAP P.38, POCKET MAP C21

81 Hudson St, between Harrison and Jay sts. Subway #1 to Franklin St. Mon–Fri 11.30am–4am, Sat & Sun noon–4am.

Far from being P. Diddy's hangout, this small dive bar serves up cheap booze without an ounce of attitude, rare in this area. Italian sandwiches are served and its cool jukebox specializes in old 45s.

Roxy Bar

MAP P.38, POCKET MAP C20

Roxy Hotel, 2 Sixth Ave, at White St. Subway A, C, E to Canal St, #1 to Franklin St. ℹ 212 965 3565. Daily 7am–2am.

Fabulous hotel bar, set at the bottom of the *Roxy*'s spacious atrium – being surrounded by twinkling lights and beautiful people (it's much more atmospheric at night) eases the pain when it's time to pay.

Sob's (Sounds of Brazil)

MAP P.38, POCKET MAP B19

204 Varick St, at W Houston St. Subway #1 to Houston St. Mon–Thurs hours vary, Fri & Sat 7pm–4am, Sun 7–11pm.

Premier place to hear hip-hop, Brazilian, West Indian, Caribbean and World Music acts in Manhattan. Vibrant and danceable, with quality music.

Terroir Tribeca

MAP P.38, POCKET MAP C21

24 Harrison St, at Greenwich St. Subway 1 to Franklin St. Mon & Tues 4pm–midnight, Wed–Sat 4pm–1am, Sun 4–11pm.

Tribeca outpost of the beloved wine bar, with more than 150 carefully curated bottles on the menu, plus eight beers on tap and select grape juices for non-drinkers. There's also a big choice of cheese, sandwiches and assorted finger foods.

Toad Hall

MAP P.38, POCKET MAP C20

57 Grand St, between W Broadway and Wooster St. Subway A, C, E to Canal St. Daily noon–4am.

With a pool table, good service and excellent bar snacks, this stylish alehouse is a little less hip and a little more of a local hangout than some of its neighbours.

Tribeca Tap House

MAP P.38, POCKET MAP C21

363 Greenwich St, between Harrison and Franklin sts. Subway #1 to Franklin St. Sun–Wed 11.30am–1am, Thurs–Sat 11.30am–2am.

Tribeca Tap House features twenty beers on tap, with plenty of microbrews on offer, as well as wine, cocktails, bar food, snacks and US sports events shown daily on big screens.

Roxy Bar

Chinatown, Little Italy and Nolita

Chinese immigrants have been coming to New York since the 1850s, making this Chinatown one of the oldest and biggest in the western hemisphere. Indeed, with over 100,000 residents, Chinatown is Manhattan's most densely populated ethnic neighbourhood. Since the 1980s it has pushed across its traditional border on Canal Street into the smaller enclave of Little Italy, and has begun to sprawl east across Division Street and East Broadway into the Lower East Side. Little Italy itself, now squeezed into a narrow strip along Mulberry Street, is far more dependent on tourists than Chinatown, but both neighbourhoods are fun places to eat, with cheap noodles, roast duck, gelato and huge plates of pasta on offer. On the northern fringes of Little Italy, the hip quarter known as Nolita ("North of Little Italy") is home to a number of chic restaurants, bars and boutiques.

Canal Street

MAP P.48, POCKET MAP D20–E20
Subway A, C, E, J, N, Q, R, Z, #1, #6 to
Canal St.

Canal Street

Canal Street is Chinatown's main all-hours artery crammed with jewellery shops and kiosks hawking sunglasses, T-shirts and fake Rolexes. At the eastern end of the thoroughfare, the majestic Byzantine dome of the former Citizen's Savings Bank (now HSBC) and the 1909 Manhattan Bridge's grand Beaux Arts entrance seem out of place amid the neon signs and market stalls.

Church of the Transfiguration

MAP P.48, POCKET MAP E21
29 Mott St. Subway J, N, Q, R, Z,
#6 to Canal St. ☏ 212 962 5157,
ⓦ transfigurationnyc.org. Sat 2–5pm,
otherwise services only. Free.
This elegant green-domed Georgian edifice is known as the "church of immigrants" for good reason. Since opening in 1801 as a Lutheran parish, it has also served Irish and Italian church-goers. Today, Mass

Grand Street

is said daily in Cantonese, English and Mandarin.

Mott Street

MAP P.48, POCKET MAP E20–21
Subway J, N, Q, R, Z, #6 to Canal St.
Mott Street is Chinatown's most touristy restaurant row, although the streets around – Canal, Pell, Bayard, Doyers and Bowery – host a glut of authentic canteens, tea and rice shops. Cantonese cuisine predominates, but many restaurants also specialize in spicier Sichuan and Hunan dishes. Most restaurants start closing around 10pm.

Grand Street

MAP P.48, POCKET MAP E20–F20
Subway B, D to Grand St.
Grand Street was the city's Main Street in the mid-1800s, and nowadays you will find outdoor fruit, vegetable and live seafood stands lining the curbs, offering bean curd, fungi and dried sea cucumbers. Ribs, whole chickens and roast ducks glisten in the storefront windows, alongside those of Chinese herbalists.

Museum of Chinese in America

MAP P.48, POCKET MAP D20
215 Centre St between Howard and Grand sts. Subway J, N, Q, R, Z, #6 to Canal St. ⓘ 212 619 4785, Ⓦ mocanyc.org. Tues–Sun 11am–6pm, Thurs 11am–9pm. $10, free first Thurs of the month.
This fascinating museum was designed by Maya Lin in 2009, its core exhibition providing an historical overview of the Chinese in the US through evocative multimedia displays, artefacts and filmed interviews. Galleries are arranged around a sun-lit courtyard reminiscent of a traditional Chinese house.

Italian American Museum and Mulberry Street

MAP P.48, POCKET MAP D20
155 Mulberry St. Subway J, N, Q, R, #6 to Canal St. ⓘ 212 965 9000, Ⓦ italianamericanmuseum.org. Fri–Sun noon–6pm. Donation $5.
Little Italy's main strip, **Mulberry Street**, is home to many of the area's cafés and restaurants – and filled with tourists. The former site of *Umberto's Clam House*, on

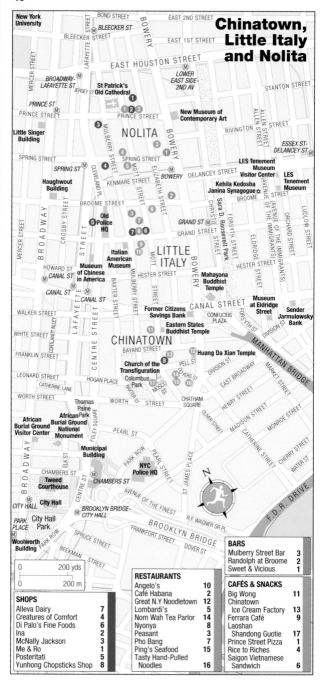

Chinatown, Little Italy and Nolita

BARS

Mulberry Street Bar	3
Randolph at Broome	2
Sweet & Vicious	1

CAFÉS & SNACKS

Big Wong	11
Chinatown Ice Cream Factory	13
Ferrara Café	9
Laoshan Shandong Guotie	17
Prince Street Pizza	1
Rice to Riches	4
Saigon Vietnamese Sandwich	6

RESTAURANTS

Angelo's	10
Café Habana	2
Great N.Y Noodletown	12
Lombardi's	5
Nom Wah Tea Parlor	14
Nyonya	8
Peasant	7
Pho Bang	3
Ping's Seafood	15
Tasty Hand-Pulled Noodles	16

SHOPS

Alleva Dairy	7
Creatures of Comfort	4
Di Palo's Fine Foods	6
Ina	2
McNally Jackson	3
Me & Ro	1
Posteritati	5
Yunhong Chopsticks Shop	8

Chinatown temples

Chinatown is a good place to observe traditional Chinese temple rituals, though the architecture is usually modern – most temples occupy converted shopfronts. **The Eastern States Buddhist Temple**, 64 Mott St (daily 8am–6pm), was established in 1962 as a social club for elderly Chinese men. The main deity here is Sakyamuni Buddha, but there's also a glass-encased gold statue of the "four-faced Buddha", a replica of the revered image in Bangkok's Erawan Shrine. Chinese influence is more obvious at the gilded and peaceful **Mahayana Buddhist Temple**, 133 Canal St (daily 8am–6pm). Candlelight and blue neon glow around the giant gold Buddha on the main altar. At the corner of Pell St and the Bowery is one of Chinatown's few Taoist temples: **Huang Daxian Temple** (daily 9am–6pm).

the corner of Mulberry and Hester streets, was once notorious as the scene of the vicious gangland murder of Joe "Crazy Joey" Gallo in 1972. On the corner of Grand Street, the **Italian American Museum**, with exhibitions on the old neighbourhood, should reopen sometime in 2019 after a major redevelopment.

St Patrick's Old Cathedral

MAP P.48, POCKET MAP D19
263 Mulberry St, at Prince St. Subway R, N to Prince St. ☎ 212 226 8075, ⓦ www. oldcathedral.org. Daily 8am–6pm. Free.
The first Catholic cathedral in the city, **St Patrick's Old Cathedral** began by serving the Irish immigrant community in 1809 and is the parent church to its much more famous offspring on Fifth Avenue and 50th Street.

New Museum of Contemporary Art and The Bowery

MAP P.48, POCKET MAP E19
235 Bowery, at Prince St. Subway R, N to Prince St, #6 to Spring St. ☎ 212 219 1222, ⓦ www.newmuseum.org. Tues, Wed & Fri–Sun 11am–6pm, Thurs 11am–9pm. $18, "pay what you wish" (suggested $2 minimum) Thurs 7–9pm.
Powerful symbol of the Bowery's rebirth, this avant-garde art gallery is housed in a stack of seven shimmering aluminium boxes.

The warehouse-like galleries are spacious, but still small enough to digest without overdosing on the diverse range of temporary exhibits inside. The **Bowery** itself was until relatively recently a byword for poverty and destitution, America's original skid row. At its peak, in 1949, around 14,000 homeless people could be found here, most dossing down in hostels known as flophouses. Today only a few flophouses remain, and the street is increasingly lined with smart, contemporary buildings, stores and bars.

New Museum of Contemporary Art

Shops

Alleva Dairy

MAP P.48, POCKET MAP D20
188 Grand St, at Mulberry St. Subway J, Z,
#6 to Canal St. Daily 9am–7pm.
The oldest Italian *formaggiaio*
(cheesemonger) and grocery in
America (1892). Makes its own
smoked mozzarella, provolone
and ricotta.

Creatures of Comfort

MAP P.48, POCKET MAP D19
205 Mulberry St, between Spring and
Kenmare sts. Subway #6 to Spring St.
Mon–Sat 11am–7pm, Sun noon–6pm.
This high-end boutique offers
beautifully presented wares – think
suede boots by Acne Studios,
colourful eyewear by Thierry Lasry
and exquisite Japanese soaps on
ropes – from its sunny, high-
ceilinged Soho digs.

Di Palo's Fine Foods

MAP P.48, POCKET MAP D20
200 Grand St, at Mott St. Subway B, D
to Grand St. Mon–Sat 9am–7pm, Sun
9am–5pm.
Charming and authoritative family-
run business, open since 1925, that
sells some of the city's best ricotta,

along with a fine selection of aged
balsamic vinegars, oils and home-
made pastas.

Ina

MAP P.48, POCKET MAP D19
21 Prince St, between Elizabeth and Mott
sts. Subway R, N, W to Prince St. Mon–Sat
noon–8pm, Sun noon–7pm.
Favourite consignment shop selling
recent season cast-offs. Full of
bargains; there's a men's branch at 19
Prince St (next door; same hours).

McNally Jackson

MAP P.48, POCKET MAP D19
52 Prince St. Subway N, R to Prince St.
Mon–Sat 10am–10pm, Sun 10am–9pm.
This independent local bookstore
has a great café and excellent
literary events. Due to move to a
new premises by the end of 2019.

Me & Ro

MAP P.48, POCKET MAP D19
241 Elizabeth St, between Houston and
Prince sts. Subway B, D, F, M to Broadway-
Lafayette, R, N to Prince St.
Tues–Sat noon–6pm.
The hottest, most distinctive
jewellery designer in Manhattan,
with tasteful Modernist designs
inspired by the traditions of China,
India and Tibet.

McNally Jackson

Posteritati

MAP P.48, POCKET MAP D20
239 Centre St, between Broome and Grand
sts. Subway #6 to Spring St. Mon–Sat
11am–7pm.

Vast selection of over nine
thousand movie posters, from
classics such as *20,000 Leagues
Under the Sea* and *Goldfinger* to
modern blockbusters like *Avatar*.

Yunhong Chopsticks Shop

MAP P.48, POCKET MAP D21
50 Mott St, between Bayard and Pell sts.
Subway A, C, E, J, N, Q, R, Z, #1, #6 to
Canal St. Daily 10.30am–8.30pm.

The only US branch of this Beijing
chopstick maker, with more than
200 different styles made from
mahogany, ebony and silver, and
hand-painted. Some feature famous
quotes from Chairman Mao.

Cafés and snacks

Big Wong

MAP P.48, POCKET MAP D20
67 Mott St, between Bayard and Canal sts.
Subway J, N, Q, R, W, Z, #6 to Canal St. Daily
7am–11pm.

This cafeteria-style Cantonese BBQ
joint serves some of Chinatown's
tastiest duck and congee (savoury
rice stew), all for $8–15.

Chinatown Ice Cream Factory

MAP P.48, POCKET MAP D21
65 Bayard St, between Mott and Elizabeth
sts. Subway J, N, Q, R, W, Z, #6 to Canal St.
Daily 11am–10pm.

An essential stop after dinner at
one of the restaurants nearby.
Specialties include green tea, ginger
and almond cookie ice cream.

Ferrara Café

MAP P.48, POCKET MAP D20
195 Grand St, between Mott and Mulberry
sts. Subway J, N, Q, R, W, Z, #6 to Canal St
B, D to Grand St. Sun–Fri 8am–midnight,
Sat 8am–1am.

The best-known and most
traditional of Little Italy's

coffeehouses, this neighbourhood
landmark has been around since
1892. Try the New York cheesecake
or, in summer, *granite* (Italian ices).
Outdoor seating is available in
warmer weather.

Laoshan Shandong Guotie

MAP P.48, POCKET MAP D21
106 Mosco St. Subway J, Z, #6 to Canal St.
Daily 8am–9pm.

Identified simply by a "Fried
Dumpling" sign in English,
this bargain hole-in-the-wall
specializes in pan-fried dumplings
characteristic of northern China
($1.25 for 5).

Prince Street Pizza

MAP P.48, POCKET MAP D19
27 Prince St, between Mott and Elizabeth
sts. Subway N, R, W to Prince St. Sun–Thurs
11.30am–11pm, Fri & Sat 11.30am–4am.

When the original Ray's closed
on this site in 2012, this pizza
joint took up the tradition,
with its game-changing, utterly
addictive SoHo Squares ($4.25),
topped with mozzarella and
"secret sauce".

Rice to Riches

MAP P.48, POCKET MAP D19
37 Spring St, between Mott and Mulberry
sts. Subway #6 to Spring St. Sun–Thurs
11am–11pm, Fri & Sat 11am–1am.

Utterly irresistible rice pudding,
served up in this fashionable space
in a variety of sweet flavours, from
peanut butter and choc chip to
mango and cinnamon. Bowls start
at $8.50.

Saigon Vietnamese Sandwich

MAP P.48, POCKET MAP D20
369 Broome St, at Mott St. Subway #6 to
Spring St. Daily 8am–6pm.

One of the best makers of
Vietnamese sandwiches (known
as *bánh mì*) in the city. The classic
is a large chunk of French bread
stuffed with pork, sausage and
pickled vegetables – all for $6.75
(cash only).

Lombardi's

Restaurants

Angelo's

MAP P.48, POCKET MAP D20
146 Mulberry St, between Hester and
Grand sts. Subway N, R, W #6 to Canal
St. Tues–Thurs & Sun noon–11.30pm, Fri
noon–12.30am, Sat noon–1am.
Little Italy's red-sauce restaurants
cater firmly to tourists these days,
but this 1902 classic is the best
place to get a sense of the area's
original style and flavours.

Café Habana

MAP P.48, POCKET MAP D19
17 Prince St, at Elizabeth St. Subway
R, W to Prince St T212 625 2001. Daily
9am–midnight.
Small and always crowded, this
Cuban–South American option
features some of the best skirt steak
and fried plantains this side of
Cuba. A takeout window next door
serves great *café con leche* (daily
11am–11pm).

Great N.Y. Noodletown

MAP P.48, POCKET MAP E21
28 Bowery, at Bayard St. Subway B, D to
Grand St, J, Z, #6 to Canal St. T 212 349
0923. Daily 9am–4am.
Despite the name, noodles aren't
the real draw at this down-to-earth
restaurant – the soft-shell crabs
(in season) are crisp, salty and
delicious. Good roast meats (try the
baby pig) and soups too.

Lombardi's

MAP P.48, POCKET MAP D19
32 Spring St, at Mott St. Subway #6 to
Spring St. T 212 941 7994. Sun–Thurs
11.30am–11pm, Fri & Sat 11.30am–
midnight.
The oldest pizzeria in the US (since
1905) serves some of the best pizzas
in town, including an amazing
clam pizza ($35); no slices, though.
Ask for roasted garlic on the side.

Nom Wah Tea Parlor

MAP P.48, POCKET MAP E21
13 Doyers St. Subway J, N, Q, R, W, Z, #6
to Canal St. T 212 962 6047. Sun–Wed
10.30am–10pm, Thurs–Sat 10.30am–11pm.
Dating back to 1920 but spruced
up in 2010, this elegant and old-
fashioned dim sum place offers a
select menu of tasty snacks, from
taro and shrimp dumplings to
salt and pepper shrimp and their
original egg roll ($7.50).

Nyonya

MAP P.48, POCKET MAP D20
199 Grand St, between Mott and Mulberry
sts. Subway B, D to Grand St, J, Z, #6 to
Canal St. ☎ 212 334 3669. Sun–Thurs
11am–11.30pm, Fri & Sat 11am–midnight.
Superb Malaysian grub at wallet-
friendly prices. Try the chicken
curry, spicy squid or clay-pot
noodles. Cash only.

Peasant

MAP P.48, POCKET MAP D19
194 Elizabeth St, between Prince and
Spring sts. Subway R, N, W to Prince St; J,
Z to Bowery, #6 to Spring St. ☎ 212 965
9511. Tues–Sat 6–11pm, Sun 6–10pm.
A bit of a hangout after hours for city
chefs, here you'll pay around $14–26
for Frank De Carlo's beautifully
crafted Italian food such as *porchetta
arrosto* (roasted suckling pig) or $16
for brick-oven-fired pizzas.

Pho Bang

MAP P.48, POCKET MAP D20
157 Mott St, between Grand and Broome sts.
Subway B, D to Grand St, J, Z, #6 to Canal St.
☎ 212 966 3797. Daily 10am–10pm.
One of the most popular
Vietnamese restaurants in the city,
often packed at weekends. The
main event is *pho*, Vietnamese
beef noodle soup, which comes
in several varieties, but the crispy
spring rolls and chicken curry are
also excellent. Cash only.

Ping's Seafood

MAP P.48, POCKET MAP E21
22 Mott St, between Chatham Square and
Pell St. Subway R, N, J, W, Z, #6 to Canal St.
☎ 212 602 9988. Mon–Fri 10.30am–11pm,
Sat & Sun 9am–11pm.
While this Hong Kong seafood
restaurant is good anytime, it's
most enjoyable at weekends for dim
sum, when carts of tasty, bite-size
delicacies whirl by for the taking
every thirty seconds. This place
offers superb bang for your buck.

Tasty Hand-Pulled Noodles

MAP P.48, POCKET MAP E21

1 Doyers St, at the Bowery. Subway J, N, Q,
R, Z, #6 to Canal St. ☎ 212 791 1817. Daily
10.30am–10.30pm.
Freshly cooked and delicious
hand-pulled noodles made
to order – choose from seven
different types, then opt for pan-
fried or boiled noodles with pork,
fish, beef, chicken, shrimp and
several other combos.

Bars

Mulberry Street Bar

MAP P.48, POCKET MAP D20
176-1/2 Mulberry St, between Broome and
Grand sts. Subway J, Z to Bowery, #6 to
Canal St. Sun–Thurs 11am–midnight, Fri &
Sat 11am–2am.
Donnie Brasco and *The Sopranos*
had scenes shot in this favourite
local dive bar, located in the heart
of Little Italy. Formerly known
as *Mare Chiaro*, the wooden bar,
subway tile floor and pressed tin
roof have barely changed since it
opened in 1908.

Randolph at Broome

MAP P.48, POCKET MAP D20
349 Broome St, between Elizabeth St and
the Bowery. Subway J, Z to Bowery, B, D to
Grand St. Mon–Fri 5pm–4am; Sat & Sun
2pm–4am.
Friendly European café that serves
artisanal cocktails and gourmet
coffee from the Brooklyn Roasting
Company (till 5pm). Happy hour
is Mon–Fri 5–8pm, and there's a
cosy outdoor patio at the front.

Sweet & Vicious

MAP P.48, POCKET MAP D19
5 Spring St, between Bowery and Elizabeth
St. Subway J, Z to Bowery. Daily 2pm–4am.
This bar is a neighbourhood
favourite and the epitome of rustic
chic, with exposed brick and
wood and antique chandeliers.
The tempting cocktail list features
berry cosmopolitans and lemon
drop martinis. A back garden
and a cosy atmosphere add to its
charm.

The Lower East Side

Historically the epitome of the American ethnic melting pot, the Lower East Side has been a revolving door for immigrants since the 1830s, when Irish and German populations moved in. The second wave came from Southern Italian and Eastern European Jewish communities arriving in the 1880s. By 1915, Jews had the largest representation in the Lower East Side, numbering more than 320,000. While a fair proportion of inhabitants today are working-class Latino or Asian, you are just as likely to find students, moneyed artsy types and other refugees from the overly-gentrified areas of Soho and the nearby East Village, a blend that makes this one of the city's most enthralling neighbourhoods and one of its hippest areas for shopping, drinking, dancing and – what else? – food.

Orchard Street

MAP P.56, POCKET MAP E19
Subway F, J, M, Z to Delancey St/Essex St,
B, D to Grand St.

The centre of the Lower East Side's so-called Bargain District,

Orchard is best visited at weekends, when filled with stalls and storefronts hawking discounted designer clothes and bags, though note that many Jewish-owned stores are closed on

Orchard Street

Exploring the Jewish Lower East Side

Though its Jewish population has dwindled, the Lower East Side retains a rich legacy of Jewish food, stores and, especially, Jewish buildings. Several synagogues are well maintained and most accept visitors Sun–Thurs. Perhaps the best preserved is the Museum at Eldridge Street (see page 56), but you can also visit the 1927 **Kehila Kedosha Janina Synagogue and Museum** (☎ 212 431 1619, ⊚ kkjsm.org. Sun 11am–4pm; free; Map page 56, Pocket Map E20) at 280 Broome Street (at Allen St), home of the Romaniote Jews from Greece, an obscure branch of Judaism with roots in the Roman era. Enthusiastic volunteers introduce Jewish art and various exhibits. Further south at 54–58 Canal St is the ornate facade of the **Sender Jarmulowsky Bank** (now being developed as office space). Founded in 1873 by a Russian peddler who made his fortune reselling ship tickets, the bank catered to the financial needs of the area's non-English-speaking immigrants (the building dates from 1912). In 1914, the bank collapsed; on its closure, thousands lost what little savings they had accumulated. At 7 Willett Street, near the junction of Grand Street and East Broadway, **Bialystoker Synagogue** (☎ 212 475 0165, ⊚ www.bialystoker.org; Mon–Thurs 7–10am, to visit you must call in advance; free; Pocket Map F19), is a trove of stained glass, gold leaf and exuberant murals of zodiac signs, all beautifully restored. For more in-depth tours, contact the Lower East Side Jewish Conservancy (☎ 212 374 4100, ⊚ nycjewishtours.org).

Saturdays. The rooms above the stores used to house sweatshops, so named because whatever the weather, a stove had to be kept warm for pressing the clothes made there. Much of the garment industry moved uptown ages ago, and the rooms are a bit less salubrious now – often home to pricey apartments.

Tenement Museum

MAP P.56, POCKET MAP E20
97 Orchard St, between Broome and Delancey sts. Subway B, D to Grand St, F, J, M, Z to Delancey St/Essex St. ☎ 212 982 8420, ⊚ www.tenement.org. $25; for tickets go to the visitor centre at 103 Orchard St (Fri–Wed 10am–6.30pm, Thurs 10am–8.30pm).

This illuminating museum offers a glimpse into the crumbling and claustrophobic interior of an 1863 tenement, with its deceptively elegant entry hall and two communal toilets for every four families. Museum guides expertly bring to life the building's past and present, aided by documents, photographs and artefacts found on-site, and concentrating on the area's multiple ethnic heritages.

Various apartments inside have been renovated with period furnishings to reflect the lives of tenants, from the mid-nineteenth century to the mid-twentieth century – when many families ran cottage industries from home.

The tenement is accessible only by themed **guided tours** (1hr, every 15–30min; daily 10.30am–5pm). These include "Hard Times", which focuses on a German-Jewish family and Italian family during the economic depressions of 1863 and 1935; "Irish Outsiders", which examines the grim life of the Irish

Moore family from 1868–69; and "Sweatshop Workers", a visit to the Levine family's garment workshop and the Rogarshevskys' Sabbath table at the turn of the twentieth century. Various two-hour tours of the neighbourhood ($25–45) complement the tenement tours.

Essex Crossing

MAP P.56, POCKET MAP E19
Centred on Essex St and Delancey St.
Subway F, J, M, Z to Delancey St/Essex St.
Ⓦ essexcrossingnyc.com.

Opening in 2018 as a vast, multi-block urban renewal development, **Essex Crossing** has transformed this corner of the Lower East Side with shiny towers and office blocks usually associated with Midtown. Historic **Essex Street Market** has been relocated here, part of a greater marketplace dubbed the Market Line, as has the

International Center of Photography Museum (Tues–Sun 10am–6pm; $14; wicP.org).

Museum at Eldridge Street

MAP P.56, POCKET MAP E20
12 Eldridge St, between Canal and Division sts. Subway B, D to Grand St, F to East Broadway. ☎ 212 219 0302, Ⓦ eldridgestreet.org. Mon–Thurs & Sun 10am–5pm, Fri 10am–3pm by tour only, every 30min (1hr); $14.

Built in 1887, this wonderfully restored synagogue is one of the neighbourhood jewels: a brick and terracotta hybrid of Moorish and Gothic influences, with rich woodwork and stained-glass windows, including the spectacular west-wing rose window. The synagogue is still in use, but tours visit the main sanctuary upstairs, while exhibits introduce the history of the building and the area.

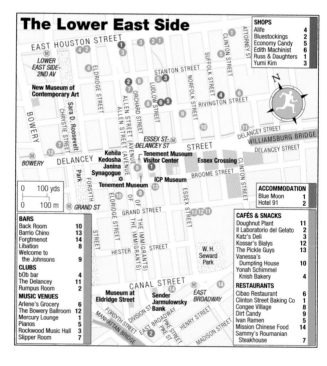

The Lower East Side

SHOPS

Alife	4
Bluestockings	2
Economy Candy	5
Edith Machinist	6
Russ & Daughters	1
Yumi Kim	3

ACCOMMODATION

Blue Moon	1
Hotel 91	2

CAFÉS & SNACKS

Doughnut Plant	11
Il Laboratorio del Gelato	2
Katz's Deli	3
Kossar's Bialys	12
The Pickle Guys	13
Vanessa's Dumpling House	10
Yonah Schimmel Knish Bakery	4

RESTAURANTS

Cibao Restaurant	6
Clinton Street Baking Co	1
Congee Village	8
Dirt Candy	9
Ivan Ramen	5
Mission Chinese Food	14
Sammy's Roumanian Steakhouse	7

BARS

Back Room	10
Barrio Chino	13
Forgtmenot	14
Libation	8
Welcome to the Johnsons	9

CLUBS

bOb bar	4
The Delancey	11
Rumpus Room	2

MUSIC VENUES

Arlene's Grocery	6
The Bowery Ballroom	12
Mercury Lounge	1
Pianos	5
Rockwood Music Hall	3
Slipper Room	7

Shops

Alife

MAP P.56, POCKET MAP F19
158 Rivington St, at Clinton St. Subway J, M, Z to Essex St, F to Delancey St. Mon–Sat noon–7pm, Sun noon–6pm.

A shrine to designer sneakers, with special-edition Nikes going for as much as $900, as well as $150 sunglasses and other accessories for sale. The hip T-shirts are "just" $42.

Bluestockings

MAP P.56, POCKET MAP E19
172 Allen St, between Rivington and Stanton sts. Subway F to Lower East Side–Second Ave. Daily 11am–11pm.

Bluestockings sells new and used books on gay and gender studies, feminism, police and prisons, democracy studies and black liberation.

Economy Candy

MAP P.56, POCKET MAP E19
108 Rivington St, between Essex and Ludlow sts. Subway J, M, Z to Essex St, F to Delancey St. Mon & Sat 10am–6pm, Tues–Fri & Sun 9am–6pm.

Old-fashioned sweet store that sells hundreds of kinds of chocolates, candies, nuts, dried fruits and halvah.

Edith Machinist

MAP P.56, POCKET MAP E19
104 Rivington St, at Ludlow St. Subway J, M, Z to Essex St, F to Delancey St. Sun, Mon & Fri noon–6pm; Tues–Thurs & Sat noon–7pm.

This trendy used clothes store holds some exceptional finds (particularly shoes and top designers) but at a fraction of their Fifth Avenue price tags.

Russ & Daughters

MAP P.56, POCKET MAP E19
179 E Houston St, between Allen and Orchard sts. Subway F to Lower East Side–Second Ave. Mon–Fri 8am–8pm, Sat 8am–7pm, Sun 8am–5.30pm.

The original Manhattan gourmet shop, it was set up in 1914 to

Russ & Daughters

sate the appetites of homesick immigrant Jews with smoked fish, pickled vegetables, cheese and amazing bagels with smoky lox ($12).

Yumi Kim

MAP P.56, POCKET MAP E19
105 Stanton St, at Ludlow St. Subway F to Delancey St, J, M, Z to Essex St. Mon–Sat noon–7.30pm.

Downtown chic clothing by New York-based Kim Phan, whose silk printed dresses, vintage bodies and flirty prints have been a big hit since launching in 2004.

Cafés and snacks

Doughnut Plant

MAP P.56, POCKET MAP F20
379 Grand St, between Essex and Norfolk sts. Subway J, M, Z to Essex St, F to Delancey St. Sun–Thurs 6.30am–8pm, Fri & Sat 6.30am–9pm.

Serious (and seriously delicious) doughnuts; make sure you sample the seasonal flavours and glazes, including pumpkin and passion fruit.

Il Laboratorio del Gelato

MAP P.56, POCKET MAP E19

188 Ludlow St, at Houston St. Subway J, Z to Essex St, F to Delancey St. Mon–Thurs 7.30am–10pm, Fri 7.30am–midnight, Sat 10am–midnight, Sun 10am–10pm.

This shrine to cream and sugar serves up over 230 flavours (48 weekly; from $4.50), from honey lavender and toasted sesame to tarragon pink pepper.

Katz's Deli

MAP P.56, POCKET MAP E19

205 E Houston St, at Ludlow St. Subway F to Lower East Side-Second Ave. Mon–Wed 8am–10.45pm, Thurs 8am–2.45am, Fri 8am–Sun 10.45pm (24hr).

Venerable Lower East Side Jewish deli since 1888, serving archetypal overstuffed pastrami ($21.45) and corned-beef sandwiches ($20.45), bagels, hot dogs and Rubens ($22.45). Famous for the faux-gasm scene from *When Harry Met Sally*.

Kossar's Bialys

MAP P.56, POCKET MAP F20

367 Grand St, between Essex and Norfolk sts. Subway J, M, Z to Essex St, F to Delancey St. Daily 6am–6pm.

A generations-old kosher treasure serves, bar none, the city's best bagels and bialys ($1), a flattened savoury dough traditionally topped with onion or garlic. Kossar's moved to this location in 1960.

The Pickle Guys

MAP P.56, POCKET MAP F20

357 Grand St, at Essex St. Subway R, N, J, Z, #6 to Canal St. Sun–Thurs 9am–6pm, Fri 9am–4pm.

Come here for fresh home-made pickles, olives and other yummy picnic staples from huge barrels of garlicky brine.

Vanessa's Dumpling House

MAP P.56, POCKET MAP E20

118A Eldridge St, between Grand and Broome sts. Subway B, D to Grand St. Mon–Sat 10.30am–10.30pm, Sun 10.30am–10pm.

This always busy Chinese restaurant knocks out various combinations of steamed or fried pork, shrimp and vegetable dumplings at the bargain price of $1.50 for 4.

Yonah Schimmel Knish Bakery

MAP P.56, POCKET MAP E19

137 E Houston St, between First and Second aves. Subway F to Lower East Side-Second Ave. Daily 9.30am–7pm.

This place has been making and selling some of New York's best knishes ($4.25) since 1910: rounds of vegetable- or fruit-stuffed dough, baked fresh on the premises, as are the wonderful bagels.

Restaurants

Cibao Restaurant

MAP P.56, POCKET MAP F19

72 Clinton St, at Rivington St. Subway J, M, Z to Essex St, F to Delancey St. ☏ 212 228 0703. Daily 7am–2am.

El Cibao is the best Dominican restaurant on the Lower East Side. Hearty portions of roast chicken ($10.50) and huge sandwiches, particularly the Cubano ($6), are bargains.

Clinton Street Baking Co

MAP P.56, POCKET MAP E19

4 Clinton St, at E Houston St. Subway F to Delancey St, J, M, Z to Essex St. ☏ 646 602 6263. Mon–Fri 8am–4pm & 5.30–11pm, Sat 9am–4pm & 5.30–11pm, Sun 9am–5pm.

This former bakery has become one of the city's most popular brunch spots (no reservations), especially noted for its delicious blueberry pancakes ($15). Dinner is just as good, however, and less crowded; try the buttermilk fried chicken and waffles ($19).

Congee Village

MAP P.56, POCKET MAP E19

100 Allen St, at Delancey St. Subway J, M, Z to Essex St, F to Delancey St. ☏ 212 941 1818. Mon–Thurs & Sun 10.30am–12.30am,

Fri & Sat 10.30am–1am.
This Cantonese restaurant is a shrine to the eponymous fragrant, soupy rice dish and a wide range of other Hong Kong favourites for less than $20.

Dirt Candy

MAP P.56, POCKET MAP E20
86 Allen St, between Grand and Broome sts. Subway F to Lower East Side-Second Ave. ☎ 212 228 7732. Tues–Fri 5.30–11pm, Sat 11am–3pm & 5.30–11pm, Sun 11am–3pm.
Inventive and beautifully presented vegetarian dishes from lauded chef Amanda Cohen; think Korean fried broccoli, Brussels sprout tacos and carrot sliders on carrot buns.

Ivan Ramen

MAP P.56, POCKET MAP F19
25 Clinton St, between Stanton and Houston sts. Subway F to Delancey St, J, M, Z to Essex St. ☎ 212 260 4555. Sun–Thurs 12.30–10pm, Fri & Sat 12.30–11pm.
Chef Ivan Orkin helms this popular ramen noodle joint adorned with a huge *papier-mâché*

mural. Menu highlights include the sesame noodles ($17), the spicy red chilli ramen ($16) and the steamed pork buns ($10).

Mission Chinese Food

MAP P.56, POCKET MAP E20
171 East Broadway. Subway F to East Broadway. ☎ 212 529 8800. Mon–Fri 5.30–10.45pm, Sat & Sun noon–4pm & 5.30–10.45pm.
Danny Bowien's cultish San Francisco Chinese fusion joint with a menu of small dishes like char siu pork cheeks ($16) and rice porridge with green tea noodles ($9), and large dishes like staff favourite thrice-cooked bacon ($19) and spicy mapo tofu ($18.50).

Sammy's Roumanian Steakhouse

MAP P.56, POCKET MAP E19
157 Chrystie St, at Delancey St. Subway B, D to Grand St, J, Z to Bowery, F to Lower East Side-Second Ave. ☎ 212 673 0330. Sun–Thurs 4–10pm, Fri & Sat 4–11pm.
This basement Jewish steakhouse gives diners more than they

THE LOWER EAST SIDE

Katz's Deli

bargained for: schmaltzy songs, delicious food (topped off by home-made *rugalach* and egg creams for dessert) and chilled vodka.

Bars

Back Room

MAP P.56, POCKET MAP F19
102 Norfolk St, between Delancey and Rivington sts. Subway F to Delancey St, J, M, Z to Essex St. Sun–Thurs 7pm–3am, Fri & Sat 7.30pm–4am.

With a hidden, back-alley entrance, this former speakeasy was reputedly once a haunt of gangster Meyer Lansky. Booze is served in teacups as a nod to its Prohibition days.

Barrio Chino

MAP P.56, POCKET MAP E20
253 Broome St, at Orchard St. Subway B, D to Grand St. Daily 9am–1am.

Don't be confused by the Chinese lanterns or drink umbrellas – the speciality here is tequila, and there are over fifty to choose from. Shots are even served with the traditional sangria chaser.

The Delancey's rooftop

Forgtmenot

MAP P.56, POCKET MAP E20
138 Division St, between Ludlow and Orchard sts. Subway F to East Broadway. Daily 10am–1am.

This quirky bar and restaurant is smothered with bumper stickers, graffiti and 1980s memorabilia, a favourite local hangout that also serves tasty pub food. Try the watermelon spicy margarita.

Libation

MAP P.56, POCKET MAP E19
137 Ludlow St, between Stanton and Rivington sts. Subway F to Delancey St, J, M, Z to Essex St. Wed 5pm–midnight, Thurs 5pm–1am, Fri 5pm–4am, Sat noon–4am, Sun noon–midnight.

A sexy lounge spanning two floors. It's a bit eclectic, with $12 cocktails, a boozy weekend brunch ($45; bottomless mimosas and bloody Marys), American-style tapas menu, and DJs spinning '80s, hip-hop and everything in between.

Welcome to the Johnsons

MAP P.56, POCKET MAP E19
123 Rivington St, between Essex and Norfolk sts. Subway F to Delancey St, J, M, Z to Essex St. Mon–Fri 3pm–4am, Sat & Sun 1–4am.

This 1970s throwback dive bar is all about rockin' out and chillin' out, and you can do both without any friction. Good beers, great bartenders.

Clubs

Bob Bar

MAP P.56, POCKET MAP E19
235 Eldridge St, between Houston and Stanton sts. Subway F to Lower East Side-Second Ave. Wed–Sat 7pm–4am, Sun 7pm–2am.

This cosy bar turns into one of the best dance parties in town after midnight, with DJs spinning a mix of hip-hop, reggae and R&B. Cover from $5.

The Delancey

MAP P.56, POCKET MAP F19

168 Delancey St, at Clinton St. Subway F to Delancey St, J, M, Z to Essex St. ⓦ www.thedelancey.com. Daily 5pm–4am.

Williamsburg hipsters meet Lower East Side chic at this rooftop lounge and nightclub. Things can get frisky in the basement, which pulsates with loud music and live acts.

Rumpus Room

MAP P.56, POCKET MAP E19

249 Eldridge St, at E Houston St. Subway F to Lower East Side-Second Ave. ☏ 212 777 5153, ⓦ rumpusroomnyc.com. Daily 10pm–4am.

The former digs of iconic Sapphire Lounge remains a popular student hangout, thanks to Smiths night on Sundays (yep, that really is Morrissey and co), and dance parties through the week. Usually no cover.

Music venues

Arlene's Grocery

MAP P.56, POCKET MAP E19

95 Stanton St, between Ludlow and Orchard sts. Subway F to Lower East Side-Second Ave. ☏ 212 358 1633, ⓦ www. arlenesgrocery.net. Daily 5pm–2am.

This intimate venue hosts free gigs by local indie talent every night. Monday (free) is "Rock and Roll Karaoke" night, when you can wail along (with a live band) to your favourite songs. Tues–Sun cover $5–10.

The Bowery Ballroom

MAP P.56, POCKET MAP E19

6 Delancey St, at the Bowery. Subway J, Z to Bowery, B, D to Grand St. ☏ 212 533 2111, ⓦ mercuryeastpresents.com. Daily from 7pm.

Great acoustics make this a favourite local venue to see well-known indie rock bands. Shows cost $15–55. Pay in cash at the *Mercury Lounge* box office (see

below), at the door or through Ticketweb.

Mercury Lounge

MAP P.56, POCKET MAP E19

217 E Houston St, between Ludlow and Essex sts. Subway F to Lower East Side-Second Ave. ☏ 212 260 4700, ⓦ www. mercuryeastpresents.com. Daily shows from 7pm.

The dark, medium-sized space showcases local, national and international pop and rock acts. Events cost around $10–25. Pay in cash at the box office, at the door or via Ticketweb.

Pianos

MAP P.56, POCKET MAP E19

158 Ludlow St, at Rivington St. Subway F to Delancey St, J, M, Z to Essex St. ☏ 212 505 3733, ⓦ www.pianosnyc.com. Daily 2pm–4am.

This converted piano factory hosts an endless roster of mostly rock bands (expect four choices nightly) in the back room ($8–10) and excellent DJs from 10pm.

Rockwood Music Hall

MAP P.56, POCKET MAP E19

196 Allen St, between Houston and Stanton sts. Subway F to Lower East Side-Second Ave. ☏ 212 614 2494, ⓦ rockwoodmusichall.com. Mon–Fri 5.30pm–4am, Sat & Sun 2.30pm–4am.

Come early: though there are no bad seats in the house. Seven nights of live music draw locals to this three-stage venue.

Slipper Room

MAP P.56, POCKET MAP E19

167 Orchard St, at Stanton St. Subway F to Second Ave. ☏ 212 253 7246, ⓦ slipperroom.com. Daily 7pm–2am.

Gilded ceilings and elaborate decor provide the backdrop for entertainment that ranges from neo-burlesque and cabaret to comedy and live music, including Seth Herzog's variety show, "Sweet" (Tues $10; cover other nights ranges $10–25).

The East Village

Once a solidly working-class refuge of immigrants, the East Village, ranging east of Broadway to Avenue D between Houston and 14th streets, became home to New York's nonconformist intelligentsia in the early part of the twentieth century; in the 1950s, it was one of the main haunts of the Beat poets – Kerouac, Burroughs, Ginsberg. By the 1980s it was home to radical artists, including Keith Haring, Jeff Koons and Jean-Michel Basquiat, while Chinese artist Ai Weiwei lived on East 7th and East 3rd streets between 1983 and 1993. During the Nineties, escalating rents forced many people out, and the East Village is no longer the hotbed of dissidence and artistry that it once was. Nevertheless, it remains one of Downtown Manhattan's most vibrant neighbourhoods, with boutiques, thrift stores, record shops, bars and restaurants, populated by old-world Ukrainians, students and Japanese hairdressers.

Astor Place

MAP P.64, POCKET MAP D18
Subway N, R, W to 8th St, #6 to Astor Place.
Astor Place marks the western fringe of the East Village, named after real-estate tycoon John Jacob Astor. Infamous for his greed, Astor was the wealthiest person in the US at the time of his death in 1848 (worth $115bn in modern terms). Beneath the replicated old-fashioned kiosk of the Astor Place subway station, the platform walls sport reliefs of beavers, recalling Astor's first big killings – in the fur trade. The teen hangout here is the balancing black steel cube *Alamo* (1967) by Tony Rosenthal, which dominates the centre of the intersection. In the 1830s, **Lafayette Street**, which runs south from Astor Place, was home to the city's wealthiest residents; **Colonnade Row**, a strip of four 1833 Greek Revival houses with Corinthian columns, is all that remains.

The stocky brownstone-and-brick building across Lafayette was once the **Astor Library**. Built with a bequest from Astor between 1853 and 1881, it was the first public library in New York. It became the Public Theater in 1967. **Astor Place Opera House** was erected on the corner of Astor Place and East 8th Street in 1847, infamous as the site of the Astor Place Riot two years later. Supporters of local stage-star Edwin Forrest tried to stop the performance of English Shakespearean actor William Macready, and in the resulting clashes 22 people died. The theatre closed in 1850.

Grace Church

MAP P.64, POCKET MAP D17
802 Broadway, at E 10th St. Subway N, R to 8th St. ☎ 212 254 2000, ⊕ www.gracechurchnyc.org. Daily noon–5pm. Free.
The lacy marble of **Grace Church** was designed and built in 1846 by James Renwick (of St Patrick's Cathedral fame) in a delicate neo-

Gothic style. Dark and aisled, with a flattened, web-vaulted ceiling, it was something of a society church in its day. Nowadays it is one of the city's most secretive escapes, and frequently offers shelter to the less fortunate.

Merchant's House Museum

MAP P.64, POCKET MAP D18
29 E 4th St, between Lafayette St and the Bowery. Subway B, D, F, M to Broadway-Lafayette, N, R, W to 8th St, #6 to Astor Place. ☎ 212 777 1089, Ⓦ merchantshouse.org. Thurs noon–8pm, Fri–Mon noon–5pm. $15.

Constructed in 1832, this elegant Federal-style row house offers a rare and intimate glimpse of domestic life in New York during the 1850s. The house was purchased by Seabury Tredwell in 1835, a successful metal merchant, when the area was an up-and-coming suburb for the middle class. Remarkably, much of the mid-nineteenth-century interior remains in pristine condition, largely thanks to Seabury's daughter Gertrude, who lived here until 1933 – it was preserved as a museum three years later. Highlights include furniture fashioned by New York's best cabinetmakers, the mahogany four-poster beds, and the tiny brass bells in the basement, used to summon the servants.

Cooper Union – Foundation Building

MAP P.64, POCKET MAP D18
7 E 7th St, Cooper Square, between Third and Fourth aves. Subway N, R to 8th St, #6 to Astor Place. ☎ 212 353 4100, Ⓦ cooper.edu.

Erected in 1859 by wealthy industrialist Peter Cooper (1791–1883) as a college for the poor, the **Foundation Building of Cooper Union** is best known as the place where, in 1860, Abraham Lincoln wowed an audience of top New Yorkers with his so-called "right makes might" speech, in which he boldly criticized the pro-slavery policies of the Southern states – an event that helped propel him to the White House later that year. In 1909 it was also the site of the first open meeting of the NAACP (National Association for the Advancement of Colored People), chaired by W.E.B. Du Bois. Today, Cooper Union is a prestigious art, engineering

The Cooper Union : Foundation Building

THE EAST VILLAGE

St. Mark's Place in the East Village

and architecture school, whose nineteenth-century glory is evoked with a statue of the benevolent Cooper by Augustus Saint-Gaudens just in front of the hall. From the entrance hall the guards normally allow you to walk downstairs to the Great Hall, where historical exhibits are displayed in the gallery outside.

St Mark's Place

MAP P.64, POCKET MAP D18–E18
Subway N, R, W to 8th St, #6 to Astor Place.
The East Village's main drag gets a name, not a number (it could have been called East 8th Street). **St Mark's Place** stretches east from Cooper Union to Tompkins Square Park. Between Third Avenue and Avenue A it's lined with souvenir stalls, punk and hippie-chic clothing shops and newly installed chain restaurants, signalling the end of the gritty atmosphere that had dominated this thoroughfare for years.

St Mark's Church in-the-Bowery

MAP P.64, POCKET MAP D17
131 E 10th St, at Second Ave. Subway N, R, W to 8th St, #6 to Astor Place. ☎ 212 674 6377, Ⓦ stmarksbowery.org.
In 1660, New Amsterdam Director-General Peter Stuyvesant built a small chapel here close to his farm, and was buried inside in 1672 (his tombstone is now set into the outer walls). The box-like Episcopalian house of worship that currently occupies this space was completed in 1799 over his tomb, and sports a Neoclassical portico that was added fifty years later. The church is still used for services and is normally locked – walk up to the office on the second floor (side door) and someone will let you in to see the vivid stained-glass windows. The church was home to Beat poetry readings in the 1950s, and in the 1960s the **St Mark's Poetry Project** (Ⓦ poetryproject.org) was founded here to ignite artistic and social change. It remains an important cultural rendezvous, with poetry readings Monday, Wednesday and Friday evenings at 8pm, dance performances by the Danspace Project (Ⓦ danspaceproject.org) and from New York Theatre Ballet (Ⓦ nytb.org).

Ukrainian Museum

MAP P.64, POCKET MAP D18
222 E 6th St, between Second and Third aves. Subway N, R, W to 8th St, #6 to Astor Place. ☎ 212 228 0110, Ⓦ ukrainianmuseum.org. Wed–Sun 11.30am–5pm. $8.
Dedicated to chronicling the history of the Ukrainian immigrant community. The varied collection contains ethnic items such as Ukrainian costumes and examples of the country's famous painted eggs; lectures are also held here.

The East Village

Russian & Turkish Baths

MAP P.64, POCKET MAP E17
268 E 10th St, between First Ave and Ave A. Subway L to First Ave. ☎ 212 674 9250, ⓦ russianturkishbaths.com. Mon, Tues, Thurs, Fri noon–10pm, Wed 10am–10pm, Sat 9am–10pm, Sun 8am–10pm. $48.

A neighbourhood landmark that's still going strong, with a an ice-cold pool, Russian sauna (filled with 20,000lbs of red-hot rocks), a modern cherry-wood sauna and a Turkish steam room, as well as massage rooms and a restaurant. Free soap, towel, robe and slippers. Check the website for details of mixed and single-sex sessions.

Tompkins Square Park

MAP P.64, POCKET MAP F17–F18
Subway L to First Ave, N, R to 8th St, #6 to Astor Place.

Fringed by avenues A and B and East 7th and East 10th streets, **Tompkins Square Park** was one of the city's great centres for political protest and homes of radical thought. In the 1960s, regular demonstrations were organized here, and during the 1980s, the park was more or less a shantytown until the homeless were kicked out

Tompkins Square Park

in 1991. Today it has a playground, dog run and a summer jazz festival. The famous saxophonist and composer Charlie "Bird" Parker lived at 151 Avenue B, a simple whitewashed 1849 house with a Gothic doorway (closed to the public). Bird lived here from 1950 until 1954, when he died of a pneumonia-related haemorrhage.

Alphabet City

MAP P.64, POCKET MAP F18
Subway L to First Ave, N, R, W to 8th St, #6 to Astor Place.

Named after the avenues known as A–D, where the island bulges east beyond the city's grid structure, **Alphabet City** was not long ago a notoriously unsafe patch, with burnt-out buildings that were well-known dens for the brisk heroin trade. Now it's one of the most dramatically revitalized areas of Manhattan: crime is down, many of the vacant lots have been made into community gardens, and the streets have become the haunt of moneyed twenty-somethings and students. These avenues have some of the coolest bars, cafés and stores in the city.

Community Gardens

MAP P.64, POCKET MAP F18
Subway L to First Ave, N, R, W to 8th St, #6 to Astor Place.

In the 1970s, pockets of the East Village burned to the ground after cuts in the city's fire-fighting budget closed many of the local firehouses. Green Thumb, founded in 1978, helped locals transform vacant lots into vibrant green spaces, turning the rubble-filled messes into some of the prettiest and most verdant spaces in lower Manhattan. Of particular note is the **East 6th Street and Avenue B** affair, overgrown with wildflowers, vegetables, trees and roses. Other gardens include the very serene **6 B/C Botanical Garden** on East 6th Street between B and C, and **Loisaida Garden** on East 4th Street between B and C.

Shops

Buffalo Exchange

MAP P.64, POCKET MAP E17
332 E 11th St, at Second Ave. Subway L
to First Ave. Mon–Sat 11am–8pm, Sun
noon–7pm.
US clothes exchange that started in
Arizona in the 1970s; bring in your
former threads for a trade-in or
cash on the spot.

Kiehl's

MAP P.64, POCKET MAP D17
109 Third Ave, at E 13th St. Subway L
to Third Ave. Mon–Sat 10am–9pm, Sun
11am–7pm.
An exclusive 160-year-old
pharmacy that sells its own range
of natural ingredient-based classic
creams, soaps and oils.

Obscura Antiques and Oddities

MAP P.64, POCKET MAP E17
207 Ave A, between E 12th and E 13th sts.
Subway L to First Ave. Daily noon–8pm.
This spooky East Village classic
specializes in antiques, rare
taxidermy and strange, freaky
artefacts – owners Mike Zohn and
Evan Michelson even have a show on
the Discovery Channel (*Oddities*).

St Mark's Comics

MAP P.64, POCKET MAP D18
11 St Mark's Place, between Second and
Third aves. Subway #6 to Astor Place.
Mon & Tues 10am–11pm, Wed 9am–1am,
Thurs–Sat 10am–1am, Sun 11am–11pm.
Pilgrimage site for comic, manga
and graphic novel fans from all
over the world, with plenty of rare
memorabilia.

Strand Bookstore

MAP P.64, POCKET MAP D17
828 Broadway, at E 12th St. Subway N, R, Q,
L, W, #4, #5, #6 to Union Square. Mon–Sat
9.30am–10.30pm, Sun 11am–10.30pm.
With about eighteen miles of
books and a stock of more than
2.5 million, this is the largest book
operation in the city.

Strand Bookstore

Tokio 7

MAP P.64, POCKET MAP E18
83 E 7th St, between First and Second
aves. Subway #6 to Astor Place. Daily
noon–8pm.
Attractive secondhand and vintage
designer consignment items;
known for its flashy, eccentric
selection – think plenty of Gaultier,
Moschino and McQueen – rather
than basic black.

Toy Tokyo

MAP P.64, POCKET MAP E18
91 Second Ave, between E 5th and E 6th
sts. Subway #6 to Astor Place. Sun–Thurs
1–9pm, Fri & Sat 12.30–9.30pm.
Dizzying ensemble of Asian toys
and cult memorabilia, mostly from
Japan and Hong Kong: action
figures, vintage robots, roto-plastic
figures and wind-ups.

Trash 'n' Vaudeville

MAP P.64, POCKET MAP E18
96 E 7th St, between First Ave and Ave
A. Subway #6 to Astor Place. Mon–Thurs
noon–8pm, Fri 11.30am–8.30pm, Sat
11.30am–9pm, Sun 1–7.30pm.
Formerly located on St Mark's
Place, this has been a Goth and
punk mecca since the 1970s. Great

clothes, new and "antique", in the true East Village spirit.

Cafés and snacks

Artichoke

MAP P.64, POCKET MAP E17
321 E 14th St, between First and Second aves. Subway L to First Ave. Daily 11am–5am.

Fabulous late-night pizza slices to take away in the early hours, with just a few choices: sumptuous cheese-laden Sicilian ($4.75), Margherita ($4.75), crab ($5) or the trademark artichoke-spinach pie, topped with a super-creamy sauce ($6).

B & H Dairy

MAP P.64, POCKET MAP E18
127 Second Ave, between E 7th St and St Mark's Place. Subway #6 to Astor Place. Mon–Fri 7am–11.30pm, Sat & Sun 7am–midnight.

Good veggie choice, this tiny luncheonette serves home-made soup, *challah* and *latkes*. You can also create your own juice combination to stay or go.

Big Gay Ice Cream Shop

MAP P.64, POCKET MAP E18
125 E 7th St, between First Ave and Ave A. Subway L to First Ave. Winter: Sun–Thurs 1–10pm, Fri & Sat 1–11pm; summer Sun–Wed 11am–11pm, Fri & Sat 11am–midnight.

The utterly addictive ice cream here has cheekily named flavours including the "salty pimp" (vanilla, dulce de leche, sea salt and chocolate dip) and the "gobbler" (pumpkin butter, maple syrup and pie pieces).

Café Mogador

MAP P.64, POCKET MAP E18
101 St Mark's Place, between First Ave and Ave A. Subway #6 to Astor Place. Sun–Thurs 9am–midnight, Fri & Sat 9am–1am.

Young hipster-types frequent this romantic, Moroccan-themed mainstay. Expect crowds and stalled service, but the food is more than worth the wait. Try the *charmoulla* with either chicken or lamb. The brunch (Sat–Sun 9am–4pm) is especially good, with a choice of delicate mains such as Moroccan Benedict (eggs in a spicy tomato sauce) served with orange juice, coffee or tea for $19.

Cafe Mogador

Crif Dogs

MAP P.64, POCKET MAP E18
113 St Mark's Place, between First Ave
and Ave A. Subway #6 to Astor Place. Sun–
Thurs noon–2am, Fri & Sat noon–4am.
Hot-dog aficionados swear by
these deep-fried, shiny wieners
bursting with flavour (from
$3.50), enjoyed Philly-steak style,
smothered in cheese, or topped
with avocado and bacon.

Otto's Tacos

MAP P.64, POCKET MAP E17
141 Second Ave, between E 9th St and
St Mark's Place. Subway #6 to Astor
Place. Sun–Thurs 11am–11pm, Fri & Sat
11am–midnight.
No frills, rustic space for delicious
corn tacos stuffed with carne
asada (beef; $4), carnitas (pork;
$3) and chicken ($3), all perfectly
seasoned and accompanied by
chips and guacamole.

Sarita's Mac & Cheese (S'Mac)

MAP P.64, POCKET MAP E17
197 First Ave, at E 12th St. Subway L to
First Ave. Sun–Thurs 11am–11pm, Fri & Sat
11am–midnight.
Indulge your macaroni and
cheese cravings at this homey
joint, with ten creative varieties
on offer, blending cheddar,
gruyère, brie and goat's cheese
with herbs and meats. Pick
your portion sizes: nosh,
major munch or mongo
($6.25–21).

Superiority Burger

MAP P.64, POCKET MAP E18
430 E 9th St, between Avenue A and First
Ave. Subway #6 to Astor Place. Daily
11.30am–10pm.
This small hole-in-the-wall, with
just six seats inside (designed
like old-fashioned school desks),
has garnered a cult following for
its creative vegetarian burgers.
The "superiority burger" (made
from grains, beans and a little
tofu) is a nutty, juicy delight with
cheese ($6).

Veselka

Veniero's Pasticceria & Caffè

MAP P.64, POCKET MAP E17
342 E 11th St, between First and Second
aves. Subway L to First Ave; #6 to Astor
Place. Sun–Thurs 8am–midnight, Fri & Sat
8am–1am.
A beloved East Village institution,
tempting the neighbourhood
with heavenly cheesecake ($4.50),
tiramisu ($5.75) and Italian pastries
since 1894 – the almond torte ($5)
is their most famous snack. Sit
inside the old-world marble-floor
café, or takeout.

Veselka

MAP P.64, POCKET MAP E17
144 Second Ave, corner of E 9th St. Subway
#6 to Astor Place. Daily 24hr.
This popular Ukrainian diner has
been an East Village institution
since the 1950s, offering fine
home-made borscht from $5.50,
kielbasa sausage ($19), *pierogi*
($8.50) and great burgers.

Restaurants

Brick Lane Curry House

MAP P.64, POCKET MAP E18

Il Posto Accanto

79 Second Ave, between E 4th and E 5th sts. Subway #6 to Astor Place. ☎ 212 979 8787. Sun–Thurs noon–11pm, Fri & Sat noon–1am.
Hands-down the best Indian in the East Village thanks to its expanded selection of traditional favourites ($16–28).

Empellón Al Pastor

MAP P.64, POCKET MAP E18
132 St Mark's Place, at Ave A. Subway L to First Ave. ☎ 646 833 7039. Mon–Thurs 4pm–midnight, Fri 4pm–2am, Sat 1pm–2am, Sun 1pm–midnight.
Part of the Alex Stupak stable, this welcoming restaurant focuses on just one dish: Mexican-style tacos al pastor ($6) made with spit-roasted pork shoulder, rubbed with chilli and dressed with salsa and pineapple, all served on house-made corn tortillas. Margaritas are $12.

Hasaki

MAP P.64, POCKET MAP D17
210 E 9th St, at Stuyvesant St. Subway #6 to Astor Place. ☎ 212 473 3327. Tues–Thurs 5.30–11pm, Fri noon–3pm & 5.30–11pm, Sat noon–4pm & 5.30–11pm, Sun noon–4pm & 5.30–10.30pm.
Some of the best sushi in the city is served at this popular but mellow

downstairs cubbyhole. Sit at the bar and the chefs will try to tempt you with a variety of improvised dishes (six pieces from $30).

Ikinari Steak

MAP P.64, POCKET MAP E17
90 E 10th St, between Third and Fourth aves. Subway #6 to Astor Place. ☎ 917 388 3546. Daily 11am–11pm.
This Japanese steakhouse chain is best known for its lack of chairs (instead there are 40 standing stations, and just 10 table seats) – lunch deals for a 10 ounce (300g) steak with salad, soup and rice are $24, with other cuts priced by the gram (a 200g or 7-ounce sirloin is just $10.50 for example).

Il Posto Accanto

MAP P.64, POCKET MAP F18
190 E 2nd Street, between aves A and B. Subway F to Lower East Side-Second Ave. ☎ 212 228 3562. Mon–Fri noon–3am, Sat & Sun noon–3.30pm & 5.30pm–3am.
Nab a spot at a high wooden table at this small, intimate wine bar and restaurant serving a vast array of Italian reds by the glass. You can easily make a meal from the excellent small plates of pasta

($14.50–19), panini ($10.50–11.50) and the like.

Ippudo

MAP P.64, POCKET MAP D17
65 Fourth Ave, between E 9th and E 10th sts. Subway #6 to Astor Place. ☎ 212 388 0088. Mon–Fri 11am–3.30pm & 5–12.30pm, Sat 11am–11.30pm, Sun 11am–10.30pm.

The first overseas outpost of Fukuoka-based "ramen king" Shigemi Kawahara, this popular Japanese ramen shop offers steaming bowls of classic *tonkotsu*-style noodles for $17, as well as tasty pork buns.

Mermaid Inn

MAP P.64, POCKET MAP E18
96 Second Ave, between E 5th and 6th sts. Subway #6 to Astor Place. ☎ 212 674 5870. Mon–Thurs 5–10pm, Fri 5–10.30pm, Sat 4–10.30pm, Sun 4–10pm.

Serious seafood restaurant serving simple and fresh dishes in a Maine boathouse atmosphere. There's an excellent raw bar, and specials change daily depending on the catch; highlights include the littleneck clams (half dozen $12) and lobster roll ($29).

Mighty Quinn's Barbeque

MAP P.64, POCKET MAP E18
103 Second Ave, at E 6th St. Subway L to Third Ave. ☎ 212 677 3733. Sun–Thurs 11.30am–11pm, Fri & Sat 11.30am–midnight.

Texas and Carolinas-inspired slow-smoked barbecue, with a no-nonsense menu of lip-smacking burnt ends ($9.85), pulled pork ($8.95) and ribs ($10.45), accompanied by burnt-end baked beans (from $3.45).

Momofuku Noodle Bar

MAP P.64, POCKET MAP E17
171 First Ave, between E 10th and E 11th sts. Subway L to First Ave, #6 to Astor Place. ☎ 212 777 7773. Mon–Thurs noon–4.30pm & 5.30–11pm, Fri noon–4.30pm & 5.30pm–1am, Sat noon–4pm & 5.30pm–1am, Sun noon–4pm & 5.30–11pm.

Celebrated chef David Chang's first restaurant, where his simplest creations are still the best: silky steamed pork buns with hoisin sauce and pickled cucumbers ($13), or steaming bowls of chicken and pork ramen noodles ($18). It's also worth checking out Christina Tosi's Momofuku offshoot the *Milk Bar* (251 E 13th St, at Second Ave; Sun–Thurs 10am–midnight, Fri & Sat 10am–1am), which serves sweet treats.

Motorino

MAP P.64, POCKET MAP E17
349 E 12th St, near First Ave. Subway L to First Ave. ☎ 212 777 2644. Mon–Thurs & Sun 11am–midnight, Fri & Sat 11am–1am.

Some of the best brick-oven pizza in the city, with a tongue-tingling Stracciatella (basil, olive oil and sea salt) and a cherry stone clam masterpiece.

Prune

MAP P.64, POCKET MAP E19
54 E 1st St, between First and Second aves. Subway F to Lower East Side-Second Ave. ☎ 212 677 6221. Mon–Fri 5.30–11pm, Sat & Sun 10am–3.30pm & 5.30–11pm.

Cramped, yet adventurous and full of surprises, this modern American bistro delivers one of the city's most exciting dining experiences, serving dishes such as sweetbreads wrapped in bacon, seared sea bass with Berber spices, and buttermilk ice cream with pistachio puff pastry. A choice of over ten Bloody Marys gives weekend brunch a bit of a kick.

Saxon & Parole

MAP P.64, POCKET MAP D19
316 Bowery, at Bleecker St. Subway #6 to Bleecker St. ☎ 212 254 0350. Mon–Thurs 6–10pm, Fri 5–11pm, Sat 10am–3pm & 5–11pm, Sun 10am–3pm & 6–10pm.

Modern American grill with amazing food; tea-smoked mussels, horseradish-whipped potatoes and whisky jelly with steaks, washed down with a celery gimlet and rounded off with the warm chocolate pudding with marshmallow and whiskey barrel smoke.

Tim Ho Wan

MAP P.64, POCKET MAP D17
85 Fourth Ave, at E 10th St. Subway #6 to Astor Place. ☎ 212 228 2800. Sun–Thurs 10am–10pm, Fri & Sat 10am–11pm.
This cult dim sum chain from Hong Kong – famed for being the world's cheapest Michelin-starred restaurant – opened here in 2016, and waits of 2–3 hours for a table (no reservations) are still the norm. It's worth the wait for aficionados, as the quality is very high and it's the closest thing to Hong Kong standards in Manhattan.

Bars

Angel's Share

MAP P.64, POCKET MAP D17
8 Stuyvesant St, between E 9th St and Third Ave. Subway #6 to Astor Place. Sun–Wed, 6pm–1.30am, Thurs 7pm–2.30am, Fri & Sat 6pm–1.30am.
This serene, Japanese-style haven is a great date spot and the cocktails are some of the best in the city. It can be hard to find, though: walk through the *Yokocho* restaurant, up the stairs.

Bar Veloce

MAP P.64, POCKET MAP E17
175 Second Ave, between E 11th and E 12th sts. Subway L to Third Ave. Mon–Thurs 5pm–1am, Fri & Sat 3pm–2am, Sun 3pm–1am.
Stylish Italian wine bar fit for the Mod Squad, with excellent hors d'oeuvres and a fine wine list (by the glass from $11).

Burp Castle

MAP P.64, POCKET MAP D18
41 E 7th St, between Second and Third aves. Subway #6 to Astor Place. Mon–Fri 5pm–midnight, Sat & Sun 4pm–2am.
Though bartenders no longer wear monks' habits and choral music is rarely piped in, you are encouraged to speak in tones below a whisper. Oh, and there are still over 550 different types of beer.

Death & Co

MAP P.64, POCKET MAP E18
433 E 6th St, between First Ave and Ave A. Subway L to First Ave. ☎ 212 388 0882. Sun–Thurs 6pm–2am, Fri & Sat 6pm–3am.
Celebrated cocktail bar with a stylish speakeasy theme (bartenders in bow ties and braces) and a huge menu of lavish drinks, from "Cloud Nine" (absinthe, rum, egg white and apple eau de vie; $23) to the "Clockwork Orange" (gin, vermouth, Mandarine Napoléon cognac and Mirabelle plum; $16).

KGB Bar

MAP P.64, POCKET MAP E18
85 E 4th St, at Second Ave. Subway F to Lower East Side-Second Ave, #6 to Astor Place. Daily 7pm–4am.
A dark bar on the second floor, which was the Ukrainian Labor Home social club in the 1950s, but is better known now for its marquee literary readings.

Manitoba's

MAP P.64, POCKET MAP F18
99 Ave B, between E 6th and 7th sts. Subway L to First Ave, #6 to Astor Place. Daily 4pm–4am.
Run by Dick Manitoba, lead singer of the punk group The Dictators, the kickin' jukebox and rough-and-tumble vibe at this spot make it a drinkers' favourite.

McSorley's Old Ale House

MAP P.64, POCKET MAP D18
15 E 7th St, between Second and Third aves. Subway #6 to Astor Place. Mon–Sat 11am–1am, Sun 1pm–1am.
Yes, it's often full of tourists and NYU students, but you'll be drinking in history at this landmark bar that opened in 1854 – it's the oldest pub in the city. Today, it only pours its own ale – light or dark.

Zum Schneider

MAP P.64, POCKET MAP F18

107 Ave C, at E 7th St. Subway L to 1st Ave, #6 to Astor Place. Mon–Thurs 5pm–1am, Fri 4pm–2am, Sat 1pm–2am, Sun 1pm–midnight.

A Bavarian beer hall (and indoor garden) with a mega-list of brews from the Fatherland, and wursts too. Cash only.

Clubs

Joe's Pub

MAP P.64, POCKET MAP D18
425 Lafayette St, between Astor Place and E 4th St. Subway #6 to Astor Place. ☎ 212 539 8770.

The word "pub" is a misnomer for this swanky nightspot that features a vast array of musical, cabaret and dramatic performances. Shows nightly at 7.30pm, 9.30pm and 11pm (tickets $20–30).

Pyramid Club

MAP P.64, POCKET MAP E18
101 Ave A, between E 6th and 7th sts. Subway L to First Ave, #6 to Astor Place. ☎ 212 228 4888. Thurs–Sat 8pm–4am, Sun 8pm–midnight

This small club has been an East Village standby for years, but it's the insanely popular 1980s Dance Parties on Thursday to Saturday that are not to be missed ($6).

Music and poetry venues

Bowery Poetry Club

MAP P.64, POCKET MAP D19
308 Bowery, at Bleecker St. Subway N, Q, R, L, #4, #5, #6 to Union Square. Poetry 3.30–10.30pm, Mon 6–11pm. ☎ 212 353 1600, ⓦ www.bowerypoetry.com.

The old Bowery Poetry Club reopened in 2013 as a joint venue with Duane Park (burlesque shows on Sat), with the poetry programme presented by Bowery Arts + Science on Sundays ($8–10) and Mondays ($15–20).

Nuyorican Poets Café

MAP P.64, POCKET MAP F18
236 E 3rd St, between aves B and C. Subway F to Lower East Side–Second Ave. ☎ 212 505 8183, ⓦ nuyorican.org. Daily noon–2am.

The godfather of all slam venues often features stars of the poetry world who pop in unannounced. SlamOpen on Wednesdays 9pm (except the first Wednesday of every month) and the Friday Night Slam (10pm) cost $10 and $13 respectively. The café was founded in 1973 by Puerto Rican poet Miguel Algarín and playwright Miguel Piñero, moving to this location in 1980.

Otto's Shrunken Head

MAP P.64, POCKET MAP F17
538 E 14th St, between aves A and B. Subway L to First Ave. ☎ 212 228 2240, ⓦ www.ottosshrunkenhead.com. Daily 2pm–4am.

This East Village joint is hard to pigeonhole; a Tiki bar that hosts live indie and punk rock bands, as well as some of the most popular club nights on the island. Weekends also see a host of rock/punk parties. Usually no cover.

Joe's Pub

The West Village

For many visitors, the West Village, Greenwich Village – or simply "the Village" – is the most-loved neighbourhood in New York. It sports refined Federal and Greek Revival townhouses and a busy late-night streetlife, while cosy restaurants, bars and cafés clutter every corner – many of the attractions that first brought bohemians here around the start of World War I. The area proved fertile ground for struggling artists and intellectuals, and the neighbourhood's clubs and off-Broadway theatres came to define Village life, laying the path for rebellious, countercultural groups and musicians in the 1960s; John Coltrane, Bob Dylan and Jimmy Hendrix all built their early careers here. Today, the central part of the Village is dominated by the sprawling New York University campus, adding a youthful edge to this fashionable, historic and increasingly expensive corner of Manhattan.

Washington Square Park

MAP P.76, POCKET MAP C18
Subway A, B, C, D, E, F to West 4th St, N, R, W to 8th St.

The natural centre of the Village is **Washington Square Park**. Memorialized in Henry James's 1880 novel *Washington Square*, the city completed an extensive renovation of the park in 2012, though only the row of elegant Greek Revival mansions on its northern edge – the "solid, honourable dwellings" that James

Washington Square Park

described – remind visitors of the area's more illustrious past.

Today, all these buildings belong to New York University (NYU). The most imposing monument in the park is Stanford White's **Washington Arch**, built in 1892 to commemorate the centenary of George Washington's presidential inauguration.

During the spring and summer months, the square becomes a combination of a running track, performance venue, giant chess tournament and social club; boiling over with life as skateboards flip, dogs run and guitar notes crash through the urgent cries of performers calling for the crowd's attention.

Church of the Ascension

MAP P.76, POCKET MAP C17
Fifth Ave and W 10th St. Subway N, Q, R, L, #4, #5, #6 to Union Square, F, L at 14th St. ① 212 254 8620, ⓦ ascensionnyc.org. Mon–Sat noon–1pm, Sun services only at 9am, 11am, 7pm. Free.

A small, restored structure originally built in 1841 by Richard Upjohn (architect of Trinity Church), the **Church of the Ascension** was later redecorated by Stanford White. Duck inside to see the gracefully toned La Farge altar painting and some fine stained glass on view.

First Presbyterian Church

MAP P.76, POCKET MAP C17
12 W 12th St, at Fifth Ave. Subway N, Q, R, L, #4, #5, #6 to Union Square, F, L at 14th St. ① 212 675 6150, ⓦ fpcnyc.org. Mon, Wed & Fri noon–12.30pm, Sun 11am service only. Free.

Continuing the Gothic theme, Joseph Wells's bulky, chocolate-brown **First Presbyterian Church**, just across 11th Street from the Church of the Ascension, was completed in 1845 with a crenellated tower modelled on the one at Magdalen College in Oxford, England. Inside, you'll find carved black-walnut pews, a soaring

altarpiece and fabulous Tiffany stained-glass windows, installed between 1893 and 1916.

Jefferson Market Courthouse and Patchin Place

MAP P.76, POCKET MAP B17
425 Sixth Ave, at W 10th St. Subway A, B, C, D, E, F, M to West 4th St, #1 to Christopher St-Sheridan Sq. ① 212 243 4334. Library open Mon–Thurs 10am–8pm, Fri & Sat 10am–5pm, Sun 1–5pm.

Known for its fanciful clock tower, the nineteenth-century **Jefferson Market Courthouse** is an imposing High Victorian-style edifice, complete with gargoyles, which first served as an indoor market but went on to be a firehouse, jail, and finally a women's detention centre before enjoying its current incarnation as a public library. Adjacent to it and opening onto West 10th Street, **Patchin Place** (closed to the public) is a tiny mews constructed in 1848, whose neat row houses were home to the reclusive Djuna Barnes for more than forty years. Patchin Place has also been home to e.e. cummings, Marlon Brando, Ezra Pound and Eugene O'Neill.

Bleecker Street

MAP P.76, POCKET MAP B18
Subway A, B, C, D, E, F to West 4th St, #1 to Christopher St-Sheridan Sq.

Cutting across from the Bowery to Hudson Street, **Bleecker Street**, with its touristy concentration of shops, bars and restaurants, is to some extent the Main Street of the Village. It has all the best reasons you come to this part of town: all-day cafés, late-night bars, cheap record stores, traditional bakeries and food shops, and the occasional good restaurant or pizzeria.

At Sixth Avenue, the Italian-Renaissance-style **Our Lady of Pompeii Church**, built in 1929, hints at the area's Italian past; *Faicco's* butchers and *Rocco's* (best known for its crunchy nut *cannoli*) are still here, as well as celebrated deli *Murray's Cheese* (see page 79). Bob Dylan lived for a time at 161 West 4th St, and the cover of his iconic 1963 *Freewheelin'* album was shot a few paces away on Jones Street, just off Bleecker.

Sheridan Square and Christopher Park

MAP P.76, POCKET MAP B18
Subway #1 to Christopher St-Sheridan Sq.
Confusingly, **Christopher Park** holds a pompous-looking statue of Civil War cavalry commander General Sheridan, though **Sheridan Square** is actually the next space down, where West 4th Street meets Washington Place. Historically, the area is better known, however, as the scene of one of the worst and bloodiest of New York's Draft Riots, when a marauding mob assembled here in 1863 and attacked members of the black community. Violence also erupted here in 1969 during the Stonewall Riots. The event is commemorated by George Segal's **Gay Liberation Monument**, unveiled in 1992. Further north, 66 Perry St, between Bleecker and West 4th Street, was used as the exterior of Carrie's apartment in *Sex and the City*, while there's almost always a queue of people waiting outside lauded *Magnolia Bakery* at Bleecker and West 11th St (see page 80). The historic *White Horse Tavern*, over at West 11th St and Hudson, is where legend claims Dylan Thomas had his last drink (see page 82).

Christopher Street

MAP P.76, POCKET MAP B18
Subway #1 to Christopher St-Sheridan Sq.
The Village's main gay artery runs from Sixth Avenue to West Street, passing by many a gay bar, sex toy shop and café. The lively

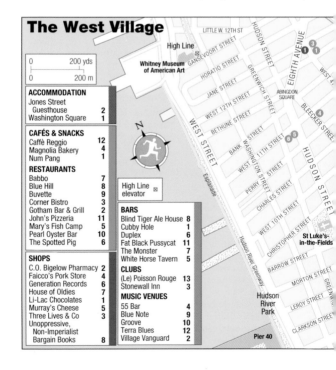

The West Village

High Line
Whitney Museum of American Art
High Line elevator

LITTLE W. 12TH ST
GANSEVOORT STREET
HORATIO STREET
JANE STREET
WEST 12TH STREET
BETHUNE STREET
BANK STREET
WEST 11TH STREET
PERRY STREET
CHARLES STREET
WEST 10TH STREET
CHRISTOPHER STREET
BARROW STREET
MORTON STREET
LEROY STREET
CLARKSON STREET

HUDSON STREET
GREENWICH STREET
ABINGDON SQUARE
EIGHTH AVENUE
WEST 4
BLEECKER STREET
HUDSON STREET
WASHINGTON STREET
GREENWICH
WEST STREET
Hudson River Greenway
Esplanade
St Luke's-in-the-Fields
Hudson River Park
Pier 40

0   200 yds
0   200 m

street's weekend cruise scene is still strong, although the domain is by no means as exclusively gay as it once was.

Bedford Street

MAP P.76, POCKET MAP B18
Subway #1 to Christopher St-Sheridan Sq.
Bedford Street runs west off Seventh Avenue to become one of the quietest and most desirable Village addresses. Edna St Vincent Millay, the young poet and playwright, lived at no. 75 1/2. At only 9ft wide, it is one of the narrowest houses in the city. The brick and clapboard structure next door at no. 77 is the **Isaacs-Hendricks House**, built in 1799; it is the oldest house in the Village. The building at no. 90, right on the corner of Grove Street (above the *Little Owl*), served as the exterior for Monica's apartment in *Friends*, though the TV series was shot entirely in L.A. studios. Opposite is 17 Grove St, one of the most

Bedford Street no. 75 1/2

complete wood-frame houses in the city, built in 1822.

Grove Street

MAP P.76, POCKET MAP B18
Subway #1 to Christopher St–Sheridan Sq.
Turn left down **Grove Street** from the *Little Owl* and you'll find Grove Court just off the street, one of the neighbourhood's most attractive and exclusive little mews. Heading back to Seventh Avenue on Grove Street, keep an eye out for *Marie's Crisis Café* at no. 59. Now a piano bar, this was the site of the rented rooms where English revolutionary writer and philosopher Thomas Paine died in 1809. Paine, who was reviled in England for his support of both the American and French revolutions, was the author of the eighteenth century's three bestselling pamphlets; *Common Sense*, published in 1776, is generally credited with turning public opinion in favour of US independence. The current building dates from 1839, the café named in part after Paine's masterful essay *The American Crisis*.

St Luke's Place

MAP P.76, POCKET MAP B18
Subway #1 to Christopher St–Sheridan Sq.
One block south of Bedford Street is a section of Leroy Street known as **St. Luke's Place**; no. 10 was used as the exterior of the Cosby house (from the beloved 1980s TV show), while no. 6 is the former residence of Jimmy Walker, an extravagant mayor of New York in the 1920s.

NY City AIDS Memorial

MAP P.76, POCKET MAP B17
St. Vincent's Hospital Park (West 12th St and Greenwich Ave). Ⓦ nycaidsmemorial.org.
Inaugurated in 2016, the **NY City AIDS Memorial** is a moving tribute to the more than 100,000 New Yorkers that have died from AIDS since the 1970s. The memorial comprises a giant steel canopy, with granite paving stones underneath designed by visual artist Jenny Holzer, featuring lines from Walt Whitman's poem *Song of Myself*.

St Luke's Place

Shops

C.O. Bigelow Pharmacy

MAP P.76, POCKET MAP C17
414 Sixth Ave, between W 8th and 9th sts.
Subway A, B, C, D, E, F, M to W 4th St; #1 to
Christopher St. Mon–Fri 7.30am–9pm, Sat
8.30am–7pm, Sun 8.30am–5.30pm.
Established in 1882, this is the
oldest apothecary in the country
– the Victorian shop-fittings
are still in place. Specializes in
homeopathic remedies.

Faicco's Pork Store

MAP P.76, POCKET MAP B18
260 Bleecker St, between Morton and Leroy
sts. Subway A, B, C, D, E, F, M to W 4th St.
Tues–Sat 9am–6pm, Sun 9am–2pm.
This old-school Italian butcher
serves some of the best-value meats,
Italian products and sandwiches in
the city.

Generation Records

MAP P.76, POCKET MAP C18
210 Thompson St, between Bleecker and
W 3rd sts. Subway A, B, C, D, E, F, M to W
4th St. Sun–Thurs noon–9pm, Fri & Sat
noon–10pm.
The focus here is on hardcore,
metal and punk, with some indie
rock thrown in. New CDs, vinyl
and records on offer.

House of Oldies

MAP P.76, POCKET MAP B18
35 Carmine St, between Bleecker St and
Bedford St. Subway A, B, C, D, E, F, M to
W 4th St; #1 to Houston St. Tues–Sat
9am–5pm.
This shop specializes in rare and
out-of-print vinyl records from the
1950s, 1960s and 1970s.

Li-Lac Chocolates

MAP P.76, POCKET MAP B17
40 Eighth Ave, at Jane St. Subway A, C, E, L,
#1, #2, #3 to 14th St. Mon–Sat 11am–8pm,
Sun 11am–7pm.
Delicious chocolates handmade on
the premises since 1923, including
fresh fudge and hand-moulded
Liberties and Empire States.

Murray's Cheese

Murray's Cheese

MAP P.76, POCKET MAP B18
254 Bleecker St, at Cornelia St. Subway
A, B, C, D, E, F, M to W 4th St, #1 to
Christopher St. Mon–Sat 8am–9pm, Sun
9am–8pm.
The exuberant and entertaining
staff make any visit to this cheese-
lovers' mecca a treat.

Three Lives & Co

MAP P.76, POCKET MAP B18
154 W 10th St, at Waverly Place. Subway
A, B, C, D, E, F, M to W 4th St, #1 to
Christopher St. Mon–Sat 10.30am–8.30pm,
Sun noon–7pm.
Excellent literary bookstore that
has an especially good selection of
books by and for women, as well as
general titles.

Unoppressive, Non-Imperialist Bargain Books

MAP P.76, POCKET MAP B18
34 Carmine St, between Bleecker and
Bedford sts. Subway A, B, C, D, E, F, M to W
4th St, #1 to Houston St. Mon–Thurs & Sun
11am–10pm, Fri & Sat 11am–midnight.
Arty overstock among a hotchpotch
of travel guides, biographies,
children's pop-up books and
spiritual titles.

Magnolia Bakery

Cafés and snacks

Caffè Reggio

MAP P.76, POCKET MAP C18

119 MacDougal St, between Bleecker and W 3rd sts. Subway A, B, C, D, E, F to W 4th St. Sun–Thurs 9am–3am, Fri & Sat 9am–4am.

Oldest coffee shop in the Village, dating back to 1927, and embellished with all sorts of Italian antiques, paintings and sculpture.

Magnolia Bakery

MAP P.76, POCKET MAP B18

401 Bleecker St, at W 11th St. Subway #1 to Christopher St. Mon–Thurs & Sun 10am–10.30pm, Fri & Sat 10am–11.30pm.

There are lots of baked goods on offer at this very popular bakery, but everyone comes for the good but slightly overrated cupcakes (celebrated in *Sex and the City*), $3.95 each.

Num Pang

MAP P.76, POCKET MAP C17

28 E 12th St, between University Place and Fifth Ave. Subway L, N, Q, R, W, #4, #5, #6 to Union Square. ☎ 646 791 0439. Mon–Sat 11am–9pm, Sun noon–8pm.

Superb Cambodian-style sandwiches served on freshly toasted semolina flour baguettes with chilli mayo and home-made pickles; try the pulled duroc pork ($10.50).

Restaurants

Babbo

MAP P.76, POCKET MAP C18

110 Waverly Place, between MacDougal St and Sixth Ave. Subway A, B, C, D, E, F, M to W 4th St, #1 to Christopher St. ☎ 212 777 0303. Mon 5–11pm, Tues–Thurs 11.30am–2pm & 5–11pm, Fri & Sat 11.30am–2pm & 5–11.30pm, Sun 4.30–11pm.

Some of the best pasta in the city; this mecca for Italian food-lovers is a must. Try the mint love letters ($23) or goose liver ravioli ($26) – they're worth the pinch on your wallet.

Blue Hill

MAP P.76, POCKET MAP C18

75 Washington Place, between Sixth Ave and Washington Square Park. Subway A, B, C, D, E, F to W 4th St, #1 to Christopher St. ☎ 212 539 1776. Mon–Sat 5–11pm, Sun 5–10pm.

Rustic American and New England fare, including parsnip soup and braised cod, made with seasonal upstate ingredients (set menus only, from $95). Don't skip the rich chocolate bread pudding.

Buvette

MAP P.76, POCKET MAP B18
42 Grove St, between Bleecker and Bedford sts. Subway A, B, C, D, E, F, M to W 4th St, #1 to Christopher St. ☎ 212 243 9579. Mon–Fri 7am–2am, Sat & Sun 8am–2am. Exquisite but casual and reasonably priced French restaurant, serving the best egg breakfasts in the city, tempting small plates like salted butter and anchovies and beautifully crafted classics like coq au vin and cassoulet (mains $14–18). Sit in the garden if it's warm enough. No reservations.

Corner Bistro

MAP P.76, POCKET MAP B17
331 W 4th St, at Jane St. Subway A, C, E, L to 14th St. ☎ 212 242 9502. Mon–Sat 11.30am–4am, Sun noon–4am. Popular no-frills tavern serving cheap beer and some of the best burgers ($9.75) in town. An excellent place to unwind and refuel in a friendly atmosphere. Cash only.

Gotham Bar & Grill

MAP P.76, POCKET MAP C17
12 E 12th St, between Fifth Ave and University Place. Subway L, N, Q, R, W, #4, #5, #6 to Union Sq. ☎ 212 620 4020. Mon–Thurs noon–2.15pm & 5.30–10pm, Fri noon–2.15pm & 5.30–11pm, Sat 5–11pm, Sun 5–10pm. One of the city's best restaurants, the *Gotham* features marvellous American food; at the very least, it's worth a drink at the bar to people-watch.

John's Pizzeria

MAP P.76, POCKET MAP B18
278 Bleecker St, between Sixth and Seventh aves. Subway A, B, C, D, E, F, M to W 4th St, #1 to Christopher St. ☎ 212 243 1680. Sun–Thurs 11.30am–11.30pm, Fri & Sat 11.30am–midnight. This full-service restaurant serves some of the city's most popular pizzas, thin with a coal-charred crust ($17–20). Be prepared to queue for a table. They don't do slices.

Mary's Fish Camp

MAP P.76, POCKET MAP B18
64 Charles St, at W 4th St. Subway #1 to Christopher St. ☎ 646 486 2185. Mon–Sat noon–3pm & 6–11pm, Sun noon–4pm. Lobster rolls, *bouillabaisse* and seasonal veggies adorn the menu at this intimate spot, where you can almost smell the salt air. Go early, as the queue lasts into the night (no reservations).

Pearl Oyster Bar

MAP P.76, POCKET MAP B18
18 Cornelia St, between Bleecker and W 4th sts. Subway A, B, C, D, E, F, M to W 4th St, #1 to Christopher St. ☎ 212 691 8211. Mon–Sat noon–2.30pm & 6–11pm. Upmarket version of a New England fish shack, best known for its lemony-fresh lobster roll. You may have to fight for a table here, but the thoughtfully executed dishes are worth it.

The Spotted Pig

MAP P.76, POCKET MAP A18
314 W 11th St, at Greenwich St. Subway #1 to Christopher St. ☎ 212 620 0393. Mon–Fri noon–2am, Sat & Sun 11am–2am. New York's first gastro-pub, courtesy of chef April Bloomfield. The menu is several steps above ordinary bar food – featuring smoked-haddock chowder and sheep's ricotta *gnudi* – and the wine list is excellent. Entrées $26–38, with lunch plates $18–$26.

Bars

Blind Tiger Ale House

MAP P.76, POCKET MAP B18
281 Bleecker St, at Jones St. Subway A, B, C, D, E, F, M to W 4th St; #1 to Christopher St. Daily 11.30am–4am.

This wood-panelled pub is the home of serious ale connoisseurs, with 28 rotating draughts (primarily US microbrews such as Sixpoint and Smuttynose for around $7–8), a couple of casks and loads of bottled beers – they also serve cheese plates from Murray's. The prime location means it tends to get packed.

Cubby Hole

MAP P.76, POCKET MAP B17
281 W 12th St, at W 4th St. Subway A, C, E, L to 14th St. Mon–Fri 4pm–4am, Sat & Sun 2pm–4am.

This pocket-sized lesbian bar is warm and welcoming, with a busy festive atmosphere and unpretentious clientele.

Duplex

MAP P.76, POCKET MAP B18
61 Christopher St, at Seventh Ave S. Subway A, B, C, D, E, F, M to W 4th St, #1 to Christopher St. Daily 4pm–4am.

A village institution, this entertaining piano bar/cabaret elevates gay bar culture to a new level. A fun place for anyone, gay or straight, to stop for a tipple.

Fat Black Pussycat

MAP P.76, POCKET MAP C18
130 W 3rd St, between Sixth Ave and MacDougal St. Subway A, B, C, D, E, F, M to W 4th St. Daily 1pm–4am.

This pub is an NYU favourite, with popular happy hours (Sun–Fri 4–8pm), cosy wooden booths, darts and billiards. The pub's original location on MacDougal Street is where Bob Dylan allegedly wrote *Blowin' in the Wind*.

The Monster

MAP P.76, POCKET MAP B18
80 Grove St, between Waverly Place and W 4th St. Subway A, B, C, D, E, F, M to W 4th St, #1 to Christopher St. ☎ 212 924 3558, ⓦ www.monsterbarnyc.com. Daily 4pm–4am, Sat & Sun 2pm–4am.

Large, campy gay bar with drag cabaret, piano and downstairs dancefloor. Very popular, especially

with tourists, yet has a strong neighbourhood feel. Cover $6–10 (Fri–Mon).

White Horse Tavern

MAP P.76, POCKET MAP A18
567 Hudson St, at W 11th St. Subway #1 to Christopher St. Daily 11am–2am.

Village institution, opening in 1880: Dylan Thomas supped his last here before being carted off to hospital with alcohol poisoning. The cheap beer and food are palatable, and there's outside seating in summer.

Clubs

(Le) Poisson Rouge

MAP P.76, POCKET MAP C18
158 Bleecker St, at Thompson St. Subway A, B, C, D, E, F, M to W 4th St. ☎ 212 505 3474, ⓦ www.lpr.com. Daily 5pm–2am, Fri & Sat till 4am.

Club and live venue (from classical to live rock, folk, pop and electronica), with dance nights most Fridays and Saturdays ("Back to the Eighties" from 11pm; $22). Cover usually ranges $15–20.

Stonewall Inn

MAP P.76, POCKET MAP B18
53 Christopher St, between Seventh Ave and Waverly Place. Subway A, B, C, D, E, F, M to W 4th St, #1 to Christopher St. ☎ 212 488 2705, ⓦ thestonewallinnnyc.com. Daily 2pm–4am.

The gay civil-rights movement began outside this bar/club in the late 1960s and despite a few revamps hasn't changed much since. The crowd is mostly tourists and men, but everyone is made welcome.

Music venues

55 Bar

MAP P.76, POCKET MAP B18
55 Christopher St, at Seventh Ave. Subway #1 to Christopher St. ⓦ 55bar.com. Daily 1pm–4am.

A gem of an underground jazz bar that's been around since the days of Prohibition, with a great jukebox, congenial clientele, and live jazz every night.

Blue Note

MAP P.76, POCKET MAP C18
131 W 3rd St, between Sixth Ave and MacDougal St. Subway A, B, C, D, E, F, M to W 4th St, #1 to Christopher St. ☎ 212 475 8592, ⊕ bluenotejazz.com/newyork. Sun–Thurs 6pm–1am, Fri & Sat 6pm–3am.
Open since 1981 (and unrelated to the record label), this jazz institution regularly hosts top international performers, the likes of B.B King and Roberta Flack ($10–45).

Groove

MAP P.76, POCKET MAP C18
125 MacDougal St, at W 3rd St. Subway A, B, C, D, E, F, M to W 4th St. ☎ 212 254 9393, ⊕ clubgroovenyc.com. Daily 4pm–4am.
This lively joint features live rhythm & blues and soul music every night; it's one of the city's best bargains. Sets at 7pm and 9.30pm. No cover Sun–Thurs.

Terra Blues

MAP P.76, POCKET MAP C18
149 Bleecker St, between Thompson St and LaGuardia Place. Subway A, B, C, D, E, F, M to W 4th St. ☎ 212 777 7776, ⊕ terrablues. com. Mon–Thurs & Sun 6.30pm–2.30am, Fri 6.30pm–3.30am, Sat 6pm–3.30am.
The last remaining exclusive blues club in the city offers acoustic blues from 7.30pm and electric blues after 10pm, for $10–20 cover; all the big national names play here, and there's an excellent house band.

Village Vanguard

MAP P.76, POCKET MAP B17
178 Seventh Ave S, between W 11th and Perry sts. Subway #1, #2, #3 to 14th St. ☎ 212 255 4037, ⊕ villagevanguard.com. Daily 7.30pm–1am.
A NYC jazz landmark, the *Village Vanguard* celebrated its seventieth anniversary in 2005. Sonny Rollins made a legendary recording here in 1957, John Coltrane followed in 1961 and there's still a regular diet of big names. Cover is $35, including a one-drink minimum ($5–16).

Village Vanguard

Chelsea and the Meatpacking District

A grid of tenements, row houses and warehouses west of Sixth Avenue between West 14th and 30th streets, Chelsea came to life with the gay community's arrival, beginning in the late 1970s. New York's art scene further transformed the neighbourhood in the 1990s with an explosion of galleries between Tenth and Twelfth avenues. These days the High Line park, the relocated Whitney Museum and a burst of new construction are responsible for the area's energy. The triangular wedge of land created by Fourteenth, Gansevoort and West streets, aka the Meatpacking District, is a trendy place for shopping and clubbing.

The Whitney Museum of American Art

MAP P.86, POCKET MAP C11
99 Gansevoort St, between Tenth and Eleventh aves. Subway A, C, E, to 14th St, L to Eighth Ave. ☎ 212 570 3600, ⓦ www.whitney.org. Mon, Wed, Thurs & Sun (and summer Tues) 10.30am–6pm, Fri & Sat 10.30am–10pm. $25, under 18 free, after 7pm Fri free. Free tours daily roughly on the hour from noon.

Transplanted from its Upper East Side home (and closer to where it began back in the 1930s, in Greenwich Village), the **Whitney Museum of American Art** debuted its Renzo Piano-designed building at the foot of the High Line in May 2015. The architecture – its industrial look, external stairs and roomy terraces – attracts nearly as much attention as the art. As for what's on display, a good chunk of the museum's permanent collection now has room to shine. Look for favourites like Alexander Calder's *Circus* and Edward Hopper's *Early Sunday Morning*; though temporary exhibitions frequently take top billing. The Whitney is, after all, most famous for its Biennial, which gives a provocative overview of contemporary American art.

The High Line

MAP P.86, POCKET MAP B10
Gansevoort St to W 30th St, roughly along Tenth Ave; entrances at Gansevoort, 14th, 16th, 18th, 20th, 23rd, 26th, 28th, 30th and 34th sts. Subway A, C, E to 14th St, C, E to 23rd St. ⓦ www.thehighline.org. Daily: April, May, Oct & Nov 7am–10pm; June–Sept 7am–11pm; Dec–March 7am–7pm.

An ambitious urban renewal project that spans the Meatpacking District and West Chelsea, the **High Line** opened in 2009. It's a stunning transformation of a disused railway that once moved goods and produce around lower Manhattan, then spent years threatened with demolition. Basically an elevated promenade-cum-public park, it pays proper homage to its history – steel rails peek out from the ground; smooth pavement and wood echo the lines of train tracks; and wild growth patches have been left intact. The first stretch, from Gansevoort to 20th Street, has a subtle water feature between 14th and 15th streets and an amphitheatre a few blocks north. Between 20th and 30th streets the walkway feels narrower; at one point it is elevated on a metal catwalk right in the

Mural by French artist JR in The High Line Park

trees. The last part, the High Line at the Rail Yards, curves around the rail terminus and finishes along 34th Street, where a massive redevelopment called Hudson Yards has taken over.

Rubin Museum of Art

MAP P.86, POCKET MAP D10
150 W 17th St, between Sixth and Seventh aves. Subway #1 to 18th St, F, M to 14th St. ⓣ 212 620 5000, Ⓦ www.rubinmuseum. org. Mon & Thurs 11am–5pm, Wed 11am–9pm, Fri 11am–10pm, Sat & Sun 11am–6pm, closed Tues. $19, free on Fri 6–10pm.

The serene **Rubin Museum** is one of the city's lesser-visited gems, a collection of a few thousand paintings, sculptures and textiles from the Himalayas and surrounding regions. The permanent exhibits on the second and third floors are organized and labelled with great care and thought essential for a subject that will be familiar to few. While a few pieces manage to stand out, the thrust is less about individual artists and objects and more about understanding how and why art is created. The ground-floor café

becomes the *K2 Lounge* on Friday nights, with DJs and cocktails.

The Chelsea Hotel

MAP P.86, POCKET MAP C10
222 W 23rd St, between Seventh and Eighth aves. Subway C, E to 23rd St. Ⓦ www. hotelchelsea.com.

Built as a luxury cooperative apartment in 1884 and converted to a hotel in 1903, the **Chelsea Hotel** has served as undisputed home to the city's harder-up literati and its musical vagabonds. Eugene O'Neill, Arthur Miller and Tennessee Williams lived here, and Brendan Behan and Dylan Thomas staggered in and out during their New York visits. Legend has it that Jack Kerouac typed *On the Road* nonstop onto a 120ft roll of paper while here, though most agree that took place at 454 W 20th Street, over a six-week period (and from existing journals, not just the top of his head). Bob Dylan wrote songs in and about the hotel, and Sid Vicious stabbed Nancy Spungen to death in 1978 in their suite, a few months before his own life ended with an overdose of heroin.

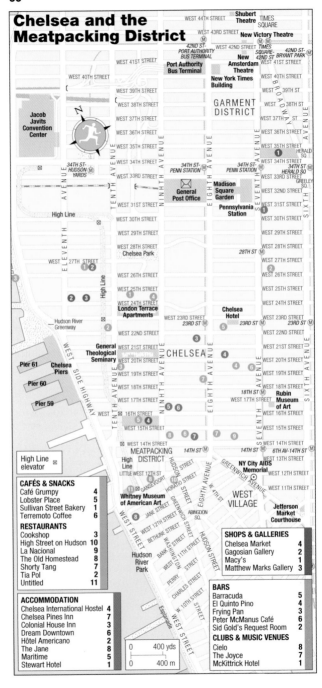

Chelsea and the Meatpacking District

CAFÉS & SNACKS

Café Grumpy	4
Lobster Place	5
Sullivan Street Bakery	1
Terremoto Coffee	6

RESTAURANTS

Cookshop	3
High Street on Hudson	10
La Nacional	9
The Old Homestead	8
Shorty Tang	7
Tia Pol	2
Untitled	11

ACCOMMODATION

Chelsea International Hostel	4
Chelsea Pines Inn	7
Colonial House Inn	3
Dream Downtown	6
Hôtel Americano	2
The Jane	8
Maritime	5
Stewart Hotel	1

SHOPS & GALLERIES

Chelsea Market	4
Gagosian Gallery	2
Macy's	1
Matthew Marks Gallery	3

BARS

Barracuda	5
El Quinto Pino	4
Frying Pan	3
Peter McManus Café	6
Sid Gold's Request Room	2

CLUBS & MUSIC VENUES

Cielo	8
The Joyce	7
McKittrick Hotel	1

0 400 yds
0 400 m

After years of closure and numerous rumours, the place is supposed to reopen in early 2019 as a boutique hotel; at least you can get a doughnut at the gourmet outlet on the ground floor.

General Theological Seminary

MAP P.86, POCKET MAP C10
440 W 21st St, between Ninth and Tenth aves. Subway C, E to 23rd St. ☎ 212 243-5150, Ⓦ www.gts.edu. Mon–Sat 10am–3pm; later in summer, but always call ahead.

Founded in 1817, this is a Chelsea secret, a harmonious assemblage of Gothic structures that feel like part of a college campus. Though the buildings still house a working Episcopalian seminary – the oldest in the US – it's possible to explore the grounds and small chapel. You'll need to get a special pass to check out their collection of Latin Bibles, one of the largest in the world.

Chelsea Piers

MAP P.86, POCKET MAP B11
W 17th to W 23rd St, along Hudson River. Subway C, E to 23rd St. ☎ 212 336 6666, Ⓦ www.chelseapiers.com. Hours vary according to activity.

First opened in 1910, this was where the great transatlantic liners would disembark their passengers (it was en route to the **Chelsea Piers** in 1912 that the *Titanic* sank). By the 1960s, however, the piers had fallen into neglect. Reopened in 1995, the new Chelsea Piers stretches between piers 59 to 62 as a sports complex, with ice rinks and open-air roller rinks, as well as a bowling alley and a golf range. There's a nice waterfront walkway and skate park at the end of **Pier 62**.

The General Post Office

MAP P.86, POCKET MAP C9
421 Eighth Ave, at W 33rd St. Subway A, C, E to 34th St. ☎ 212 330 3296. Mon–Fri 7am–10pm, Sat 9am–9pm, Sun 11am–7pm.

The 1913 **General Post Office**, officially the James A Farley Station (named after a well-regarded postmaster general), is a relic from when municipal pride was all about making statements. Twenty huge columns stand beneath the sonorous inscription: "Neither snow nor rain nor heat nor gloom of night stays these couriers from the swift completion of their appointed rounds." The McKim, Mead, and White building is being refitted to serve as an entrance to Amtrak and LIRR trains at Penn Station; it is currently used for fashion events and other happenings.

James A Farley Building, formally General Post Office Building

Shops and galleries

CHELSEA AND THE MEATPACKING DISTRICT

Chelsea Market

MAP P.86, POCKET MAP A17
75 Ninth Ave, between W 15th and 16th sts. Subway A, C, E to 14th St. Mon–Sat 7am–10pm, Sun 8am–9pm.

Food markets, cooking shops, bakeries and restaurants line this former Nabisco factory warehouse's ground floor, which led the way in the city's food hall fad and has become a crowded attraction (as well as lunch spot for Google workers). It's got all the bases covered: espresso drinks, *pad thai*, panini, tacos, sinful brownies, fresh oysters, wines by the glass, kitchenware, art installations. … tours are available too.

Gagosian Gallery

MAP P.86, POCKET MAP B10
555 W 24th St, between Tenth and Eleventh aves, other locations at 522 W 21st St and 980 Madison Ave. Subway C, E to 23rd St. ☎ 212 741 1111, Ⓦ www.gagosian.com.

Winter Tues–Sat 10am–6pm; summer Mon–Fri 10am–6pm.
This art world powerbroker shows heavyweights such as Richard Serra and Damien Hirst.

Macy's

MAP P.86, POCKET MAP D9
151 Broadway, at W 34th St at Herald Square. Subway B, D, F, M, N, Q, R to 34th St. Mon–Sat 10am–10pm, Sun 10am–9pm.
One of the world's largest department stores, Macy's stocks fairly mediocre brands (except for the excellent Cellar houseware department). If you're from abroad, head to the Visitor Center (Balcony Level) to receive a ten percent discount; bring your passport.

Matthew Marks Gallery

MAP P.86, POCKET MAP B10
522 W 22nd St, between Tenth and Eleventh aves, with two other branches in Chelsea. Subway C, E to 23rd St. ☎ 212 243 0200, Ⓦ www.matthewmarks.com. Tues–Sat 10am–6pm, summer Mon–Fri 10am–6pm.
The centrepiece of Chelsea's art scene, showcasing pieces by artists such as Cy Twombly and Ellsworth Kelly.

Chelsea Market

Cafés and snacks

Café Grumpy

MAP P.86, POCKET MAP C10
224 W 20th St, between Seventh and Eighth
aves; three other city locations. Subway
C, E to 23rd St. Mon–Fri 7am–8pm, Sat
7.30am–8pm, Sun 7.30am–7.30pm.
It's uncertain which will take
longer, choosing a coffee – the
selections described as if they
were wines – or getting your fix,
as each cup comes made to order.
But you'll be able to taste the
difference; it's as good as it gets.
The original *Grumpy* is over in
Brooklyn's Greenpoint.

Lobster Place

MAP P.86, POCKET MAP C11
75 Ninth Ave, between 15th and 16th
sts. Subway A, C, E to 14th St. Mon–Sat
9.30am–9pm, Sun 10am–8pm.
This Chelsea Market fishmonger
has a large sushi and oyster bar
in its center. You can take a seat
there; order chowder (small portion
$4.95), fresh sushi meal or picnic
box ($13.95–21.50) to takeaway
up to the High Line for lunch;
or go to the attached. seafood
restaurant, *Cull and Pistol*, for
something more refined.

Sullivan Street Bakery

MAP P.86, POCKET MAP C10
236 Ninth Ave between W 24th and W 25th
sts. Subway C, E to 23rd St. ☏ 212 929
5900, ⓦ sullivanstreetbakery.com. Mon–Fri
7am–4pm, Sat & Sun 7.30am–6pm.
A lovely array of crispy breads is
on display, though you can also
indulge in panini, smoked salmon
tartine and pizza slices.

Terremoto Coffee

MAP P.86, POCKET MAP C11
328 W. 15th St, between Eighth and Ninth
aves. Subway A, C, E to 4th St. ☏ 212 243
4399. Mon–Fri 7am–7pm, Sat 8am–7pm,
Sun 9am–6pm.
This shoebox-size café serves up
delicious espresso-based drinks
(starting at $3.50) made from
single-source beans. Pour-overs
are available too, as are a limited
number of pastries.

Restaurants

Cookshop

MAP P.86, POCKET MAP C10
156 Tenth Ave, at 20th St. Subway C, E to
23rd St. ☏ 212 924 4440. Mon–Fri 8am–4pm
& 5.30–11.30pm, Sat 10am–4pm & 5.30–
11.30pm, Sun 10am–4pm & 5.30–10pm.
Part of the Marc Meyer stable, with
ever-busy street-side tables and a
menu of seasonal, contemporary
American fare – dishes always
showcase the food's provenance;
entrées might include pheasant
pasta, grilled rabbit from the
Hudson Valley and Vermont
suckling pig (most $25–30); there
are interesting brunch options and
inventive bloody Marys, too.

High Street on Hudson

MAP P.86, POCKET MAP C11
637 Hudson St, at Horatio St. Subway A, C,
E, L to 14th St. ☏ 917 388 3944. Mon–Thurs
& Sun 8am–9pm, Sat & Sun 8am–10pm.
Known for its house-baked breads,
this bright Philly import keeps
folks coming back for eggs on a
biscuit, avocado toast and homey
entrees (a half-chicken with
mustard greens, $24). It's right by
the Whitney and High Line.

La Nacional

MAP P.86, POCKET MAP B17
239 W 14th St, between Seventh and Eighth
aves. Subway: A, C, E, L to 14th St. ☏ 917
388 2888. Tues & Wed 5–10pm, Thurs–Sat
5–11pm.
After having been dormant for a
few years, the bar-restaurant arm
of the Spanish Benevolent Society
has reopened with its traditional
array of tapas (croquettes, garlic
shrimp), paella, Spanish wines and
festive happy hours. It's easy to pass
by without noticing, imagining
it's just another historic building
in a neighborhood full of them.
Thursdays are tango night.

Old Homestead Steakhouse

Tia Pol

MAP P.86, POCKET MAP B10
205 Tenth Ave, between W 22nd and 23rd sts. Subway C, E to 23rd St. ☎ 212 675 8805. Mon 5.30–11pm, Tues–Thurs noon–11pm, Fri noon–midnight, Sat 11am–midnight, Sun 11am–10.30pm.

The narrow space in this popular tapas bar-restaurant is frequently full. Graze on bar snacks like croquetas ($4/$8) or choose octopus salad ($14) and shrimp *al ajillo* ($12); wash it all back with the easy-drinking house-made sangria ($9 glass).

Untitled

MAP P.86, POCKET MAP A17
99 Gansevoort St, at Washington St. Subway: A, C, E, L to 14th St–Eighth Ave. ☎ 212 570 3670, ⓦ www.untitledatthewhitney.com. Mon–Thurs noon–3pm & 5–9pm, Fri noon–3pm & 5–10pm, Sat 11am–3.30pm & 5–10pm, Sun 11am–3.30pm & 5–9pm.

The main restaurant at the Whitney is more than just a place for refined salads and snacky avocado toast; it offers lovely New American cooking – think lamb meatballs ($15), roasted striped bass ($26) and grilled pork rib ($27).

The Old Homestead

MAP P.86, POCKET MAP A17
56 Ninth Ave, between W 14th and 15th sts. Subway A, C, E to 14th St. ☎ 212 242 9040. Mon–Thurs noon–10.45pm, Fri noon–11.45pm, Sat 1–11.45pm, Sun 1–9.45pm.

Steak. Period. But really gorgeous steak, served in an almost comically old-fashioned walnut dining room by waiters in black vests. Huge portions, but expensive – roughly $50–60.

Shorty Tang

MAP P.86, POCKET MAP C11
98 W Eighth Ave, between W 14th and W 15th sts. Subway A, C, E, L to Eighth Ave 14th St. ☎ 646 896 1883, ⓦ shortytang.com. Daily 11am–10.30pm.

The signature cold sesame noodles ($8), which the owner's grandfather popularized in NYC decades ago, are the main draw, but the dumplings, scallion pancakes, sautéed vegetables and noodle soups are also worth exploring. It's a casual place, good for lunch.

Bars

Barracuda

MAP P.86, POCKET MAP C10
275 W 22nd St, between Seventh and Eighth aves. Subway C, E, #1 to 23rd St. Daily 4pm–4am.

A favourite bar in New York's gay scene, and pretty laidback for Chelsea, though drag shows and DJs perk things up in the later hours.

El Quinto Pino

MAP P.86, POCKET MAP C10
401 W 24th St at Ninth Ave. Subway C, E to 23rd St. Mon–Thurs 5.30–11.30pm, Fri 5pm–midnight, Sat 11.30am–3.30pm & 5pm–midnight, Sun 11.30am–3.30pm & 5.30–10.30pm.

Nibble on croquettes ($5) and an uncanny sea urchin sandwich ($15) in this elegant tapas bar. There's also a dining room that serves the foods of Spain, concentrating on specific regions.

Frying Pan

MAP P. 86, POCKET MAP B10
Pier 66, at West 26th St. Subway C, E to 23rd St. May–Sept daily noon–midnight, Apr & Oct weather dependent.
This disused lightship, docked on the Hudson River, serves as a seasonal, atmospheric spot for drinks and standard bar food.

Peter McManus Café

MAP P.86, POCKET MAP C11
152 Seventh Ave, at 19th St. Subway #1 to 18th St. Mon–Sat 11am–4am, Sun noon–4am.
Unlike many Irish pubs in the city, this is the real deal, moving to this location in 1936 and appearing in episodes of *Seinfeld* and *Law & Order*. The worn oak bar adds character, along with the in-house ale, decent burgers ($13) and old-style telephone booths inside.

Sid Gold's Request Room

MAP P.86, POCKET MAP D10
165 W 26th St, between Sixth and Seventh aves. Subway #1 to 28th St. Mon–Fri 5pm–2am, Sat 7pm–2am.
The place for a sing-a-long, some old-school cocktails and snacks, and the stylings of local music legend Joe McGinty. Fabulously retro.

Clubs and music venues

Cielo

MAP P.86, POCKET MAP A17
18 Little W 12th St, at Ninth Ave. Subway A, C, E to 14th St. ☎ 212 645 5700, ⓦ www.cieloclub. com. Mon & Wed–Sat 10pm–4am. $20–25.
Expect velvet rope-burn at this super-exclusive place: there's only room for 250 people.

The Joyce

MAP P.86, POCKET MAP C11
175 Eighth Ave, at W 19th St. Subway #1 to 18th St; C, E to 23rd St. ☎ 212 691 9740, ⓦ www.joyce.org.
Touring companies both local and from around the world keep this Art Deco-style theatre in brisk business.

McKittrick Hotel

MAP P.86, POCKET MAP B10
530 W 27th St, between Tenth and Eleventh aves. ☎ 212 904 1883, ⓦ mckittrickhotel. com.
Not a hotel nor a traditional nightlife venue, this converted warehouse hosts the interactive theater sensation Sleep No More – a kind of mystery-filled version of Macbeth, with actors spread out in rooms over a number of floors – as well as a post-show bar, a rooftop bar (Gallows Green) and a host of temporary theatrical performances. Book ahead for pretty much everything.

McKittrick Hotel

Union Square, Gramercy Park and the Flatiron District

For a glimpse of well-preserved nineteenth-century New York, it's definitely worth a jaunt around the more genteel parts of the east-side neighbourhoods that surround Union Square and Gramercy Park. Madison Square Park and the decidedly anorexic Flatiron Building anchor the amorphous area of the Flatiron District, which veers up and down Broadway and takes in a number of elegant facades; things take on more of a high-rise, Midtown flavour the closer you get to the Empire State Building. Some of the best and most expensive restaurants in the city call this stretch home; wander east to the high 20s around Lexington Avenue, a little Indian area called Curry Hill, for wallet relief in the kosher vegetarian restaurants and chaat cafés frequented by taxi drivers.

Union Square

MAP P.94, POCKET MAP D11
Bordered by Broadway, Park Avenue S, 14th and 17th sts. Subway L, N, Q, R, #4, #5, #6 to Union Square.

Founded as a park in 1813, **Union Square** lies between E 14th and E 17th streets, interrupting Broadway's diagonal path. The park was the site of many political protests and workers' rallies between the Civil War and the early twentieth century. Later, the area evolved into an elegant theatre and shopping district. The leafy and bench-lined square is best known for its **Farmers' Market**, held Monday, Wednesday, Friday and

Union Square

Saturday from 8am to 6pm; there's tons of local produce, cheese, meat, even wine. Craft vendors, none too special, line the southwest side, though they're taken over by a popular holiday market as Christmas approaches.

Irving Place

MAP P.94, POCKET MAP E11
Subway L, N, Q, R, #4, #5, #6 to Union Square.

This graceful six-block stretch was named after author Washington Irving, though the claims that he lived at no. 49 are spurious; he did, at the least, frequently visit a nephew who lived in the area. Regardless, it's a lovely walk from the Con Ed building at the south end up to Gramercy Park; the intersection with 19th Street – and that side street itself – is especially evocative.

Theodore Roosevelt Birthplace

MAP P.94, POCKET MAP D10
28 E 20th St, between Park Ave S and Broadway. Subway R, W, #6 to 23rd St.
☎ 212 260 1616. Wed–Sat 9am–5pm, room tours on the hour 10am–4pm (except noon). Free.

Theodore Roosevelt's birthplace was restored in 1923 to the way it would have been when he was born there in 1858; the family moved uptown when he was fourteen. The rather sombre mansion contains mostly original furnishings – a brilliant chandelier in the parlour and "Teddie's" crib – viewable on an obligatory guided tour; it doesn't take more than fifteen minutes to see it all. You might spend as much time in the attached galleries looking at hunting trophies and documents from Roosevelt's life.

Gramercy Park

MAP P.94, POCKET MAP E10
Irving Place, between 20th and 21st sts. Subway #6 to 23rd St.

A former "little crooked swamp", **Gramercy Park** is one of the city's

Theodore Roosevelt's Birthplace

prettiest squares. The city's last private park, it is accessible only to those rich or fortunate enough to live here – or those staying at the nearby *Gramercy Park Hotel* (see page 170). Inside the gates stands a statue of the actor Edwin Booth, brother of Lincoln's assassin, John Wilkes Booth. The private **Players Club**, at 15 Gramercy Park, was founded by Booth and sits next door to the prestigious **National Arts Club** at no. 16, another members-oriented place, though you can sneak inside in the afternoons for the free art exhibits. The brick-red structure at no. 34 was one of the city's very first building cooperatives.

The Flatiron Building

MAP P.94, POCKET MAP D10
At Broadway, Fifth Ave and 23rd St. Subway R, W to 23rd St.

Set on a triangular, or iron-shaped, plot of land, the lofty, elegant 1902 **Flatiron Building** is covered with terracotta Medusa heads and other striking ornamentation. The uncommonly thin, tapered shape of this Daniel Burnham-designed skyscraper (tall for the time, at 307ft) caused consternation regarding its stability and wind-tunnel effects, but it has more than survived the years – it's become a New York symbol.

Madison Square Park

MAP P.94, POCKET MAP D10

E 23rd and 26th sts and Madison Ave and Broadway. Subway R, W to 23rd St.

Perhaps because of the stateliness of its buildings and the park-space in the middle, **Madison Square** possesses a grandiosity that Union Square has long since lost. Next to the Art Deco Metropolitan Life Company's building and clock tower on the eastern side, the Corinthian-columned marble facade of the Appellate Division of the **New York State Supreme Court** is resolutely righteous with its statues of Justice, Wisdom and Peace, though the chamber where arguments are heard (Tues–Thurs 2pm) is well-nigh Rococo in its detail. The grand structure behind that, the 1928 **New York Life Building**, was the work of Cass Gilbert, creator of the Woolworth Building (see page 33).

There are plenty of places to sit and relax in and around the park, including a pedestrianized triangle on its western side. In the southeast corner is the original outpost of Danny Meyer's popular *Shake Shack* (see page 97), and at the northwest corner of 23rd and Broadway, the celebrity-chef-owned *Eataly* (see page 96).

National Museum of Mathematics

MAP P.94, POCKET MAP D10

11 E 26th St, between Fifth and Madison aves. Subway R, W, #6 to 23rd St or 28th St. ☎ 212 542 0566, ⦿ www.momath.org. Daily 10am–5pm. $17, children 12 and under $11.

Somewhere between a high-minded institution and an interactive romper room, the **Museum of Mathematics** debuted in late 2012 with the goal of making maths fun

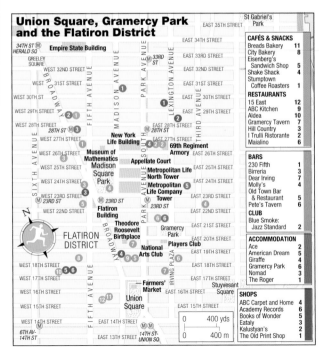

Union Square, Gramercy Park and the Flatiron District

CAFÉS & SNACKS	
Breads Bakery	11
City Bakery	8
Eisenberg's Sandwich Shop	5
Shake Shack	4
Stumptown Coffee Roasters	1

RESTAURANTS	
15 East	12
ABC Kitchen	9
Aldea	10
Gramercy Tavern	7
Hill Country	3
I Trulli Ristorante	2
Maialino	6

BARS	
230 Fifth	1
Birreria	3
Dear Irving	7
Molly's	4
Old Town Bar & Restaurant	5
Pete's Tavern	6

CLUB	
Blue Smoke: Jazz Standard	2

ACCOMMODATION	
Ace	2
American Dream	5
Giraffe	4
Gramercy Park	6
Nomad	3
The Roger	1

SHOPS	
ABC Carpet and Home	4
Academy Records	6
Books of Wonder	5
Eataly	3
Kalustyan's	2
The Old Print Shop	1

Empire State Building

and accessible to kids – and adults. Featuring roughly thirty exhibits on two floors, the gallery puts a focus on experience and engagement over understanding, with the idea that the latter will naturally follow; highlights include the square-wheeled tricycle and the Human Tree exhibit.

69th Regiment Armory

MAP P.94, POCKET MAP E10
68 Lexington Ave, between 25th and 26th sts. Subway #6 to 23rd or 28th sts.
Ⓦ www.sixtyninth.net.

The lumbering but landmarked **69th Regiment Armory** building, with its mansard roof and arched drill shed, was the site of the famous Armory Show of 1913, which brought modern art to New York; it was also, briefly, a very early home to the Knicks' basketball team. These days it retains its original function as the headquarters of the National Guard's "Fighting Sixth-Ninth", though its drill hall is still used for events and exhibitions.

The Empire State Building

MAP P.94, POCKET MAP D9
Fifth Ave and 34th St. Subway B, D, F, M, N, Q, R, W to 34th St. ☏ 212 736 3100,
Ⓦ www.esbnyc.com. Daily 8am–2am, last trip 1.15am. $37, $31 for ages 6 to 12, additional $20 for ticket to 102nd-floor Observatory.

The 1931 **Empire State Building**, easily the city's most evocative symbol, was New York's tallest skyscraper for years until being topped by the original World Trade Center; after 9/11 it was the tallest once more, before being overtaken again by the new One World Trade Center in 2012. It stands at 102 floors and 1454ft – toe to TV mast – but its height is deceptive, rising in stately tiers with steady panache. Standing on Fifth Avenue below, it's easy to walk by without seeing it. From elsewhere, it can seem ubiquitous, especially at night, when it's lit in various colours. Admire the immaculately restored Art Deco lobby and ceiling before the elevators take you to the main **86th-floor Observatory**. The views from the outside walkways here are as stunning as you'd expect; on a clear day visibility is up to eighty miles. A second set of elevators can take you to the smallish **102nd-floor Observatory**, at the base of the radio and TV antennas; the extra price makes it more for completists.

Shops

ABC Carpet and Home

MAP P.94, POCKET MAP D11
888 Broadway, at E 19th St. Subway R, W
to 23rd St. Mon–Wed & Fri–Sat 10am–7pm,
Thurs 10am–8pm, Sun 11am–6.30pm.
Six floors of antiques and country
furniture, knick-knacks, linens and,
of course, carpets. The grandiose,
museum-like setup is half the fun.

Academy Records

MAP P.94, POCKET MAP D11
12 W 18th St, between Fifth and Sixth aves.
Subway F, M to 14th St. Daily 11am–7pm.
Used, rare and hard-to-find music
is the focus; this outlet has an
exceptional selection for classical
music fans.

Books of Wonder

MAP P.94, POCKET MAP D11
18 W 18th St, between Fifth and Sixth aves.
Subway #1 to 18th St, F, M to 14th St, L, N,
Q, R, #4, #5, #6 to Union Square. Mon–Sat
10am–7pm, Sun 11am–6pm.

Kalustyan's

There's no better place in the city
for kids' books. Helpful staff,
regular story times and frequent
author readings make coming here
a pleasure. They've got another
location at 217 W 84th St on the
Upper West Side.

Eataly

MAP P.94, POCKET MAP D10
200 Fifth Ave, at W 23rd St. Subway R, W
to 23rd St, #6 to Astor Place. Market daily
9am–11pm, retailer hours vary.
This vast and wildly popular
culinary landmark is part Italian
café/restaurant complex, part food
market. There is an incredible range
of delicious wine, cheese, meat,
bread and seafood for sale, sourced
locally or flown in from Italy, and
a wide choice of places to stop and
try the tempting offerings – plus a
rooftop beer bar (see page 99).
Keep an eye out for tastings, classes
and tours. A second Eataly has
opened up in the Financial District,
at Brookfield Place.

Kalustyan's

MAP P.94, POCKET MAP E10
123 Lexington Ave, between E 28th and
29th sts. Subway #6 to 28th St. Mon–Sat
10am–8pm, Sun 11am–7pm.
This heavenly scented store has
been selling a variety of Indian
food products, spices and hard-
to-find ingredients since 1944.
Today its selection covers a range
of foods from around the globe.
The building was once home to
President Chester A. Arthur.

The Old Print Shop

MAP P.94, POCKET MAP E10
150 Lexington Ave, between 29th & 30th
sts. Subway #6 to 28th St. Sept–May Tues–
Fri 9am–5pm, Sat 9am–4pm, June–Aug
Mon–Thurs 9am–5pm, Fri 9am–4pm.
This fascinating and long-
established shop is by far the
best place to find yourself a
great old map of a New York
neighbourhood, a rare first-edition
art book or a historic print from an
old edition of *Harper's Weekly*.

Cafés and snacks

Breads Bakery

MAP P.94, POCKET MAP D11
18 E 16th St, between Broadway and Fifth
Ave. Subway L, N, Q, R, W, #4, #5, #6 to
14th St-Union Sq. Mon–Fri 6.30am–9pm,
Sat 6.30am–8pm, Sun 7.30am–8pm.
You can't go wrong with the
fresh-made breads, quiches or
sandwiches, but it's the chocolate
babka that draws raves as the city's
best. At the back is a sit-down cafe.

City Bakery

MAP P.94, POCKET MAP D11
3 W 18th St, between Fifth and Sixth
aves. Subway F, M to 14th St. Mon–Fri
7.30am–6pm, Sat 8am–6pm.
A smart stop for a satisfying lunch
or a sweet-tooth craving. The
vast array of pastries is head and
shoulders above most in the city.
Try a cookie or pretzel croissant
with a hot chocolate.

Eisenberg's Sandwich Shop

MAP P.94, POCKET MAP D10
174 Fifth Ave, between E 22nd and 23rd sts.
Subway R, W to 23rd St. Mon–Fri 7.30am–
8pm, Sat 9am–5pm, Sun 10am–3pm.
A colourful luncheonette, this
slice of NY life serves great tuna
sandwiches ($7.50), matzoh ball
soup ($4) and old-fashioned
fountain sodas ($2).

Shake Shack

MAP P.94, POCKET MAP D10
Madison Square Park, near Madison Ave
and E 23rd St; other locations across the
city. Subway R, W, #6 to 23rd St. Mon–Fri
7.30am–11pm, Sat & Sun 8am–11pm.
Danny Meyer's leafy food kiosk
has become a phenomenon, with
a long wait for tables pretty much
all day (try to avoid prime lunch
and evening hours) and spawning
offshoots all over town (and
beyond), including at the Mets'
Citi Field. Folks come for perfectly
grilled burgers and frozen custard
shakes; everything is under $9.

Stumptown Coffee Roasters

MAP P.94, POCKET MAP D10
18 W 29th St, between Broadway and Fifth
Ave, in the Ace Hotel. Subway R, W to 28th
St. Mon–Fri 6am–8pm, Sat & Sun 7am–8pm.
One of the country's most
renowned coffee roasters brings its
brews to a hip hotel; you'll have
your latte methodically made by
knowledgeable baristas. Pastries and
bagels are also available.

Restaurants

15 East

MAP P.94, POCKET MAP C17
15 E 15th St, between Fifth Ave and
Broadway. Subway L, N, Q, R, W, #4, #5,
#6 to 14th St-Union Square. ☎ 212 647
0015. Mon–Fri noon–1.45pm & 6–10.30pm,
Sat noon–1.45pm & 6–11pm, Sun
5.30–9.30pm.
The attention given to both
cooked dishes (diver scallops
$36, sea urchin risotto $34)
and fresh sushi/sashimi (chef's
selection $65) elevates this stylish
Japanese restaurant.

ABC Kitchen

MAP P.94, POCKET MAP D11
35 E 18th St, between Park Ave S and
Broadway. Subway L, N, Q, R, W, #4, #5, #6
to 14th St-Union Square. ☎ 212 475 5829.
Mon–Wed noon–3pm & 5.30–10.30pm,
Thurs noon–3pm & 5.30–11pm, Fri noon–
3pm & 5.30–11.30pm, Sat 11am–3pm
& 5.30–11.30pm, Sun 11am–3pm &
5.30–10pm.
Inside the ABC store (see page
96), this upscale resto from Jean-
Georges Vongerichten focuses on
market-fresh, seasonal ingredients.
Get the crab toast ($16) to start.

Aldea

MAP P.94, POCKET MAP D11
31 W 17th St, between Fifth and Sixth aves.
Subway F, M to 14th St. ☎ 212 675 7223.
Mon 6–9pm, Tues–Thurs 5.30–11pm, Fri &
Sat 5.30–11.30pm.
In a cool, relaxed dining room,
Portuguese-accented dishes come

Maialino

exquisitely prepared and full of flavour. Entrees $27–347, four-course prix fixe $89.

Gramercy Tavern

MAP P.94, POCKET MAP D10

42 E 20th St, between Broadway and Park Ave S. Subway R, W, #6 to 23rd St. ☎ 212 477 0777. Main dining room: Mon–Thurs 11.30am–2pm & 5–9.45pm, Fri 11,39am–2pm & 5.30–10.30pm, Sat noon–1.30pm & 5.30–10.30pm, Sun 5.30–9.45pm; Front tavern: 11.30am–11pm, midnight at weekends.

One of NYC's best restaurants; its neo-colonial decor, exquisite New American cuisine and perfect service make for a memorable meal. The seasonal tasting menus are well worth the steep prices ($184 three-course prix fixe $134, gratuity included), but you can also drop in for a drink or cheaper meal in the casual front room.

Hill Country

MAP P.94. POCKET MAP D10

30 W 26th St, between Broadway and Sixth Ave. Subway R, W to 28th St, F to 23rd St. ☎ 212 255 4544. Daily 11.30am–2am, though kitchen closes 10pm Sun–Wed, 11pm Thurs and midnight Fri & Sat.

This Texas-style pioneer serves some of the best barbecue in the city, especially the moist, fatty brisket ($28.50/lb). Grab a table, then order your meats (all priced by the pound or half pound) and sides from the counters.

I Trulli Ristorante

MAP P.94, POCKET MAP E10

122 E 27th St, between Lexington and Park aves. Subway #6 to 28th St. ☎ 212 481 7372. Mon–Thurs noon–3pm & 5.30–10pm, Fri noon–3pm & 5.30–11pm, Sat 5–11pm, Sun 3:30–9pm.

Find quality southern Italian food mingled with a bit of a French flair; the Italian wine list is extensive.

Maialino

MAP P.94, POCKET MAP E10

Gramercy Park Hotel, 2 Lexington Ave. Subway #6 to 23rd St. ☎ 212 777 2410. Mon–Thurs 7.30–10am, noon–2pm & 5.30–10pm, Fri 7.30–10am, noon–2pm & 5.30–10.30pm, Sat 10am–2.30pm & 5.30–10.30pm, Sun 10am–2.30pm & 5.30–10pm.

Danny Meyer's attractive Roman trattoria, looking out on Gramercy Park, is both rustic and refined. Much of the focus is on the hog (which gives the place its name) – the special is roast suckling pig. Reservations recommended, though the bar is open all day.

Bars

230 Fifth

MAP P.94, POCKET MAP D10

230 Fifth Ave. Subway R, W, #6 to 23rd St.
Mon–Fri 2pm–4am, Sat & Sun 10am–4am.
Classy lounge bar with the biggest
roof garden in the city – blankets
and heaters are provided in winter.
Drinks and snacks are reasonably
priced for the experience (Martinis
from $14; no cover). No sneakers/
trainers or T-shirts for men.

Birreria

MAP P.94, POCKET MAP D10

Eataly, 200 Fifth Ave, at 23rd St. Subway
R, W, #6 to 23rd St. ☎ 212 937 8910. Daily
11.30am–11pm.
A sprawling rooftop bar, *Birreria*
is a modern twist on the beer
garden with handcrafted ales and
home-made sausages on offer. It's
also a restaurant that changes its
theme seasonally.

Dear Irving

MAP P.94, POCKET MAP E11

55 Irving Plaza, between E 17th and 18th
sts. Subway L, N, Q, R, #4, #5, #6 to 14th
St-Union Square. Mon–Sat 5pm–2am, Sun
5pm–1am.
Up a flight of stairs and behind an
innocuous door, this speakeasy-
lounge offers expertly made
cocktails and attentive service.

Molly's

MAP P.94, POCKET MAP E10

287 Third Ave, between E 22nd and
23rd sts. Subway #6 to 23rd St. Daily
11am–4am.
While the city trends move toward
gastropubs and handcrafted
cocktails, the friendly bartenders
at *Molly's* pour the best pints of
Guinness around.

Old Town Bar & Restaurant

MAP P.94, POCKET MAP D11

45 E 18th St, between Broadway and Park
Ave S. Subway L, N, Q, R,#4, #5, #6 to 14th
St-Union Square. Mon–Fri 11.30am–2am,
Sat noon–2am, Sun 1pm–midnight.

This atmospheric and spacious
bar is popular with publishing
types, models and photographers.
Great burgers.

Pete's Tavern

MAP P.94, POCKET MAP E11

129 E 18th St, at Irving Place. Subway L, N,
Q, R, #4, #5, #6 to 14th St-Union Square.
Mon–Wed & Sun 11am–2.30am, Thurs
11am–3am, Fri & Sat 11am–4am.
Former speakeasy that claims to
be the oldest bar in New York – it
opened in 1864. These days it
inevitably trades on its history,
though its well-worn counter
and outdoor seating are convivial
enough. There are some good menu
deals (full dinners are available)
during the week.

Club

Blue Smoke: Jazz Standard

MAP P.94, POCKET MAP E10

116 E 27th St, between Park and Lexington
aves. Subway #6 to 28th St. ☎ 212 576
2232, ⊛ www.jazzstandard.com. Sets at
7.30pm and 9.30pm Mon–Thurs & Sun, with
an extra set at 11.30pm Fri & Sat. Cover
$20–35.
This gourmet club books all
flavours of jazz and serves sublime
BBQ, the best in-club grub
in town.

Pete's Tavern

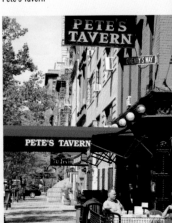

Midtown

The largely corporate and commercial area east of Sixth Avenue all the way to the river, from the 40s through the 50s, is known as Midtown. You'll find the city's sniffiest boutiques, best Art Deco facades and exemplary Modernist skyscrapers scattered primarily along E 42nd and E 57th streets and Fifth, Madison and Park avenues. Fifth is the grand sight- and store-studded spine of Manhattan; the sidewalks nearly reach a standstill at Christmas, with shoppers stalled at elaborate window displays. Cornelius Vanderbilt's Beaux Arts train station, Grand Central Terminal, anchors Park Avenue, while major museums and city symbols such as the Museum of Modern Art, Rockefeller Center and the United Nations dot the rest of the landscape.

The Morgan Library and Museum

MAP P.102, POCKET MAP D9
225 Madison Ave, between E 36th and 37th sts. Subway #6 to 33rd St. ☎ 212 685 0008, ⓦ www.themorgan.org. Tues–Thurs 10.30am–5pm, Fri 10.30am–9pm, Sat 10am–6pm, Sun 11am–6pm. $20, free Fri 7–9pm.

The Morgan Library and Museum

The uplifting **Morgan Library** in Murray Hill was originally built to hold the fruits of financier J.P. Morgan's collecting sprees during frequent trips abroad; he claimed keen interest in "all the beautiful things in the world", in this case, illuminated manuscripts, paintings, prints and furniture. A stunning

Midtown monoliths

The city, especially Midtown, is filled with far too many landmark, innovative or just plain unusual buildings to list in these pages. If you're interested in the subject of architecture, try to catch the following in addition to the ones described in this chapter: the **Ford Foundation Building**, 320 E 43rd St, between First and Second avenues, whose atrium is one of New York's great indoor/outdoor experiences; Philip Johnson's **Lipstick Building**, 885 Third Ave, between E 53rd and 54th streets, named for its curved, telescoping shape; and the right-angle steel and glass slabs of the **Lever House**, 390 Park Ave, also between E 53rd and 54th streets.

Renzo Piano-designed gathering space brings together Morgan's library, annex and Morgan Jr's nineteenth-century brownstone. The collection of nearly 10,000 drawings and prints, including works by Da Vinci, Degas and Dürer, is augmented by the rare literary manuscripts of Dickens, Jane Austen and Thoreau, as well as hand-written correspondence between Ernest Hemingway and George Plimpton and musical scribblings by everyone from Haydn to Dylan. Morgan's personal library and study, part of the McKim building at the core of the complex, are also on view.

Grand Central Terminal

MAP P.102, POCKET MAP E8
E 42nd St, between Lexington and Vanderbilt aves. Subway S, #4, #5, #6, #7 to 42nd St–Grand Central. ☎ 212 935 3960 or ☎ 212 883 2420 for tours, ⓦ www.grandcentralterminal.com.

Grand Central Depot opened in 1871 under the direction of Cornelius Vanderbilt, but the current masterly piece of urban planning that replaced it, **Grand Central Terminal**, was built in 1913. With a basic iron frame and dramatic Beaux-Arts skin, the main train station's concourse is a sight to behold – 470ft long and 150ft high, it boasts a barrel-vaulted ceiling speckled like a Baroque church with a painted

representation of the winter night sky. The station's more esoteric reaches include a lower concourse brimming with takeout options as well as the landmark *Oyster Bar and Restaurant* (see page 112). Daily tours ($30; 75min) of the station begin at 12.30pm from the main information booth; a 12.30pm tour on Fridays (free; 90min) takes in some of the neighbouring area as well and starts across the street in the glass atrium of 120 Park Avenue. You can also embark on an informative, self-guided audio tour (daily 9am–6pm; $9) by picking up a device at one of the windows marked "GCT Tour", on the main concourse.

The Chrysler Building

MAP P.102, POCKET MAP E8
405 Lexington Ave, between E 42nd and E 43rd sts. Subway S, #4, #5, #6, #7 to 42nd St–Grand Central. Lobby Mon–Fri 8am–6pm.

One of Manhattan's best-loved structures, the **Chrysler Building** dates from a time (1928–30) when architects married prestige with grace and style. The car-motif friezes, jutting gargoyles and arched stainless-steel pinnacle give the solemn Midtown skyline a welcome whimsical touch. The lobby, once a car showroom, is all you can see of the building's interior – still worth it to get a look at the walls covered in

African marble, murals depicting aeroplanes, machines and the brawny builders who worked on the tower, and showy elevator doors with inlaid wood.

The United Nations

MAP P.102, POCKET MAP F8
First Ave, at E 46th St. Subway S, #4, #5, #6, #7 to 42nd St-Grand Central. ☎ 212 963 8687, ⓦ www.visit.un.org. Guided tours (45min) Mon–Fri 9.am–4.45pm. $22, $13 children 5–12.

A must-visit only for those obsessed by global goings-on, the **United Nations complex** comprises the glass-curtained Secretariat, the curving sweep of the General Assembly and, connecting them, the low-rising Conference Wing. Tours – bring ID for security purposes and arrive early – take in the UN conference chambers and its constituent parts. Even more revealing than the stately rooms are its thoughtful

exhibition spaces and country gifts on view.

The Met Life Building

MAP P.102, POCKET MAP E8
200 Park Ave, between E 44th and E 45th sts. Subway S, #4, #5, #6, #7 to 42nd St-Grand Central.

The unsubtle bulk of the **Met Life Building**, looming over the southern end of Park Avenue before its interruption by Grand Central, steals the thunder of many of the more delicate structures around it. Bauhaus guru Walter Gropius had a hand in the design, and the critical consensus is that he could have done better. As the headquarters of the now-defunct Pan Am airline, the building, in profile, was meant to suggest an aircraft wing. The blue-grey mass certainly adds drama to the cityscape, even as it seals the avenue at 44th Street.

Waldorf Astoria New York

Waldorf Astoria Hotel

MAP P.102, POCKET MAP E8
301 Park Ave, between E 49th and E 50th
sts. Subway #6 to 51st St.

The solid mass of the 1931
Waldorf Astoria Hotel helps
contribute to the conspicuous
wealth of Park Avenue. It's
undergoing a long-term
renovation that won't see it reopen
until 2021, so you'll have to
admire its blocking grandeur from
the outside.

St Bartholomew's Church

MAP P.102, POCKET MAP E8
325 Park Ave, at E 51st St. Subway #6
to 51st St. Ⓦ www.stbarts.org. Daily
9am–6pm, choir service Sun 11am.

The Episcopalian **St
Bartholomew's Church** is a
low-slung Romanesque hybrid
with portals designed by McKim,
Mead, and White. Adding
immeasurably to the street, it
gives the lumbering skyscrapers a
much-needed sense of scale. Due
to the fact that it's on some of the
city's most valuable real estate, the
church fought against developers
for years and ultimately became
a test case for New York City's
landmark preservation law.

The Seagram Building

MAP P.102, POCKET MAP E7
375 Park Ave, between E 52nd and E 53rd
sts. Subway E, M Lexington Ave/53rd St,
#6 to 51st St.

Designed by Mies van der Rohe
with Philip Johnson, the 1958
Seagram Building was the
seminal curtain-wall skyscraper.
Its floors are supported internally,
allowing for a skin of smoky glass
and whisky-bronze metal. Every
interior detail – from the fixtures
to the lettering on the mailboxes
– was specially designed. The
plaza, an open forecourt designed
to set the building apart from its
neighbours, was such a success that
the city revised the zoning laws to
encourage other high-rise builders
to supply similar public spaces.

Citigroup Center

MAP P.102, POCKET MAP E7
601 Lexington Ave, between E 53rd and E
54th sts. Subway #6 to 51st St.

Opened in 1978, the chisel-
topped **Citigroup Center**

The New York Public Library

(formerly the Citicorp Center) is one of Manhattan's most conspicuous landmarks. The slanted roof was designed to house solar panels to provide power for the building, and it adopted the distinctive building-top as a corporate logo. Inside lies small **St Peter's Church**, known as "the Jazz Church" for being the venue of many a jazz musician's funeral; jazz vespers are held on Sundays at 5pm.

The Sony Building

MAP P.102, POCKET MAP D7
550 Madison Ave, between E 55th and E 56th sts. Subway E, M to 5th Ave/53rd St or Lexington Ave/53rd St.

Philip Johnson's 38-storey **Sony Building** (1978–84) follows the Postmodernist theory of eclectic borrowing from historical styles: a Modernist skyscraper sandwiched between a Chippendale top and a Renaissance base. Even though the first floor is well worth ducking into to soak in the brute grandeur, some speculate Johnson should have followed the advice of his teacher, Mies van der Rohe: "It's better to

build a good building than an original one." Though sold for $1 billion a few years back, it had its exterior landmarked in 2018 – putting the brakes on a planned renovation. It's more or less empty.

The New York Public Library

MAP P.102, POCKET MAP D8
E 42nd St and Fifth Ave. Subway B, D, F, M, #4, #5, #6 to 42nd St. ☎ 917 275 6975, Ⓦ www.nypl.org. Mon & Thurs–Sat 10am–6pm, Tues & Wed 10am–8pm, Sun 1–5pm (except in summer), building tours Mon–Sat 11am & 2pm, Sun 2pm.

This monumental Beaux Arts building, faced in brilliant white marble (and recently restored for the library's centennial), is the headquarters of the largest public-library system in the world. Plenty of folks meet at the **NYPL**'s steps, framed by two majestic reclining lions, to while away the time; head inside to explore the place on your own or to take a free guided tour. The latter gives a good all-round picture of the building, taking in the **Map Room** and evocative **Periodicals Room**, with its stunning faux-wood ceiling and paintings of old New York. The undisputed highlight, however, is the large, coffered 636-seat **Reading Room** on the third floor, which was restored in 2016. Authors Norman Mailer and E.L. Doctorow worked here, as did Leon Trotsky during his brief sojourn in New York just prior to the 1917 Russian Revolution. It was also here that Chester Carlson came up with the idea for the Xerox copier and Norbert Pearlroth whiled away the better part of 52 years researching columns for "Ripley's Believe It or Not." More than anything, you may find the building familiar from its roles in all kinds of movies, including *Ghostbusters* and *Breakfast at Tiffany's*.

Bryant Park

MAP P.102, POCKET MAP D8
Sixth Ave, between W 40th and 42nd
sts. Subway B, D, F, M to 42nd St. ☎ 212
768 4242, ⓦ www.bryantpark.org. Daily
7am–10pm, later May–Sept.

Right behind the public library,
Bryant Park is a grassy, square
block filled with slender trees,
flowerbeds, a small carousel
and inviting chairs. It officially
became a park in 1847 and is
named after a newspaper editor
– William Cullen Bryant of the
New York Post, also famed as a
poet and instigator of Central
Park. Bryant Park was the site of
the first American World's Fair
in 1853, with a Crystal Palace,
modelled on the famed London
Crystal Palace, on its grounds –
an edifice that burned down in
1858. Summertime brings a lively
scene to the park all day long:
free jazz and yoga classes, table
tennis and free outdoor movies
on Monday evenings; come
winter there's a holiday market
and an ice-skating rink (roughly
Nov–Feb; free entry, skate rentals
extra). A tiny carousel ($3)
operates year-round.

Diamond Row

MAP P.102, POCKET MAP D8
W 47th St, between Fifth and Sixth
aves. Subway B, D, F, M to 47–50th St-
Rockefeller Center.

You'll know **Diamond Row** by the
diamond-shaped lamps mounted
on pylons at either end. This strip,
where you can get jewellery fixed at
reasonable prices, features wholesale
and retail shops chock-full of
gems and was first established in
the 1920s. These stores are largely
managed by Hasidic Jews, and
the workaday vibe feels more like
the Garment District or the old
Lower East Side than a part of
tourist Midtown.

Rockefeller Center

MAP P.102, POCKET MAP D8
From Fifth to Sixth aves, between W
48th and W 51st sts. Subway B, D, F, M to
47–50th St/Rockefeller Center. ☎ 212 332
6868, ⓦ www.rockefellercenter.com. Tours
daily 10am–7.30pm, every 30min, $25
(☎ 212 698 2000 ext 5).

The heart of Midtown's glamour,
Rockefeller Center was built
between 1932 and 1940 by John
D. Rockefeller Jr, son of the
oil magnate, and is one of the

Rockefeller Center

finest pieces of urban planning anywhere, balancing office space with cafés, underground concourses and rooftop gardens that work together with a rare intelligence and grace. At its centre, the **Lower Plaza** holds a sunken restaurant in the summer months. It's a great place for afternoon cocktails beneath Paul Manship's golden *Prometheus* sculpture. In winter this area becomes an ice rink for skaters, and every Christmas since 1931, a huge tree has been on display above the statue; its lighting, with accompanying musical entertainment, draws throngs in early December.

The GE Building

MAP P.102, POCKET MAP D8
30 Rockefeller Plaza, between W 49th and W 50th sts. Subway B, D, F, M to 47–50th St/Rockefeller Center. NBC studio tours daily 8.30am–5pm, Ⓦ www.thetouratnbcstudios.com. ☎ 212 664 3700. $33, children 6–12 $29. Tapings ☎ 212 664 3056, Ⓦ nbc.com/tickets.

Perhaps the apogee of Art Deco styling, the **GE Building** (or **30 Rock**) rises 850ft, its symmetrical monumental lines matching the scale of Manhattan itself. In the GE lobby, José Maria Sert's murals, *American Progress* and

Time, are in tune with the 1930s Art Deco ambience – though paintings by Diego Rivera were scrapped after the artist refused to remove an image glorifying Lenin. Among the building's many offices are the **NBC Studios**, which produce the long-running comedy hit *Saturday Night Live* and *The Tonight Show Starring Jimmy Fallon*. Studio tours and tapings of select shows (limited availability) should satisfy most curiosity seekers.

Top of the Rock Observation Deck

MAP P.102, POCKET MAP D8
30 Rockefeller Plaza at W 50th St. Subway B, D, F, M to 47–50th St/Rockefeller Center. ☎ 212 698 2000, Ⓦ www.topoftherocknyc.com. Daily 8am–midnight, last elevator at 11pm. $36, children 6–12 $30.

It's a lot to pay for a view, but what a view. Arguably as grand as that from the Empire State Building (with the added bonus of being able to see the Empire State), the panorama from the top of the **GE Building** lets you examine the layout of Central Park and how built-up downtown is compared to uptown, offers a vertiginous look at St Patrick's Cathedral and looks out to the George Washington Bridge and

City views

Top of the Rock and the Empire State Building are the obvious places to go for panoramic views of New York, but you can save a bit of money and find unique angles on the city at any of the following:

The mid-point of **Brooklyn Bridge** (P.42), to see the Financial District.

The **High Line** (P.92), for a look up Tenth Avenue.

General Worth Square next to Madison Square Park (P.102), for a look at the Flatiron, Metlife tower, the park and a lot of whizzing traffic.

The Roof Garden Café at the Met (P.145), for views of Central Park.

Empire Fulton Ferry in Dumbo (P.161), for glimpses of the Brooklyn and Manhattan bridges.

Radio City Music Hall

beyond. The film that introduces a bit of history on Rockefeller Center is missable; just head to the elevator that whisks you up to floor 67, with additional decks on floors 69 and 70 accessible by stairs.

Radio City Music Hall

MAP P.102, POCKET MAP D8
1260 Sixth Ave, at W 50th St. Subway B, D, F, M to 47–50th St/Rockefeller Center. Tickets ☏ 1 866 858 0008, tours ☏ 212 247 4777, Ⓦ msg.com/radio-city-music-hall. Daily 9.30am–5pm. Tour $30, children 12 and under $26, ticket prices for concerts vary.

Heralded by one of the most familiar marquees in New York, the world-famous concert hall **Radio City** is the last word in 1930s luxury. If you're not taking in a show – greats such as Sinatra used to grace the stage here, but these days it's better-known for its "Christmas Spectacular" than for any major bookings – you'll need to join one of the hour-long "Stage Door" behind-the-scenes walking tours to see it. The staircase is resplendent, with the world's largest chandeliers, while

the huge auditorium looks like an extravagant scalloped shell. The movable parts of the stage hold some fascination, and there's a brief meeting with (and photo of) a Rockette too.

St Patrick's Cathedral

MAP P.102, POCKET MAP D8
50th St and Fifth Ave. Subway B, D, F, M to 47–50th St/Rockefeller Center. ☏ 212 753 2261, Ⓦ www.saintpatrickscathedral.org. Daily 6.30am–8.45pm, services throughout the day.

Designed by James Renwick and completed in 1888, **St Patrick's Cathedral** is the result of a painstaking academic tour of the Gothic cathedrals of Europe – perfect in detail, yet rather lifeless in spirit, with a sterility made all the more striking by the glass-black **Olympic Tower** next door, an exclusive apartment block where Jackie Kennedy Onassis once lived.

Paley Center for Media

MAP P.102, POCKET MAP D7
25 W 52nd St, between Fifth and Sixth aves. Subway B, D, F, M to 47–50th St/Rockefeller Center, E, M to Fifth Ave/53rd St. ☏ 212 621

MoMA

6800, Ⓦ www.paleycenter.org/visit. Wed &
Fri–Sun noon–6pm, Thurs noon–8pm. $10,
under 14 $5.

The former Museum of Television
and Radio still largely centres on
its extensive archive of American
TV and radio broadcasts, so if
you want to view episodes of
beloved but short-lived series like
Freaks and Geeks or old classics
like *Dragnet* or the *Honeymooners*,
this is the place. An excellent
computerized reference system lets
you have a show at your fingertips
in no time.

The Museum of Modern Art

MAP P.102, POCKET MAP D7
11 W 53rd St between Fifth and Sixth aves.
Subway B, D, F, M to 47–50th St/Rockefeller
Center, E, M to Fifth St/53rd St. ☎ 212
708 9400, Ⓦ www.moma.org. Mon, Wed,
Thurs, Sat & Sun 10.30am–5.30pm, Fri
10.30am–8pm. $25, children 16 and under
free, free Fri 4–8pm.

The Museum of Modern Art –
MoMA to its friends – offers the
finest and most complete account
of late nineteenth- and twentieth-
century art you're likely to find
in the world. More than 100,000
paintings, sculptures, drawings,
prints, photographs, architectural
models and design objects
make up the collection, along
with a world-class film archive.
Note that the specifics below
represent what is typically on
display. Pieces rotate with some
regularity, though the biggest
names can always be found. The
museum has been undergoing
a major redevelopment which
will result in almost a third more
gallery space and a performance
area; that means by sometime
in 2019, a good deal more of
the permanent collection should
be visible.

The core is the **Collection
Galleries 1880–1950**, which
occupies the fifth floor. The
display starts with Cézanne,
Gauguin and the Post-
Impressionists of the late
nineteenth century, takes in
Picasso, Braque and Matisse

(who has his own dedicated room, highlighted by the self-referential *Red Studio* and odd perspective of *The Dance*), moves through De Chirico, Duchamp and Mondrian, follows with the surrealists Miró, Magritte and Dalí and finishes with Abstract Expressionists like Pollock, Rothko and Barnett Newman. Familiar works from the more modern canon – Jasper Johns' *Flag*, Robert Rauschenberg's mixed media paintings – may be here too.

The remaining floors hold thematic or temporary exhibitions, so you may see all kinds of things from MoMA's holdings: Warhol's soup cans, Roy Lichtenstein's cartoons, every imaginable aspect of design from the mid-nineteenth century on (including the original set of emoji pictographs), as well as drawings and contemporary art The film screenings pick up on all kinds of themes and present a compelling draw as well. If you need to refuel, the second-floor café, *Café 2*, serves very good,

slickly presented Italian-style food. *Terrace 5*, on the fifth floor, is a more formal option, and provides nice views of the ground-level sculpture garden (which opens early, perfect for a morning stroll). A swanky restaurant, *The Modern*, sits on the first floor.

Trump Tower

MAP P.102, POCKET MAP D7
**725 Fifth Ave, between 56th and 57th sts.
Subway F to 57th St.**
New York real-estate developer, reality TV show personality, and President of the United States, Donald Trump claims an outrageously overdone high-rise and atrium, **Trump Tower**, as his own. It's just short of repellent to many — perfumed air, polished marble panelling and a five-storey waterfall are calculated to knock you senseless. The building is clever, a neat little outdoor garden is squeezed high in a corner, and each of the 230 apartments above the atrium provides views in three directions. The outside is heavily guarded and the site of occasional protests.

Trump Tower

Shops

Apple Store

MAP P.102, POCKET MAP D7
767 Fifth Ave, between 58th and 59th sts;
other locations. Subway N, R, W to 5th
Ave/59th St. Daily 24hr.

There are now nine Apple stores in
town, though this is the only 24hr
one – one that's returning after a
renovation that doubled the size.
A giant glass cube rises from the
sidewalk to herald the entrance;
descend the spiral staircase within
to see the latest in gadgets and
to take part in free demos and
workshops.

Bergdorf Goodman

MAP P.102, POCKET MAP D7
754 and 745 Fifth Ave, at 58th St. Subway
F to 57th St, N, R, W to Fifth Ave/59th St.
Mon–Sat 10am–8pm, Sun 11am–7pm.

This venerable department store
caters to the city's wealthiest
shoppers and, in an unusual setup,
flanks Fifth Avenue. Haute couture
designers fill both buildings,
one for men, one for women. Its
holiday windows are among the
flashiest in town.

Bloomingdale's

MAP P.102, POCKET MAP E7
1000 Third Ave, at E 59th St. Subway
N, R, W, #4, #5, #6 to 59th St. Mon–Sat
10am–8.30pm, Sun 11am–7pm.

One of Manhattan's most famous
department stores, packed with
designer clothiers, perfume
concessions and housewares.

Saks Fifth Avenue

MAP P.102, POCKET MAP D8
611 Fifth Ave, at 50th St. Subway E, M to
53rd St, B, D, F, M to 47–50th St/Rockefeller
Center. Mon–Sat 10am–8.30pm, Sun
11am–7pm.

Every bit as glamorous as it was
when it opened in 1922, Saks
remains virtually synonymous with
style and quality.

Tannen's Magic

MAP P.102, POCKET MAP D9
45 W 34th St, Suite 608, between Fifth
and Sixth aves. Subway B, D, F, M, N, Q,
R, W to 34th St-Herald Square. Mon–Fri
11am–6pm, Sat 10am–4pm.

Your kids will never forget a visit
to the largest magic shop in the
world, full of props, tricks and
magic sets, and staff who can
demonstrate tricks.

Bloomingdales

Tiffany & Co.

MAP P.102, POCKET MAP D7
727 Fifth Ave, at E 57th St. Subway N, R, W
to Fifth Ave/59th St. Mon–Sat 10am–7pm,
Sun noon–6pm.

Tiffany's soothing green marble
and weathered wood interior is
perhaps best described by Truman
Capote's fictional Holly Golightly:
"It calms me down right away…
nothing very bad could happen to
you there."

Cafés and snacks

Lucid Café

MAP P.102, POCKET MAP E9
311 Lexington Ave, at 38th St. Subway
#4, #5, #6, #7 to 42nd St-Grand Central.
Mon–Fri 7am–5pm, Sat 8am–5pm, Sun
8am–3pm.

You'd do well to grab one of the
two window seats and enjoy a
strong shot of espresso ($2.75)
or a cortado ($3.75) alongside
a buttery croissant at this tiny,
charming spot.

The Plaza Food Hall

MAP P.102, POCKET MAP D7
1 W 58th St, Concourse Level of The Plaza.
Subway N, R, W to Fifth Ave-59th St. Mon–
Sat 8am–9.30pm, Sun 11am–8pm.

On the lower level of this venerable
hotel, outlets of *No. 7 Sub*, *Luke's
Lobster* and others have set up shop;
there's also the Todd English Food
Hall (daily 11am–10pm) within
the food hall, where the celebrity
chef offers raw shellfish, wood-fired
pizza and grilled meats.

Restaurants

Ai Fiori

MAP P.102, POCKET MAP D9
400 Fifth Ave, between 36th and 37th sts
in the Langham Place hotel. Subway B, D,
F, M, N, Q, R, W to 34th St-Herald Square;
#6 to 33rd St. ☎ 212 613 8660. Mon–Thurs
7–10.30am, noon–2.30pm & 5.30–10pm,
Fri 7–10.30am, noon–2.30pm & 5–10pm,
Sat 8am–2.15pm & 5–10.15pm, Sun

Aquavit

8am–2.15pm & 5.30–9.30pm.

The decor and atmosphere are
unmemorable, but the elegant
French-Italian dishes are anything
but. Splurge on the four-course
prix-fixe menu ($108), which
allows you to choose your dishes
(butter-poached lobster, for
example) from the outstanding
regular menu.

Aquavit

MAP P.102, POCKET MAP D7
65 E 55th St, between Madison and Park
aves. Subway #6 to 51st St. ☎ 212 307
7311. Mon–Thurs 11.45am–2.30pm &
5.30–10pm, Fri 11.45am–2.30pm &
5.30–10.30pm, Sat 5.30–10.30pm.

Go for a blowout in the main
dining room (three courses run
to about $115) or a more casual
meal in the bar-lounge. Either
way, you'll sample Scandi food at
its finest: silky gravlax, herring,
Swedish meatballs and, of course,
a home-made version of the
eponymous spirit.

Cho Dang Gol

MAP P.102, POCKET MAP D9
55 W 35th St, between Fifth and Sixth aves.
Subway B, D, F, M, N, Q, R, W to 34th St.
☎ 212 695 8222. Daily noon–10pm.

Korean restaurants proliferate on
32nd Street between Fifth and
Sixth; this one, a little off the

The Grand Central Oyster Bar & Restaurant

path, specializes in home-made tofu every which way. There's more, though, like simmered pork belly served as part of a spicy lettuce wrap.

Hatsuhana

MAP P.102, POCKET MAP D8
17 E 48th St, between Fifth and Madison aves. Subway #6 to 51st St. ☎ 212 355 3345; another branch at 237 Park Ave. Mon–Fri noon–2.30pm & 5.30–10pm, Sat 5–10pm.

A longtime favourite of local sushi lovers, this place is not cheap but won't break the bank – and the freshness of the fish compensates in any case.

Keens Steakhouse

MAP P.102, POCKET MAP D9
72 W 36th St, between Fifth and Sixth aves. Subway B, D, F, M, N, Q, R, W to 34th St-Herald Square. ☎ 212 947 3636. Mon–Fri 11.45am–10.30pm, Sat 5–10.30pm, Sun 5–9.30pm.

This 130-year-old chophouse is a classic; the bustling pub makes a great place for a Martini and junior-sized mutton chop (an off-menu item), or you can go all out on the larger cuts served in the rambling dining room.

La Grenouille

MAP P.102, POCKET MAP D7
3 E 52nd St, between Fifth and Madison aves. Subway E, M to Fifth Ave–53rd St. ☎ 212 752 1495. Tues–Fri noon–2.30pm & 5–10pm, Sat 5–10pm.

The haute French cuisine here has melted hearts and tantalized palates since 1962. All the classics are done to perfection, and the service is gracious. Its prix-fixe lunch is $68, and dinner is $172 per person. Jacket required.

The Modern

MAP P.102, POCKET MAP D7
9 W 53rd St. Subway E, M to Fifth Ave–53rd St. ☎ 212 333 1220. Mon–Fri noon–2pm & 5–10.30pm, Sat 5–10.30pm, Bar Room only on Sun 11.30am–9.30pm.

MoMA's fine-dining offering is elegant without trying too hard. Seasonal ingredients are artfully combined to yield unexpected dishes: say, chorizo-crusted codfish with white cocoa-bean purée. Four-course set meals cost from $128. The *Bar Room at the Modern* offers more casual dining.

Oyster Bar

MAP P.102, POCKET MAP E8
Lower level, Grand Central Terminal, at

42nd St and Park Ave. Subway S, #4, #5, #6, #7 to 42nd St-Grand Central. ☎ 212 490 6650. Mon–Sat 11.30am–9.30pm.

Down in the vaulted cellars of Grand Central, the fabled (and just restored) *Oyster Bar* draws Midtown office workers for lunch and seafood-lovers for dinner, who choose from a staggering list of daily catches including barramundi and steamed Maine lobster. Prices are moderate to expensive, but you can always choose chowder, a pan roast or a sandwich from the counter.

Sarge's Deli

MAP P.102, POCKET MAP E9
548 Third Ave, between 36th and 37th sts. Subway #6 to 33rd St. ☎ 212 679 0442. Daily 24hr.

Want a classic NYC deli without the hype of the over-touristed spots? Come for a pile of pastrami (or whatever you like) at this friendly Murray Hill place that's run by a former police officer.

Bars

Campbell Bar

MAP P.102, POCKET MAP E8
Grand Central Terminal, southwest balcony, E 42nd St. Subway S, #7, #4, #5, #6 to 42nd St-Grand Central. ☎ 212 297 1781. Daily noon–2am.

Once home of businessman John W. Campbell, who oversaw the construction of Grand Central, this majestic space was sealed up for years. Now, it's one of New York's most distinctive bars. Dress relatively nicely; Sunday night is jazz night.

King Cole Bar

MAP P.102, POCKET MAP D7
2 E 55th St, between Fifth and Madison aves, in the St Regis Hotel. Subway E, M to Fifth Ave-53rd St, F to 57th St. Mon–Sat 11.30am–1am, Sun noon–midnight. Dress smart and be prepared to spend at the reputed home of the Bloody Mary (here known as

the Red Snapper), but sipping a cocktail under the Maxfield Parrish mural at the bar, you'll surely feel like a million bucks.

Overlook Bar

MAP P.102, POCKET MAP E8
225 E 44th St, between Second and Third aves. Subway 4, 5, 6, 7 to Grand Central Terminal. Daily 11am–3pm.

It may not look like much from the outside, but this sports pub holds a treasure of public art: an illustrated wall executed by some of the leading cartoonists of the 1970s—done largely in exchange for drinks back in the days when the establishment was known as Costello's.

PJ Clarke's

MAP P.102, POCKET MAP E7
915 Third Ave, at E 55th St. Subway #6 to 51st St, E, M to Lexington Ave/53rd St. ☎ 212 317 1616. Daily 11.30am–1am, Sat & Sun 10am–1am .

One of the city's most famous watering holes, *PJ Clarke's* alehouse serves good beers, but only Guinness comes in a pint serving. Tables with red-and-white-checked cloths await diners in the back, where you can choose from a classic American menu. You may recognize it as the setting of the film *The Lost Weekend*.

PJ Clarke's

Times Square and the Theater District

The towering signs and flashing lights of Times Square, the blocks just north of 42nd Street where Seventh Avenue intersects with Broadway, bring a whole new meaning to the term "sensory overload". More than 300,000 people pass through daily, and on New Year's Eve hundreds of thousands more come to watch the apple drop at midnight. The seedy days are gone, but ostentatious displays of media and commercialism still reign. The adjoining Theater District and its million-dollar Broadway productions draw crowds, while Hell's Kitchen to the west offers innumerable restaurants as well as an array of bars and LGBTQ nightlife. You may wind up spending a decent amount of time here – it's a major hotel base and you'll probably want to take in a show or two – but there are few, if any, must-see sights (other than the sheer spectacle).

Times Square

MAP P.116, POCKET MAP D8
Broadway, Seventh Ave and 42nd St. Subway N, Q, R, W, #1, #2, #3 to Times Square–42nd St. Ⓦ www.timessquarenyc.org.

If not always so in the public imagination, **Times Square** is now a largely sanitized universe of popular consumption. It takes its name from the *New York Times* offices built in 1904 (the current *Times* building, a Renzo Piano creation, is at Eighth Avenue between 40th and 41st streets); publisher Adolph Ochs staged a New Year's celebration here in honour of their opening. This tradition continues today: hundreds of thousands arrive early to pack the streets, party (as best they can without being able to purchase or publicly consume alcohol) and watch the giant Waterford Crystal Ball drop on One Times Square. The neon, so much a signature of the square, was initially confined to

the theatres and spawned the term "the Great White Way", but myriad ads for hundreds of products now form one of the world's most garish nocturnal displays; indeed, Broadway buildings here are required to have a certain amount of signage. A number of glitzy attractions have opened in the area in recent years, including the Spy Museum (what you'd imagine) and Gulliver's Gate (miniature models of the great buildings, cities and landscapes of the world) – good but pricey if you're looking for some family entertainment.

Hell's Kitchen

MAP P.116, POCKET MAP C8
Between 34th and 59th streets west of Eighth Avenue, **Hell's Kitchen** mostly centres on the engaging slash of restaurants, bars, ethnic delis and food shops of Ninth Avenue (which has begun to extend farther

west) – the staging set for the excellent **Ninth Avenue International Food Festival** (Ⓦ ninthavenuefoodfestival. com) each May. Once one of New York's most violent and lurid neighbourhoods, it was first populated by Irish and Eastern European immigrants, who were soon joined by Greeks, Puerto Ricans and blacks. The rough-and-tumble area was popularized in the 1957 musical *West Side Story*. But things have changed quite a bit: the odd tatty block is now countered by trim residential streets, and construction and renovation of luxury apartments and hotels occurs at sometimes breakneck speed. Along with other gentrifiers, there's now a substantial gay community, with nearly as many gay bars and nightspots as in Chelsea or the West Village.

The Intrepid Sea, Air & Space Museum
MAP P.116, POCKET MAP B8

The Intrepid Sea, Air & Space Museum

Pier 86, at W 46th St and Twelfth Ave. Subway A, C, E to 42nd St, C, E to 50th St. ☏ 212 245 0072, Ⓦ www.intrepidmuseum.org. April–Oct Mon–Fri 10am–5pm, Sat & Sun 10am–6pm; Nov–March daily 10am–5pm. $26, ages 7–17 $19, add $7/$5 for Space Shuttle Pavilion.

This impressive, 900ft-long old aircraft carrier has picked up capsules from the Mercury and Gemini space missions and made several trips to Vietnam. It holds an array of modern and vintage air- and seacraft, including the A-12 Blackbird, the world's fastest spy plane, and the USS *Growler*, the only guided missile submarine open to the public. Interactive exhibits dominate the interior hangar, but make sure to explore further into the bowels of the carrier, where you can see the crew's dining and sleeping quarters, the anchor room and lots of navigational gadgets. The museum is also home to the retired *Concorde* and, in its Space Shuttle Pavilion, *Enterprise* (just a

test vehicle – it never made it to outer space).

Ed Sullivan Theater

MAP P.116, POCKET MAP C7
1697 Broadway, between 53rd and 54th sts. Subway B, D, E to Seventh Ave. For taping information. ⓦ colbert.1iota.com.

Come afternoon, a queue can usually be seen outside this building; it's where Stephen Colbert hosts CBS's popular *Late Show*. Book well ahead (two per reservation; tickets are free) to try to catch a taping in the domed interior.

Carnegie Hall

MAP P.116, POCKET MAP D7
154 W 57th St, at Seventh Ave. Subway N, Q, R, W to 57th St. ☎ 212 903 9600, tickets ☎ 212 247 7800, ⓦ www.carnegiehall.org. Tours Oct–June usually Mon–Fri 11.30am, 12.30pm, 2pm & 3pm, Sat 11.30am & 12.30pm, Sun 12.30pm. $17, children aged under 13 $12.

One of the world's great concert venues, stately Renaissance-inspired **Carnegie Hall** was built by steel magnate Andrew Carnegie for $1 million in 1891. Tchaikovsky conducted on opening night, and Mahler, Rachmaninov, Toscanini, Frank Sinatra, Duke Ellington and Judy Garland have all played here. The superb acoustics help to ensure full houses most of the year; those craving a behind-the-scenes glimpse should take the excellent tours. The second-floor Rose Museum is free and open to the public.

Columbus Circle

MAP P.116, POCKET MAP C7
Intersection of Broadway, Central Park West and 59th St. Subway A, B, C, D, #1 to 59th St-Columbus Circle.

A rare Manhattan roundabout that separates Midtown from the Upper West Side, **Columbus**

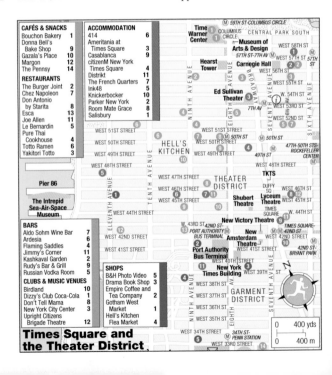

Times Square and the Theater District

The Theater District

West of Broadway and north of 42nd Street, the Theater District helps light up Times Square. Of the great old palaces still in existence, the **New Amsterdam**, at 214 W 42nd Street, and family-oriented **New Victory**, at 209 W 42nd Street, have been refurbished to their original splendour. **The Lyceum**, at 149 W 45th Street, has its original facade, while the **Shubert Theater**, at 225 W 44th Street, has a magnificent landmark interior that belies its simple outward appearance.

If you want to see a **show**, check out the TKTS booth at 47th Street in Times Square (there are other booths at the South Street Seaport and Lincoln Center), which sells half-price, same-day tickets for Broadway shows (Mon & Wed–Sat 3–8pm, Tues 2–8pm for evening shows, also Wed, Thurs & Sat 10am–2pm, Sun 11am–3pm for matinees). The booth has available at least one pair of tickets for each performance of every Broadway and off-Broadway show, at 20 to 50 percent off (plus a $4.50 per ticket service charge). Also, many theatre box offices sell greatly reduced "standing room only" tickets the day of the show. See also Ⓦ www.tdf.org.

Circle is best experienced from its centre island underneath the statue of Columbus himself, who stands uncomfortably atop a lone column. From there you can look out at the horse and carriages off Central Park and some striking buildings, like the Hearst Tower, Time Warner Center and Two Columbus Circle. Off the circle at the Central Park entrance is the **USS Maine Monument**, a large stone column with the prow of a ship jutting out from its base; a dazzlingly bright gilded statue of Columbia Triumphant tops it off. The monument is dedicated to the 260 seamen who died in an explosion that helped propel the Spanish–American War.

Hearst Tower

MAP P.116, POCKET MAP C7
300 W 57th St, at Eighth Ave. Subway A, B, C, D, #1 to 59th St–Columbus Circle.
The limestone base of the **Hearst Tower** waited for a skyscraper to top it since the Great Depression. Finally completed in 2006, the glass-and-steel geometry of the Hearst Tower sits ingeniously

– and somewhat incongruously – inside the shell of that base. It's certified as one of the most environmentally friendly high-rises ever constructed and was the first skyscraper to begin construction post 9/11.

Hearst Tower

TIMES SQUARE AND THE THEATER DISTRICT

Museum of Arts and Design

MAP P.116, POCKET MAP C7
2 Columbus Circle. Subway A, B, C, D, #1 to
59th St-Columbus Circle. ☎ 212 299 7777,
Ⓦ www.madmuseum.org. Tues, Wed &
Fri–Sun 10am–6pm, Thurs 10am–9pm. $16,
visitors 18 and under free, Thurs 6–9pm
pay what you wish.

The story of the building that
arcs along the south side of
Columbus Circle is as interesting
as the holdings of the **Museum
of Arts and Design** that occupy
it. Built in the 1960s to house
the Gallery of Modern Art, 2
Columbus Circle was regarded as
an architectural folly (and a failure
as a museum), yet after years of
abandonment and disrepair, the
building became the subject of
an epic battle over its significance
and status. Noted architects like
Robert A.M. Stern fought for
its preservation but eventually
failed, and the Museum of Arts
and Design (the former American
Crafts Museum) had the building

totally redesigned. Gone are the
portholes and white marble;
in their place, slots, ceramic
and glass that seem to form
letter shapes on the facade. The
eclectic collection inside features
everything from blown-glass
objets d'art to contemporary
jewellery; the temporary exhibits
frequently take centre stage.

Time Warner Center

MAP P.116, POCKET MAP C7
10 Columbus Circle. Subway A, B, C, D,
#1 to 59th St-Columbus Circle. Ⓦ www.
shopsatcolumbuscircle.com.

The glassy, curving **Time Warner
Center**, a massive, $1.7 billion
building with a shopping complex
on its lower levels (Mon–Sat
10am–9pm, Sun 11am–7pm),
opened in 2004. The timing
and design make it hard not to
think of it as a more modern,
less-loved variation of the Twin
Towers. Some of the city's priciest
restaurants (*Per Se*, *Masa*) dish it
out here.

Time Warner Center

Shops

B&H Photo Video

MAP P.116, POCKET MAP C9
420 Ninth Ave, at 34th St. Subway A, C, E
to 34th St. ☎ 212 444 6615. Mon–Thurs
9am–6pm, Fri 9am–2pm, Sun 10am–5pm.
You'll find a staggering array of
cameras, camcorders, blu-ray
players and every other kind of
home electronic you might want or
need; there's a used-goods section
upstairs. Closed on Saturdays and
Jewish holidays.

Drama Book Shop

MAP P.116, POCKET MAP C9
250 W 40th St, between Seventh and
Eighth aves. Subway A, C, E, N, Q, R, W,
#1, #2, #3, #7 to 42nd St. Mon–Wed &
Fri–Sat 10am–7pm, Thurs 10am–8pm, Sun
noon–6pm.
A long-running shop that
stocks theatre books, scripts and
publications on all manner of
drama-related subjects.

Empire Coffee and Tea Company

MAP P.116, POCKET MAP C8
568 Ninth Ave, between 41st and 42nd
aves. Subway A, C, E to 42nd St. Mon–Fri
7.30am–7pm, Sat 9am–6.30pm, Sun
10am–6pm.
One-hundred-year-old coffee
roaster that looks and smells
authentic. There are lots of exotic
teas, too.

Gotham West Market

MAP P.116, POCKET MAP B8
600 Eleventh Ave, between 44th and 45th
sts. Subway A, C, E to 42nd St. Mon–Fri
7am–11pm, Sat & Sun 8am–11pm.
One of the latest in the city's
haute food markets, this one
offers the *Ivan Ramen Slurp Shop*
as well as Ample Hills ice cream,
food counters for tacos, pizza and
charcuterie… even a bike shop.
Each place has its own hours.

Hell's Kitchen Flea Market

MAP P.116, POCKET MAP C9

W 39th St, between Ninth and Tenth aves.
Subway A, C, E to 42nd St. Sat & Sun
9am–5pm.
While there's still an indoor flea
market in Chelsea, the outdoor
version relocated to Hell's Kitchen;
you'll find a mishmash of home
decorations, antique jewellery,
electronics and other odds
and ends.

Cafés and snacks

Bouchon Bakery

MAP P.116, POCKET MAP C7
10 Columbus Circle, Third Floor, Time
Warner Center; another location in
Rockefeller Center. Subway A, B, C, D, #1 to
59th St–Columbus Circle. Bakery Mon–Sat
8am–8pm, Sun 8am–7pm, café Mon–Fri
8am–5pm, Sat–Sun 10am–5pm.
At this Thomas Keller
establishment you can get
something to go or sit at a table
and gaze onto the corner of
leafy Central Park, grazing on a
sandwich, decadent pastry, salad
or charcuterie.

Donna Bell's Bake Shop

MAP P.116, POCKET MAP C8
301 W 49th St, between Eighth and Ninth
aves. Subway C, E to 50th St. Mon–Fri
6am–7pm, Sat 9am–7pm, Sun 9am–3pm.
Tiny Southern-style bakery –
cupcakes, biscuits, delicious bread
pudding and some savoury dishes –
opened by a TV star from the show
NCIS. No seating.

Gazala's Place

MAP P.116, POCKET MAP C8
709 Ninth Ave, between 48th and 49th
sts. Subway C, E to 50th St. Mon–Thurs
& Sun 11am–10.30pm, Fri & Sat
11am–11.30pm.
Supposedly the only Druze (a
Middle Eastern sect) restaurant in
the States – besides the outpost
at 380 Columbus Ave – Gazala's
serves dinner, but is best known
for its good lunch deals and flaky
bourekas ($9.50),– giant stuffed
savoury pastries.

Margon

MAP P.116, POCKET MAP D8
136 W 46th St, between Sixth and Seventh
aves. Subway B, D, F, M to 47–50th sts/
Rockefeller Center, N, Q, R to 49th St.
☎ 212 354 5013. Mon–Fri 6am–5pm, Sat
7am–3pm.

This narrow Cuban lunch counter
is nearly always packed; savoury
Cuban sandwiches ($10 with
rice and beans), garlicky *pernil*
(roast pork; Wed special, $10) and
brightly seasoned octopus salad
($12) top the choices.

The Pennsy

MAP P.116, POCKET MAP C9
2 Penn Plaza, 33rd St, at Seventh Ave.
Subway 1, 2, 3, A, C, E to 34th St/Penn
Station. ☎ 917 475 1830. Daily 11am–2am..
Yes, it's a posh food hall attached
to workaday Penn Station. Get Pat
LaFrieda steak sandwiches ($15),
vegan treats from *Cinnamon
Snail* and craft cocktails from *The
Pennsy Bar*.

Restaurants

The Burger Joint

MAP P.116, POCKET MAP D7
119 W 56th St, between Sixth and Seventh
aves, in Le Parker Meridien. Subway F,
N, Q, R, W to 57th St. ☎ 212 708 7414,
Ⓦ burgerjointny.com. Mon–Thurs &
Sun 11am–11.30pm, Fri & Sat 11am to
midnight.

The secret has long been out on
the retro hamburger stand hidden
in a swish Midtown hotel. Good
for late-night eating (burgers from
around $9); you might have to wait
for a table, though.

Chez Napoleon

MAP P.116, POCKET MAP C8
365 W 50th St, between Eighth and Ninth
aves. Subway C, E to 50th St. ☎ 212 265
6980, Ⓦ cheznapoleon.com. Mon–Fri
noon–2pm & 5–9.30pm, Sat 5–9.30pm.
One of several highly authentic
Gallic eateries that sprang up
around here in the 1940s and
1950s, *Chez Napoleon*, a friendly,

family-run bistro, is kind of
stuck in a time warp – in a good
way. There's a good-value prix
fixe ($35), and the wines are
well priced.

Don Antonio by Starita

MAP P.116, POCKET MAP C8
309 W 50th St, between Eighth and Ninth
aves. Subway C, E to 50th St. ☎ 646 719
1043, Ⓦ www.donantoniopizza.com. Mon–
Thurs 11.30am–11pm, Fri & Sat 11.30am–
midnight, Sun 11.30am–10.30pm.
The progeny of two celebrated
Neopolitan pizza mavens, busy *Don
Antonio* showcases a few different
styles of pie; traditional margheritas
($14) share the menu with the
signature Montanara ($16) – which
is light, smoky and chewy and
comes by way of the deep fryer and
the brick oven.

Esca

MAP P.116, POCKET MAP C8
402 W 43rd St, at Ninth Ave. Subway A, C,
E to 42nd St-Port Authority. ☎ 212 564
7272, Ⓦ escanyc.com. Mon noon–2.30pm
& 5–10pm, Tues–Thurs noon–2.30pm
& 4.30–10.30pm, Fri–Sat noon–2.30 &
4.30–11.30pm, Sun 4.30–10pm.
Chef-owner Dave Pasternack has a
passion for fresh fish that is evident.
Lots of crudo ($20–25) and whole
fish grilled or salt-baked (entrées
$36–42).

Joe Allen

MAP P.116, POCKET MAP C8
326 W 46th St, between Eighth and
Ninth aves. Subway A, C, E to 42nd St.
☎ 212 581 6464, Ⓦ joeallenrestaurant.
com. Mon noon–11pm, Tues, Thurs & Fri
noon–11.45pm, Thurs noon–11.45, Sat
11.30am–11.45pm, Sun 11.30am–11pm.
The tried-and-true formula of
checked tablecloths, old-fashioned
bar-room feel, and reliable
American food at moderate prices
(entrées $20–39) works well at
this pre-theatre spot. Make a
reservation.

Le Bernardin

MAP P.116, POCKET MAP D8

Le Bernardin

155 W 51st St, between Sixth and Seventh aves. Subway B, D, F, M to 47–50th St/Rockefeller Center or #1 to 50th St. ☎ 212 554 1515, ⓦ le-bernardin.com. Mon–Thurs noon–2.30pm & 5.15–10.30pm, Fri noon–2.30pm & 5.15–11pm, Sat 5.15–11pm.
One of the finest and priciest ($160 prix fixe) French restaurants in the city (though the lounge offers a la carte dishes $24–44). Award-winning chef, Eric Ripert, offers inventive takes on every kind of fish and seafood imaginable. His sauces are not to be believed.

Pure Thai Cookhouse

MAP P.116, POCKET MAP C7
766 Ninth Ave, between 51st and 52nd sts. Subway C, E to 50th St. ☎ 212 581 0999, ⓦ purethaicookhouse.com. Mon–Thurs noon–10.30pm, Fri & Sat noon–11.30pm, Sun noon–10.15pm.
Wok-induced smoke fills the air at this rough-hewn Thai spot, which does excellent stir-fries and noodles, some a bit more daring than elsewhere (crab and pork dry noodles, $14; chilli turmeric with beef, $14).

Totto Ramen

MAP P.116, POCKET MAP C8
366 W 52nd St, between Eighth and Ninth aves. Other locations in Hell's Kitchen and Midtown. Subway C, E to 50th St. ☎ 212 582 0082. Mon–Sat noon–4.30pm & 5.30pm–midnight, Sun 4–11pm.
This narrow spot (mainly counter seating) is one of the top places to get ramen – preferably with char siu pork and spicy sesame oil. The queue forms quickly; it's slightly easier to score a table at the location a block further west (464 W 51 St).

Yakitori Totto

MAP P.116, POCKET MAP C7
251 W 55th St, between Broadway and Eighth Ave. Subway A, B, C, D, #1 to 59th-St–Columbus Circle, N, Q, R, W to 57th St, B, D, E to Seventh Ave. ☎ 212 245 4555, ⓦ tottonyc.com. Mon–Thurs 11.30am–2pm & 5.30pm–midnight, Fri 11.30am–2pm & 5.30pm–1am, Sat 5.30pm–1am, Sun 5.30–11pm.
This popular upstairs hideaway is perfect for late-night snacking – though you may miss out on some of the more esoteric grilled skewers (soft knee bone served rare, anyone?), which can be gone by then. Chicken heart, skirt steak and chicken thigh with scallion

all burst with flavour (most $3–5 each). Reasonable set lunches, too ($11–14).

Bars

Aldo Sohm Wine Bar

MAP P.116, POCKET MAP D8
151 W 51st St, between Sixth and Seventh aves. Subway B, D, F, M to 47–50th Sts/Rockefeller Center. Mon–Thurs 11.45am–2.30pm & 4.30–11.30pm, Fri 11.45am–2.30pm & 4.30pm–midnight, Sat 4.30pm–midnight.

Run by the sommelier from *Le Bernardin* (see page 120), this comfortably upscale bar offers one of the best wine lists in town, accompanied by an array of charcuterie and small bites.

Ardesia

MAP P.116, POCKET MAP B7
510 W 52nd St, between Tenth and Eleventh aves. Subway C, E to 50th St. Mon–Wed 4pm–midnight, Thurs, Fri & Sat 4pm–2am, Sun 2–11pm. ☎ 212 247 9191, ⓦ www. ardesia-ny.com.

A sleek but comfortable wine bar with a bold snack menu (home-made pretzels, quail-egg toast,

Jimmy's Corner

house-cured meats) and a diverse selection of vintages, thirty of which are available by the glass ($9–16).

Flaming Saddles

MAP P.116, POCKET MAP C7
793 Ninth Ave, between 52nd and 53rd sts. Subway C, E to 50th St. ⓦ www. flamingsaddles.com. Mon–Fri 3pm–4am, Sat & Sun noon–4am.

This LGBTQ hangout comes with a Texas twist: there's dancing on the bar, a Western vibe and drink specials (Texas Tea, with sweet tea and vodka) all day and most of the night.

Jimmy's Corner

MAP P.116, POCKET MAP D8
140 W 44th St, between Broadway and Sixth Ave. Subway B, D, F, M, N, Q, R, W, #1, #2, #3 to 42nd St. Mon–Sat 11.30am–4am, Sun 3pm–4am.

The walls of this long, narrow corridor of a bar, owned by an ex-fighter/trainer, make up a virtual Boxing Hall of Fame. You'd be hard pressed to find a more characterful dive and cheaper drinks – or a better jazz/R&B jukebox.

Kashkaval Garden

MAP P.116, POCKET MAP C7
852 Ninth Ave, between 55th and 56th sts. Subway A, B, C, D, #1 to 59th St/ Columbus Circle. Mon–Thurs noon–1am, Fri noon–2am, Sat 11am–2am, Sun 11am–11pm.

This cosy wine and cheese bar serves up tasty bites, including excellent cheese and meat plates, cold tapas and fondues.

Rudy's Bar & Grill

MAP P.116, POCKET MAP C8
627 Ninth Ave, between W 44th and 45th sts. Subway A, C, E to 42nd St-Port Authority. Mon–Sat 8am–4am, Sun Noon–4am.

One of New York's cheapest, friendliest and liveliest dive bars, Rudy's is a favourite with local musicians. A giant plastic pig greets you at the door; there are also free hot dogs and a great backyard.

Russian Vodka Room

MAP P.116, POCKET MAP C7
265 W 52nd St, between Broadway and Eighth Ave. Subway C, E, #1 to 50th St. Mon–Wed & Sun 4pm–2am, Thurs–Sat 4pm–4am.
They serve more than fifty types of vodka here, including their own fruit-flavoured and sublime garlic-infused concoctions; there's also caviar and plenty of small plates. Whatever you do, don't ask for a mixer with your shot.

Clubs and music venues

Birdland

MAP P.116, POCKET MAP C8
315 W 44th St, between Eighth and Ninth aves. Subway A, C, E to 42nd St–Port Authority. ☎ 212 581 3080, ⓦ www.birdlandjazz.com. Cover $25–50, $10 food/drink minimum. Shows generally at 8.30pm & 11pm.
Celebrated alto saxophonist Charlie "Bird" Parker served as the inspiration for this jazz venue, which has existed in some incarnation for 70 years. The menu – with a Cajun twist – is decent. A more intimate downstairs theatre, with Italian food and additional shows, opened in 2018.

Dizzy's Club Coca-Cola

MAP P.116, POCKET MAP C7
Time Warner Center, Broadway, at W 60th St, 5th floor. Subway A, B, C, D, #1 to 59th St–Columbus Circle. ☎ 212 258 9595, ⓦ www.jazz.org. Shows at 7.30pm, 9.30pm & 11.30pm. $20–45 cover, $10 minimum at tables.
Part of Jazz at Lincoln Center's home within the Time Warner Center, this room named in honour of Dizzy Gillespie is the only great jazz venue in town with a view – that of Central Park. Book a table for dinner or just drinks and enjoy hot acts.

Don't Tell Mama

MAP P.116, POCKET MAP C8
343 W 46th St, between Eighth and Ninth

Kevin Eubanks performs at Birdland

aves. Subway A, C, E to 42nd St–Port Authority or 50th St. ☎ 212 757 0788, ⓦ www.donttellmamanyc.com. Cover $10–25.
The lively, convivial piano bar and cabaret features rising stars. Two-drink minimum in cabaret rooms; showtimes vary.

New York City Center

MAP P.116, POCKET MAP D7
131 W 55th St, at Seventh Ave. Subway B, D, E to Seventh Ave, F to 57th St, N, Q, R, W to 57th St–Seventh Ave. ☎ 212 581 1212, ⓦ www.nycitycenter.org.
This large, restored venue – once a temple – revives long-forgotten musicals, hosts the Manhattan Theatre Club and features the Alvin Ailey American Dance Theater.

Upright Citizens Brigade Theatre

MAP P.116, POCKET MAP B8
555 W 42nd St, at Eleventh Ave. Subway A, C, E to 42nd St–Port Authority. ☎ 212 366 9176, ⓦ ucbtheatre.com. Cover free–$12.
Consistently hilarious sketch-based and improv comedy, seven nights a week. Sunday's ASSSSCAT 3000 is a longtime favourite (and the later of its two shows is free). You may see some Saturday Night Live alums on stage.

Central Park

"All radiant in the magic atmosphere of art and taste", enthused Harper's magazine upon the opening in 1876 of Central Park, the first landscaped park in the US. Today, few New Yorkers could imagine life without it. Set smack in the middle of Manhattan, extending from 59th to 110th streets, it provides residents (and street-weary tourists) with a much-needed refuge from the arduousness of big-city life. The two architects commissioned to transform 843 swampy acres, Frederick Law Olmsted and Calvert Vaux, were inspired by classic English landscape gardening. They designed 36 elegant bridges, each unique, and planned a revolutionary system of four sunken transverse roads to keep traffic out of sight. Although some of the open space has been turned into asphalted playgrounds, the intended sense of captured nature largely survives.

Wollman Memorial Ice Skating Rink

MAP P.126, POCKET MAP D6
830 Fifth Ave, at E 63rd St. Subway N, R to Fifth Ave–59th St. ⓣ 212 439 6900, ⓦ www. wollmanskatingrink.com. Oct–early April Mon & Tues 10am–2.30pm, Wed & Thurs 10am–10pm, Fri & Sat 10am–11pm, Sun 10am–9pm. Mon–Thurs $12, Fri–Sun $19, children $6, skate rentals $9, spectator fee $5.

Get in the rink for some of the city's most atmospheric ice skating; you're surrounded by onlookers, trees and, beyond that, a brilliant view of Central Park South's skyline. In summer, **Wollman Rink** becomes **Victorian Gardens**, a small amusement park.

Snow leopard at Central Park Zoo

Central Park Zoo

MAP P.126, POCKET MAP D6
Enter at Fifth Ave and E 64th St. Subway N, R to Fifth Ave–59th St. ⓣ 212 439 6500, ⓦ www.centralparkzoo.com. April–Oct Mon–Fri 10am–5pm, Sat & Sun 10am–5.30pm, Nov–March daily 10am–4.30pm. $12, ages 3–12 $7.

This small zoo contains over 150 species in largely natural-looking homes with the animals as close to the viewer as possible: the penguins, for example, swim around at eye level in Plexiglas pools. Other highlights include giant polar bears, snow leopards and a humid tropical zone filled with exotic birds. The complex also features the **Tisch Children's Zoo**, with a petting zoo.

The Carousel

MAP P.126, POCKET MAP D6
Mid-park, at 64th St. Subway A, B, C, D, #1, to 59th St-Columbus Circle. ☏ 212 439 6900 ext 4. Daily: April–Oct 10am–6pm; Nov–March roughly same hours, weather permitting; call ahead. $3.

Built in 1908 and moved to the park from Coney Island in 1951, this hand-carved, wooden **carousel** is one of around 150 such specimens left in the country.

The Mall

MAP P.126, POCKET MAP D6
Roughly mid-park, from 66th to 72nd sts. Subway #6 to 68th St, B, C to 72nd St.

If the weather's nice, head straight to the **Mall**, where you'll find every manner of street performer. Flanked by statues of Robert Burns and a pensive Sir Walter Scott, with Shakespeare nearby (all part of the so-called literary walk), the Mall is the park's most formal, but by no means quiet, stretch.

The Sheep Meadow

MAP P.126, POCKET MAP C6
Between 66th and 69th sts on the western side. Subway #1 to 66th St-Lincoln Center. Mid-April to mid-Oct dawn to dusk. This swathe of green, named after the fifteen acres of commons where sheep grazed until 1934, is crowded in the summer with picnic blankets.

Two grass courts used for lawn bowling and croquet are found on a hill near the meadow's northwest corner; to the southeast lie volleyball courts. On warm weekends, the area between the **Sheep Meadow** and the north end of the Mall is filled with colourfully attired rollerbladers.

Strawberry Fields

MAP P.126, POCKET MAP C5

Rowing in Central Park

W 72nd St and Central Park W. Subway B, C to 72nd St.

This peaceful pocket of the park is dedicated to the memory of John Lennon, who was murdered in 1980 in front of his home, the **Dakota Building** (see page 138). The tragic event is memorialized with a round Italian mosaic with the word "Imagine" at its centre, donated by Lennon's widow, Yoko Ono.

Bethesda Terrace and Fountain

MAP P.126, POCKET MAP D5
Roughly mid-park, at 72nd St. Subway B, C to 72nd St.

The only formal element of the original Olmsted and Vaux plan, the **Bethesda Terrace** overlooks the lake; beneath the terrace is an elaborate arcade with tiled floors. The crowning centrepiece of the **Bethesda Fountain** is the *Angel of the Waters* sculpture.

Loeb Boathouse

MAP P.126, POCKET MAP D5
Mid-park, near 74th st. Subway B, C

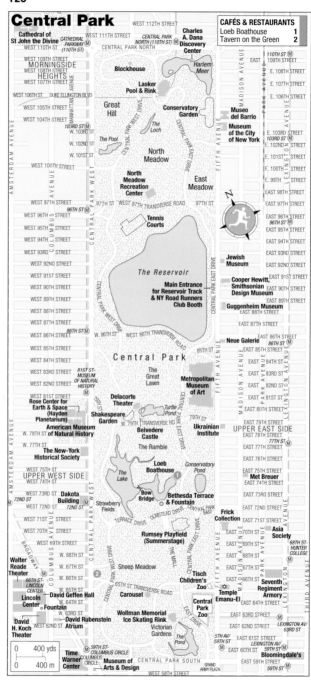

Central Park

CAFÉS & RESTAURANTS
Loeb Boathouse	1
Tavern on the Green	2

WEST 112TH STREET

Cathedral of
St John the Divine
WEST 110TH ST
CATHEDRAL
PARKWAY
(110TH ST)

WEST 111TH STREET

CENTRAL PARK
NORTH (110TH ST)

Charles
A. Dana
Discovery
Center

CENTRAL PARK NORTH

110TH ST
109TH STREET

MORNINGSIDE
HEIGHTS
WEST 108TH STREET
WEST 107TH STREET

EAST 108TH STREET

E. 107TH STREET

WEST 106TH ST DUKE ELLINGTON BLVD

Blockhouse

E. 106TH STREET

Lasker
Pool & Rink

WEST 105TH STREET

WEST 104TH STREET

Great
Hill

Conservatory
Garden

Museo
del Barrio

E. 103RD STREET

103RD ST
W. 103RD ST

The Pool

E. 102ND STREET

W. 102ND ST

North
Meadow

Museum
of the City
of New York

W. 101ST ST

E. 101ST STREET

WEST 100TH STREET

E. 100TH STREET

North
Meadow
Recreation
Center

E. 99TH STREET

WEST 97TH STREET

East
Meadow

E. 98TH STREET

97TH ST WEST 97TH TRANSVERSE ROAD

97TH ST

EAST 97TH STREET

WEST 96TH STREET
96TH ST

EAST 96TH STREET
96TH ST

WEST 95TH STREET

Tennis
Courts

EAST 95TH STREET

WEST 94TH STREET

EAST 94TH STREET

WEST 93RD STREET

EAST 93RD STREET

WEST 92ND STREET

Jewish
Museum

EAST 92ND STREET

WEST 91ST STREET

The Reservoir

Cooper Hewitt,
Smithsonian
Design Museum

EAST 91ST STREET

WEST 90TH STREET

EAST 90TH STREET

Main Entrance
for Reservoir Track
& NY Road Runners
Club Booth

Guggenheim Museum

WEST 89TH STREET

EAST 89TH STREET

WEST 88TH STREET

EAST 88TH STREET

WEST 87TH STREET

EAST 87TH STREET

WEST 86TH STREET
86TH ST

Neue Galerie

EAST 86TH STREET
86TH ST

W. 86TH ST WEST 86TH TRANSVERSE ROAD

EAST 85TH STREET

WEST 85TH STREET

85TH ST

WEST 84TH STREET

C e n t r a l   P a r k

EAST 84TH STREET

WEST 83RD STREET
81ST ST-
MUSEUM
OF NATURAL
HISTORY

The
Great
Lawn

EAST 83RD STREET

WEST 82ND STREET

Metropolitan
Museum
of Art

EAST 82ND STREET

WEST 81ST STREET
Rose Center for
Earth & Space
(Hayden
Planetarium)

Delacorte
Theater
79TH ST

EAST 81ST STREET

EAST 80TH STREET

Shakespeare
Garden W. 79TH TRANSVERSE RD

Turtle
Pond
79TH ST

American Museum
of Natural History
W. 78TH ST

Belvedere
Castle

Ukrainian
Institute

UPPER EAST SIDE

EAST 78TH STREET

W. 77TH ST

The Ramble

The New-York
Historical Society

77TH ST

EAST 77TH STREET

EAST 76TH STREET

WEST 75TH STREET

Loeb
Boathouse

Conservatory
Pond

Met Breuer

EAST 75TH STREET

UPPER WEST SIDE
WEST 74TH STREET

The
Lake

EAST 74TH STREET

WEST 73RD STREET Dakota
72ND ST   Building

Bow
Bridge

Bethesda Terrace
& Fountain

EAST 73RD STREET

WEST 72ND STREET
72ND ST

Strawberry
Fields

Frick
Collection

EAST 72ND STREET

WEST 71ST STREET

TERRACE DRIVE

Asia
Society

EAST 71ST STREET

EAST 70TH STREET

WEST 70TH STREET

OLMSTEAD DRIVE

Rumsey Playfield
(Summerstage)

CENTRAL PARK EAST

68TH ST-
HUNTER
COLLEGE

WEST 69TH STREET

EAST 69TH STREET

Walter
Reade
Theater

Sheep Meadow

EAST 68TH STREET

W. 68TH STREET

EAST 67TH STREET

W. 67TH STREET

Seventh
Regiment
Armory

66TH ST-
LINCOLN
CENTER

W. 66TH STREET

Tisch
Children's
Zoo

Lincoln
Center

David Geffen Hall
W. 64TH STREET

65TH ST TRANSVERSE ROAD

Carousel

Temple
Emanu-El

EAST 66TH STREET

Fountain

EAST 65TH STREET

David
H. Koch
Theater

WEST 62ND STREET

David Rubenstein
Atrium

Wollman Memorial
Ice Skating Rink

Central
Park
Zoo

EAST 64TH STREET

WEST 63RD STREET

EAST 63RD STREET

Victorian
Gardens

EAST 62ND STREET

LEXINGTON AV/
63RD ST

59TH ST-
COLUMBUS CIRCLE

The
Pond

5TH AV/
59TH ST

EAST 61ST STREET
LEXINGTON AV/
59TH ST

0		400 yds
0		400 m

Time
Warner
Center

COLUMBUS
CIRCLE

Museum of
Arts & Design

CENTRAL PARK SOUTH

EAST 60TH STREET

59TH ST

WEST 58TH STREET

GRAND
ARMY PLAZA

Bloomingdale's

EAST 59TH STREET

Cafés and restaurants

Besides vendors and a few cafés, there are only two eating destinations in the park. *Loeb Boathouse* (see page 125) offers both upscale dining and casual bar-and-grill fare. *Tavern on the Green*, at Central Park West and 67th Street (☎ 212 877 8684), is a reincarnation of a storied restaurant and focuses on seasonal food – like the Boathouse, the setting is half the point.

to 72nd St. ☎ 212 517 2233, Ⓦ www.thecentralparkboathouse.com. April–Oct Mon–Fri 10am–6pm, Sat & Sun 9am–6pm, weather permitting; $15 for the first hour, and $4/15min after, $20 deposit required.

You can go for a Venetian-style gondola ride ($45/30min) or rent a rowing boat ($34/30min) from the **Loeb Boathouse** on the lake's eastern bank.

The Great Lawn

MAP P.126, POCKET MAP D4
Mid-park, from 79th to 85th sts. Subway B, C to 81st or 86th sts.

The **Great Lawn** hosts free New York Philharmonic and Metropolitan Opera summertime concerts, holds eight softball fields, basketball and volleyball courts, and a running track. At the southern end, **Turtle Pond** is a fine place to view turtles and birds.

Belvedere Castle

MAP P.126, POCKET MAP D5
Mid-park, at 79th St. ☎ 212 772 0288.
Visitor Center daily 10am–5pm. Regular walking tours, birdwatching excursions and educational programmes on offer.

The highest point in the park (and a splendid viewpoint), **Belvedere Castle**, designed by park architect Vaux and his assistant, houses the New York Meteorological Observatory's **weather centre** and the **Henry Luce Nature Observatory**. Closed for restoration in 2018, the castle has refashioned a tower from its original design among other changes.

Delacorte Theater

MAP P.126, POCKET MAP D5
Mid-park, at 80th St. Subway B, C to 81st St.

☎ 212 539 8750, Ⓦ www.publictheater.org.
This performance space is most notably home to **Shakespeare in the Park** in the summer. Tickets are free but go quickly; visit the website for details.

Conservatory Garden

MAP P.126, POCKET MAP D2
East side from 104th to 106th sts, entrance at Fifth Ave and 105th St. Subway #6 to 103rd St.

If you see nothing else above 86th Street in the park, don't miss the **Conservatory Garden**, the park's only formal garden, featuring English, Italian and French styles.

Conservatory Garden

The Upper East Side

The defining characteristic of Manhattan's Upper East Side is wealth. While other neighbourhoods were penetrated by immigrant groups and artistic trends, the area has remained primarily a privileged enclave of the well off, with high-end shops, clean and relatively safe streets, well-preserved buildings and landmarks, most of the city's finest museums, and some of its most famous boulevards: Fifth, Madison and Park avenues. Madison Avenue is lined with designer clothes stores, while primarily residential Park Avenue is solidly comfortable and often elegant, sweeping down the spine of upper Manhattan. It has awe-inspiring views south, as the avenue coasts down to Grand Central and the Met Life Building. Shedding its stuffy image somewhat, an influx of young professionals has sparked a mini surge in gastropubs and cocktail bars in the last few years.

Fifth Avenue

MAP P.130, POCKET MAP D3–D7
Subway F to Lexington Ave/63rd St, N, R, W to Lexington Ave/59th St, #4, #5, #6 to 59th St, #6 to 68th St, 77th St, 86th St or 96th St.

Fifth Avenue

The haughty patrician face of Manhattan since the 1876 opening of Central Park along which it runs, **Fifth Avenue** lured the Carnegies, Astors, Vanderbilts, Whitneys and others north to

build their fashionable Neoclassical residences. In the late nineteenth century, fanciful mansions were built at vast expense, but lasted only ten or fifteen years before being demolished for even wilder extravagances or, more commonly, grand apartment buildings. As Fifth Avenue progresses north, it turns into the **Museum Mile**.

Temple Emanu-El

MAP P.130, POCKET MAP D6
1 E 65th St, at Fifth Ave. Subway F to Lexington Ave/63rd St, #6 to 68th St. ☎ 212 744 1400, Ⓦ emanuelnyc.org. Synagogue and museum Sun–Thurs 10am–4.30pm. Free.

America's largest reform synagogue, the **Temple Emanu-El**, is a brooding, Romanesque–Byzantine cavern. The on-site museum houses a fascinating collection of Judaica.

Frick Collection

MAP P.130, POCKET MAP D6
1 E 70th St, at Fifth Ave. Subway #6 to 68th St. ☎ 212 288 0700, Ⓦ frick.org. Tues–Sat 10am–6pm, Sun 11am–5pm. $22; pay what you wish Wed 2–6pm.

Built in 1914 for Henry Clay Frick, probably the most ruthless of New York's robber barons, this handsome pile is now the tranquil home of the **Frick Collection**, displaying artwork from the Middle Ages to the nineteenth century. Opened in 1935, the museum has been largely kept as it looked when the Fricks lived there. Much of the furniture is heavy eighteenth-century French, but what sets it apart from most galleries – and the reason many rate the Frick so highly – is that it strives hard to be as unlike a museum as possible. There is no wall text describing the pictures, though you can dial up info on each work using hand-held guides.

This legacy of Frick's self-aggrandizement affords a revealing glimpse into the sumptuous life enjoyed by the city's big industrialists, while the collection

Frick Collection

includes paintings by Constable, Reynolds, Hogarth, Gainsborough, Goya, Bellini, El Greco, Titian and Vermeer. The **West Gallery** holds Frick's greatest prizes: two Turners, views of Cologne and Dieppe; and a set of piercing self-portraits by Rembrandt, along with his enigmatic *Polish Rider*. Also unmissable are Holbein's famous portraits of Thomas More and Thomas Cromwell in the **Living Hall**, and Vermeer's stunning *Officer and a Laughing Girl*.

At the far end of the West Gallery you will find a tiny chamber called the **Enamel Room**, named after the exquisite set of mostly sixteenth-century Limoges enamels on display.

Metropolitan Museum of Art

MAP P.130, POCKET MAP D5
1000 Fifth Ave, at E 82nd St. Subway #4, #5, #6 to 86th St. ☎ 212 535 7710, Ⓦ metmuseum.org. Sun–Thurs 10am–5.30pm, Fri & Sat 10am–9pm. $25.

The foremost art museum in America, the **Metropolitan Museum of Art** (or the Met) takes in over two million works and

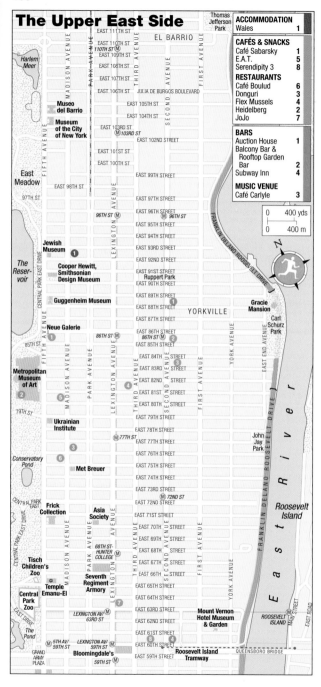

The Upper East Side

Thomas Jefferson Park

ACCOMMODATION	
Wales	1

CAFÉS & SNACKS	
Café Sabarsky	1
E.A.T.	5
Serendipity 3	8

RESTAURANTS	
Café Boulud	6
Donguri	3
Flex Mussels	4
Heidelberg	2
JoJo	7

BARS	
Auction House	1
Balcony Bar & Rooftop Garden Bar	2
Subway Inn	4

MUSIC VENUE	
Café Carlyle	3

EL BARRIO

Harlem Meer

Museo del Barrio

Museum of the City of New York

East Meadow

Jewish Museum

The Reservoir

Cooper Hewitt, Smithsonian Design Museum

Ruppert Park

Guggenheim Museum

YORKVILLE

Gracie Mansion

Neue Galerie

Carl Schurz Park

Metropolitan Museum of Art

Ukrainian Institute

Conservatory Pond

Met Breuer

John Jay Park

Roosevelt Island

Frick Collection

Asia Society

68TH ST-HUNTER COLLEGE

Tisch Children's Zoo

Seventh Regiment Armory

Central Park Zoo

Temple Emanu-El

The Pond

GRAND ARMY PLAZA

Bloomingdale's

Mount Vernon Hotel Museum & Garden

Roosevelt Island Tramway

ROOSEVELT ISLAND

Queensboro Bridge

East River

0   400 yds
0   400 m

spans the cultures of America, Europe, Africa, the Far East, and the classical and Egyptian worlds.

You enter at the **Great Hall**, where you can consult floor plans and check tour times. From here the Grand Staircase leads to the museum's greatest attraction – the **European Painting galleries**. Dutch painting is particularly strong, embracing an impressive range of Rembrandts, Hals and Vermeers – his *Young Woman with a Water Jug* is a perfect example of his skill in composition and tonal gradation, combined with an uncannily naturalistic sense of lighting; you'll also find such masters as Goya, Velázquez, and a room of freaky, dazzling canvases by El Greco, each of which underscores the jarring modernism of his approach.

Highlights of the popular **Nineteenth-Century galleries** include stunning Rodin sculptures and a lauded collection of Impressionists; Manet, Monet, Cézanne and Renoir are all well represented, and there are mesmerizing works by Van Gogh and Gauguin nearby.

The Museum's Asian art section is justly celebrated for its Japanese screens and Buddhist statues, and the Chinese Garden Court, a serene, minimalist retreat; a pagoda, small waterfall and stocked goldfish pond landscaped with limestone rocks, trees and shrubs create a sense of peace.

Close to being a museum in its own right, the **American Wing** is a thorough introduction to the development of fine art in America, with a vast collection of paintings, period furniture, glass, silverware and ceramics. The undeniable standout of the Egyptian collection is the **Temple of Dendur**, built by the emperor Augustus in 15 BC and moved here en masse as a gift of the Egyptian government during the construction of the Aswan High Dam in 1965.

Thanks to a magnificent renovation completed in 2007, one of the largest collections of Roman and Greek art in the world occupies some of the most attractive wings of the museum; check out the wonderfully bright **Greek Sculpture Court**, a fittingly elegant setting for sixth- to fourth-century BC marble sculptures.

Whatever you do choose to see, between May and October be sure to ascend to the **Roof Garden Bar** (see page 137) for incredible views and changing contemporary sculpture exhibits.

Neue Galerie

MAP P.130, POCKET MAP D4
1048 Fifth Ave, at E 86th St. Subway #4, #5, #6 to 86th St. ☎ 212 628 6200, ⓦ neuegalerie.org. **Thurs–Mon 11am–6pm. $20.**
Dedicated to early twentieth-century art from Austria and Germany, the **Neue Galerie** occupies an ornate Beaux Arts mansion built in 1914. It's a relatively small space and the exhibits tend to rotate, but the collection contains some real gems.

Neue Galerie

The Guggenheim Museum

The galleries begin on the second floor, where the undoubted star is Gustav Klimt's *Portrait of Adele Bloch-Bauer I* (1907), a resplendent gold portrait from Klimt's "Golden Period". The Bloch-Bauers were one of Vienna's richest Jewish families; the painting was looted by the Nazis in 1938, but descendants sued the Austrian government and had the painting returned in 2006 – the gallery is said to have paid $135 million for it soon after. On this floor you'll also find exceptional work by Egon Schiele and Max Oppenheimer, while the third floor is usually reserved for rotating works of German Expressionism: look out for Paul Klee, Ernst Ludwig Kirchner and Otto Dix.

Guggenheim Museum

MAP P.130, POCKET MAP D4
L 1071 Fifth Ave, at E 89th St. Subway #4, #5, #6 to 86th St. ☎ 212 423 3500, Ⓦ guggenheim.org. Sun–Wed & Fri 10am–5.45pm, Sat 10am–7.45pm. $25; pay what you wish Sat 5.45–7.45pm.
Designed by Frank Lloyd Wright, the 1959 **Guggenheim Museum** is better known for the building in which it's housed than its collection. Its centripetal spiral ramp, which winds all the way to its top floor, is an exhilarating space, and some still favour Wright's talents over those of the artists exhibited. Nevertheless, the museum boasts an awe-inspiring ensemble of art, not least its fabulous stash of Kandinsky paintings gathered by Solomon Guggenheim (1861–1949), the mining millionaire who laid the foundations for the museum.

Temporary exhibits, often linked to pieces in the permanent collection, take up most of the galleries, but you'll always see plenty of Kandinsky's exuberant work: look out particularly for the jarring *Komposition 8* and the abstract *Blue Mountain*.

The Level 2 and 3 annexes also contain permanent displays: highlights include Picasso's haunting *Woman Ironing*, Van Gogh's vivid *Roadway with Underpass*, Cézanne's magnificent *Man with Crossed Arms* and *Dancers in Green and Yellow* by Degas. The museum also owns notable paintings by Chagall, Gauguin, Kirchner, Matisse and Monet, as well as contemporary work by artists such as Roni Horn.

Ukrainian Institute

MAP P.130, POCKET MAP D5
2 East 79th St, at Fifth Ave. Subway #4, #5, #6 to 86th St. ☎ 212 288 8660, Ⓦ ukrainianinstitute.org. Tues–Sun noon–6pm. $8.
Inevitably overshadowed by the Met just up the road, the Ukrainian Institute boasts a small but intriguing art collection – temporary exhibits from modern Ukrainian artists take up the second floor, but the upper levels contain some real gems. Still life from Sergei Belik, abstract work from Alexander Archipenko and paintings from David Burliuk,

the one-eyed "father of Russian Futurism", plus some huge Soviet Socialist Realist canvases, saved from destruction in the 1990s by collector Jurii Maniichuk and on loan here till 2018. The opulent building was completed in 1899 and served as the home of scandal-prone oilman Harry Sinclair in the 1920s.

Cooper Hewitt, Smithsonian Design Museum

MAP P.130, POCKET MAP D4
2 East 91st St, at Fifth Ave. Subway #6 to 96th St. ☎ 212 849 8400, ⓦ cooperhewitt. org. Sun–Fri 10am–6pm, Sat 10am–9pm. $18; pay what you wish Sat 6–9pm.

Housed in an elegant mansion completed for millionaire industrialist Andrew Carnegie in 1902, this museum blends modern galleries with an original interior – don't miss the old Carnegie Library on the second floor, adorned with intricate Indian-style teak carvings. Much of the museum comprises temporary or rotating exhibits with a design theme, though some version of "Making Design", showcasing the permanent

collection, should be on display, plus one of the largest collections of work from artists Winslow Homer and Frederic Edwin Church.

Jewish Museum

MAP P.130, POCKET MAP D4
1109 Fifth Ave, at E 92nd St. Subway #6 to 96th St. ☎ 212 423 3200, ⓦ thejewishmuseum.org. Fri–Tues 11am–5.45pm, Thurs 11am–8pm. $18, Sat free.

With over 28,000 items, this is the largest museum of Judaica outside Israel. Highlights of the permanent exhibition, "Culture and Continuity: The Jewish Journey", include a large and rare collection of Hanukkah lamps, the oldest dating from eighteenth-century Eastern Europe and Germany; you'll also find absorbing temporary displays of works by major international Jewish artists, such as Chagall and Man Ray.

Museum of the City of New York

MAP P.130, POCKET MAP D2
1220 Fifth Ave, at E 103rd St. Subway #6 to 103rd St. ☎ 212 534 1672, ⓦ mcny.org. Daily 10am–6pm. Suggested donation $18.

Jewish Museum

Housed in a grand neo-Georgian building purpose-built in 1930, the **Museum of the City of New York** has been transformed by major renovations in recent years. Most of the galleries feature temporary exhibits – subjects delve into all sorts of New York-related topics, from affordable housing and Currier & Ives prints (the museum has one of the world's largest collections) to World Fairs and the Gilded Age. The enlightening "Timescape" audiovisual presentation (25min; 15min and 45min past the hour) on the second floor, which tackles the history of the city from the Lenape Indians to 9/11, is permanent, as is the **Activist New York gallery**, a thought-provoking journey through the city's most contentious protest movements, from defending the Quakers in the 1650s to modern debates on gay rights.

Museo del Barrio

MAP P.130, POCKET MAP D2
1230 Fifth Ave, at E 104th St. Subway #6 to 103rd St. ☎ 212 831 7272, ⓦ elmuseo. org. Tues–Sat 11am–6pm, Sun noon–5pm. Suggested donation $9 (free every 3rd Sat of month).

Literally translated as "the neighbourhood museum", **Museo del Barrio** has largely a Puerto Rican emphasis in its traditional and contemporary collections, but the museum embraces the whole of Latin American and Caribbean cultures; its location places it on the edge of East Harlem, also known as "*El Barrio*" or Spanish Harlem. The pre-Columbian collection includes intricately carved vomiting sticks (used to purify the body with the hallucinogen cohoba before sacred rites).

Met Breuer

MAP P.130, POCKET MAP D5
945 Madison Ave, at E 75th St. Subway #6 to 77th St. ☎ 212 748 8600, ⓦ metmuseum.org. Tues–Thurs & Sun 10am–5.30pm, Fri & Sat 10am–9pm. $25.
The Whitney Museum relocated to new premises in 2015 (see page 84), and its old home now serves as the **Met Breuer**, an extension of the Met displaying modern and contemporary art. Galleries show temporary exhibitions from artists such as Indian modernist Nasreen Mohamedi, photographer Diane Arbus and painter Kerry James Marshall. The Marcel Breuer-designed building originally opened in 1966; the Brutalist design was initially a controversial addition to the Upper East Side, but in a sign of how beloved the structure became, plans to wreck its integrity with a Neoclassical addition were shouted down in the late 1980s.

Asia Society Museum

MAP P.130, POCKET MAP E6
725 Park Ave, at E 70th St. Subway #6 to 68th St. ☎ 212 288 6400, ⓦ asiasociety. org. Tues–Sun 11am–6pm, Fri until 9pm (Sept–June only). $12, free Fri 6–9pm (Sept–June only).
A prominent educational resource on Asia founded by John D. Rockefeller 3rd, the **Asia Society** offers an exhibition space

Asia Society Museum

Gracie Mansion

dedicated to both traditional and contemporary art from all over Asia. Exhibits are revolving, but often draw from the society's extensive permanent collection; exhibitions have included the arts of ancient Vietnam and South Indian Chola bronze sculptures. Intriguing performances, political roundtables, lectures, films and free events are frequently held.

Mount Vernon Hotel Museum & Garden

MAP P.130, POCKET MAP F7
421 E 61st St, between First and York aves.
Subway F, Q to Lexington Ave/63rd St, N, R, W to Lexington Ave/59th St, #4, #5, #6 to 59th St. ☎ 212 838 6878, ⓦ mvhm.org.
Tues–Sun 11am–4pm. $8.

Inside this fine stone house is a series of period rooms from the 1820s, meticulously restored by the Colonial Dames of America (an association of women who can trace their ancestry back to colonial times). The Dames were attracted by a connection with Abigail Adams Smith (daughter of President John Adams), though recent research has revealed this to be tenuous; the property was part

of an estate bought by Abigail and husband in 1795, but the family soon went bankrupt, and it was only completed as a carriage house in 1799 by the new owner. The house served as a hotel between 1826 and 1833.

Gracie Mansion

MAP P.130, POCKET MAP F4
East End Ave, at E 88th St. Subway #4, #5, #6, Q to 86th St. ☎ 311 or 212 676 3060 (outside NYC). Tours (45min) on Mon 10am, 11am & 5pm. Free; reservations required on-line at ⓦ 1.nyc.gov/site/gracie/visit.

One of the city's best-preserved colonial buildings, the 1799 **Gracie Mansion** has served as the official residence of the mayor of New York City since 1942; billionaire Michael Bloomberg opted not to live at the mansion, but current mayor Bill de Blasio has continued the tradition. The mansion was meticulously restored in 2002, but other than a few antiques and the bold murals in the dining room, the house itself isn't particularly compelling, and the tours are most interesting for the effusive guides and the stories of past mayors.

Cafés and snacks

Café Sabarsky

MAP P.130, POCKET MAP D4
1048 Fifth Ave, at E 86th St. Subway #4,
#5, #6 to 86th St. Mon & Wed 9am–6pm,
Thurs–Sun 9am–9pm.
Try to get a table by the window
at this sumptuous Viennese café
with great pastries and coffees.
Conveniently located in the
Neue Galerie.

E.A.T.

MAP P.130, POCKET MAP D5
1064 Madison Ave, between E 80th and E
81st sts. Subway #6 to 77th St. ☎ 212 772
0022. Daily 7am–10pm.
Expensive and crowded but the
food at this New York deli is
excellent (celebrated restaurateur
and gourmet grocer Eli Zabar is the
owner). Try the soups and breads,
or the heavenly mozzarella, basil
and tomato sandwiches.

Serendipity 3

MAP P.130, POCKET MAP E7
225 E 60th St, between Second and Third
aves. Subway N, R, W, #4, #5, #6 to 59th

St. Sun–Thurs 11.30am–midnight, Fri & Sat
11.30am–1am.
Adorned with Tiffany lamps, this
long-established eatery/ice cream
parlour is celebrated for its frozen
hot chocolate, which is out of this
world; there's a wealth of sundaes
(from $14.95) too, with everything
from cinnamon fudge to fresh
fruit and "Forbidden Broadway"
(chocolate blackout cake, ice
cream, hot fudge topped with
whipped cream).

Restaurants

Café Boulud

MAP P.130, POCKET MAP D5
20 E 76th St, between Madison and Fifth
Ave, at the Surrey Hotel. Subway #6 to 77th
St. ☎ 212 772 2600. Mon–Fri 7am–
10.30am, noon–2.30pm & 5.30–10.30pm,
Sat 8am–10.30am, 11.30am–2.30pm
& 5.30–10.30pm, Sun 8am–10.30am,
11.30am–3pm & 5.45–10pm.
Exceptional French–American
cuisine directed by celebrated chef
Daniel Boulud, a slightly more
casual version of his swanky *Daniel*
(entrées $28–48).

Café Sabarsky

Donguri

MAP P.130, POCKET MAP E4
309 E 83rd St, between First and Second
aves. Subway Q to 86th St. ☏ 212 7373
5656. Tues–Sun 5.30–9.30pm.
Hidden Japanese gem, not far from
the Met, serving exquisite sushi
dinners in a tiny five-table space;
superb seafood.

Flex Mussels

MAP P.130, POCKET MAP E5
174 E 82nd St, between Third and
Lexington aves. Subway #4, #5, #6, Q to
86th St. ☏ 212 717 7772. Mon–Thurs 5.30–
10pm, Fri 5.30–11pm, Sat 11.30am–11pm,
Sun 11.30am–10pm.
Serves mussels fresh from Prince
Edward Island (Canada) with
various sauces, from Dijon to
Thai, ranging from $25–30. Don't
miss the cornmeal-crusted clam
strips ($12).

Heidelberg

MAP P.130, POCKET MAP E4
1648 Second Ave, between E 85th and E
86th sts. Subway Q to 86th St. ☏ 212 628
2332. Mon & Tues 5–10pm, Wed & Thurs
11am–10pm, Fri & Sat 11am–11pm, Sun
11am–10pm.
The atmosphere here is Mittel-
European kitsch, with gingerbread
trim and staff sporting traditional
dirndls and lederhosen. The food is
the real deal, too.

JoJo

MAP P.130, POCKET MAP E6
160 E 64th St, between Lexington and
Third aves. Subway F, Q to Lexington
Ave/63rd St. ☏ 212 223 5656. Mon–Thurs
5.30–10.30pm, Fri & Sat 5.30–11pm, Sun
5.30–10pm.
Lavish townhouse restaurant
created by feted chef Jean-Georges
Vongerichten, serving excellent
French fusion cuisine with the
freshest ingredients.

Bars

Auction House

MAP P.130, POCKET MAP E4

300 E 89th St, between First and Second
aves. Subway Q to 86th St. Mon–Wed & Sun
7.30pm–2am, Thurs–Sat 7.30pm–4am.
This is a cosier, smarter alternative
to the frat-boy pubs that dominate
this part of town. The two quiet
candlelit rooms decked out like
Victorian parlours are perfect
for couples.

Balcony Bar & Rooftop Garden Bar

MAP P.130, POCKET MAP D5
Metropolitan Museum of Art, 1000 Fifth
Ave, at E 82nd St. Subway #4, #5, #6 to
86th St. Rooftop Garden Bar Sun–Thurs
11am–4.30pm, Fri & Sat 11am–8.15pm.
It's hard to imagine a more
romantic spot to sip a glass of wine,
whether on the *Rooftop Garden Bar*
(open mid-April to Oct), which has
some of the best views in the city,
or in the *Balcony Bar* overlooking
the Great Hall (Fri–Sat 4–8.30pm).

Subway Inn

MAP P.130, POCKET MAP F7
1140 Second Ave, at E 60th St. Subway N,
R, W, #4, #5, #6 to Lexington Ave/59th St.
Mon–Sat 11am–4am, Sun noon–4am.
A neighbourhood anomaly since
1937, this downscale dive bar is
great for a late-afternoon beer –
and the perfect retreat after a visit
to Bloomingdale's.

Music venue

Café Carlyle

MAP P.130, POCKET MAP D5
The Carlyle Hotel, 35 E 76th St, at Madison
Ave. Subway #6 to 77th St. ☏ 212 570
7175, ⊛ cafecarlylenewyork.com. Mon–Sat
6.30pm–midnight.
This stalwart venue is home to
Woody Allen, who plays the
clarinet with his jazz band here
on Monday nights (Jan–June;
cover: general seating $165; bar
seating $120 plus $25 drink/food
minimum). Other shows cost $55–
140, but it's free if you book a table
for dinner. Sets are at 8.45pm (plus
10.45pm Sat). Jacket required.

THE UPPER EAST SIDE

The Upper West Side

The Upper West Side has traditionally exuded a more unbuttoned vibe than its counterpart across Central Park, though there is plenty of money in evidence, especially in the dazzling late nineteenth-century apartment buildings along the lower stretches of Central Park West and Riverside Drive, and at Lincoln Center, New York's palace of culture. This is generally less true further north, though gorgeous – and occasionally landmarked – blocks pop up in the 80s, 90s and 100s. Along the way a few museums, most significantly the Natural History Museum, are worth your time. At its northern edge, marked by the monolithic Cathedral of St John the Divine, Morningside Heights is a diverse area with a youthful buzz from Columbia University; most action revolves around Broadway.

Lincoln Center for the Performing Arts

MAP P.140, POCKET MAP C6
W 62nd St to W 66th St, between Broadway, Amsterdam and Columbus aves. Subway #1 to 66th St-Lincoln Center. ☎ 212 875 5000, ⓦ www.lincolncenter.org.
This marble assembly of early 1960s buildings, which received a substantial facelift for its 50th birthday, hosts New York's most prestigious performing arts groups. At the centre of the complex, the world-class **Metropolitan Opera House** is an impressive marble and glass building, with murals by Marc Chagall. Flanking the Met are **David Geffen Hall** (formerly Avery Fisher Hall), home to the New York Philharmonic, and Philip Johnson's elegant **David H Koch Theater**, home to the New York City Ballet. The fountain in the middle serves as a meeting place; other spaces include an arts library, multiple theatres, and parks and plazas for summer events. Informative tours (75min, 2–7 tours daily, 10.30am–4.30pm; $25; ☎ 212 875 5350)

leave from the attractive Atrium, on Broadway between 62nd and 63rd streets.

The Dakota Building

MAP P.140, POCKET MAP C5
1 W 72nd St, at Central Park West. Subway B, C to 72nd St.
An early co-op finished in 1884, this grandiose German Renaissance-style mansion is best known as the home of John Lennon and his wife Yoko Ono (who still lives here). It was outside the Dakota, on the night of December 8, 1980, that the Beatle member was shot.

The New-York Historical Society

MAP P.140, POCKET MAP C5
170 Central Park West, at W 77th St. Subway B, C to 81st St. ☎ 212 873 3400, ⓦ www.nyhistory.org. Tues–Thurs & Sat 10am–6pm, Fri 10am–8pm, Sun 11am–5pm. $21, children 5–13 $6, Fri 6–8pm free.
The **New-York Historical Society** holds an extensive collection of books, prints, drawings, portraits and manuscripts. Among the

highlights are all 435 existing original watercolours of James Audubon's landmark *Birds of America* (a selection of them is exhibited periodically). Elsewhere you'll find a broad cross section of nineteenth-century American painting, notably Thomas Cole's Course of Empire series. The **Henry Luce Center** contains cultural and historical odds and ends, while the Center for Women's History is an educational and research-focused mission that has as its highlight the Billie Jean King archive – dedicated to the memorabilia of the LGBTQ tennis-playing pioneer. The lowest level holds the **DiMenna Children's History Museum**, which teaches history to children through the history *of* children.

American Museum of Natural History

MAP P.140, POCKET MAP C5
Central Park West, at W 79th St. Subway B, C to 81st St. ☎ 212 769 5100, ⓦ www. amnh.org. Daily 10am–5.45pm. Suggested admission $23, children 2–12 $13, IMAX films, space show & special exhibits extra ($10, children $7, to cover all).

This elegant giant fills four blocks with a strange architectural melange of heavy Neoclassical and rustic Romanesque styles that was built in several stages, the first by Calvert Vaux and Jacob Wrey Mould in 1872. The museum boasts 32 million items in its holdings, superb nature dioramas and anthropological collections, interactive and multimedia displays, and an awesome assemblage of bones, fossils and models. Top billing goes to the crowded **Dinosaur Halls**. **The Hall of Diversity** focuses on both the ecological and evolutionary aspects of nature, while other delights include the massive totems in the **Hall of Northwest Coast Indians**, the taxidermal marvels in North American Mammals and the giant whale suspended in the **Hall of Ocean Life**.

The **Hall of Planet Earth** takes on the formation of planets, earthquake tracking and carbon dating. You can watch the earth via satellite on its **Dynamic Earth Globe**.

Housed inside a metal and glass sphere, the **Hayden Planetarium**

Hall of Biodiversity at the American Museum of Natural History

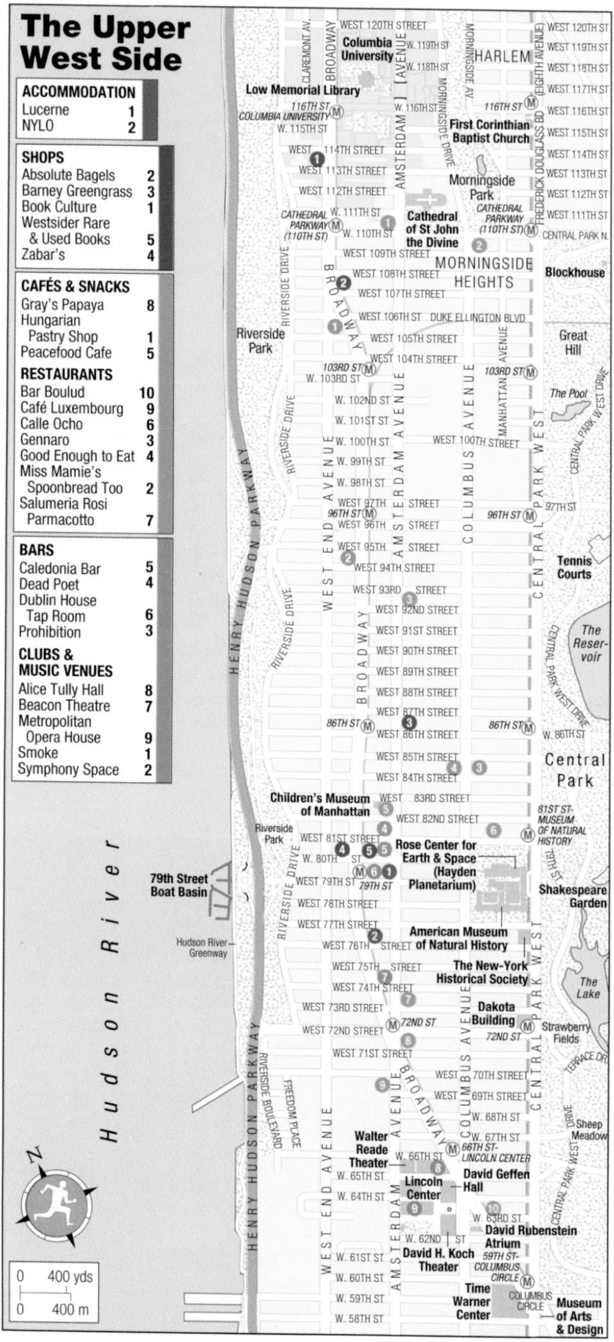

The Upper West Side

ACCOMMODATION
Lucerne	1
NYLO	2

SHOPS
Absolute Bagels	2
Barney Greengrass	3
Book Culture	1
Westsider Rare & Used Books	5
Zabar's	4

CAFÉS & SNACKS
Gray's Papaya	8
Hungarian Pastry Shop	1
Peacefood Cafe	5

RESTAURANTS
Bar Boulud	10
Café Luxembourg	9
Calle Ocho	6
Gennaro	3
Good Enough to Eat	4
Miss Mamie's Spoonbread Too	2
Salumeria Rosi Parmacotto	7

BARS
Caledonia Bar	5
Dead Poet	4
Dublin House Tap Room	6
Prohibition	3

CLUBS & MUSIC VENUES
Alice Tully Hall	8
Beacon Theatre	7
Metropolitan Opera House	9
Smoke	1
Symphony Space	2

Columbia University
Low Memorial Library
HARLEM
First Corinthian Baptist Church
Morningside Park
Cathedral of St John the Divine
MORNINGSIDE HEIGHTS
Blockhouse
Great Hill
Riverside Park
The Pool
Hudson River
79th Street Boat Basin
Hudson River Greenway
Children's Museum of Manhattan
Riverside Park
Rose Center for Earth & Space (Hayden Planetarium)
81ST ST-MUSEUM OF NATURAL HISTORY
American Museum of Natural History
The New-York Historical Society
Shakespeare Garden
The Lake
Dakota Building
Central Park
Tennis Courts
The Reservoir
Strawberry Fields
Walter Reade Theater
Lincoln Center
David Geffen Hall
David Rubenstein Atrium
David H. Koch Theater
Sheep Meadow
Time Warner Center
COLUMBUS CIRCLE
Museum of Arts & Design

0	400 yds
0	400 m

Columbia University

is one of the prime features of the **Rose Center for Earth and Space**; it regularly screens a 3D movie and the space show *Dark Universe* about the past century of space discovery.

The Cathedral of St John the Divine

MAP P.140, POCKET MAP C2
1047 Amsterdam Ave, at W 112th St. Subway B, C, #1 to 110th St. ☎ 212 316 7490, tour info ☎ 212 932 7540, Ⓦ www. stjohndivine.org. Daily prayer and meditation 7.30am–6pm, visitation Mon–Sat 9am–5pm, Sun 1–3pm, $10.

The largest Anglican church in the world holds that title despite being only two-thirds finished. A curious mix of Romanesque and Gothic styles, **St John the Divine** was begun in 1892, but its full 601ft length was completed only in 1941, after which construction stopped, to proceed sporadically between the late 1970s and 1997. As it stands, St John is big enough to swallow Notre Dame and Chartres whole.

Inside, note the intricately carved wood Altar for Peace, the Poets' Corner, the octagonal baptistry and the triptych by Keith Haring – his final finished work. The amazing stained-glass windows include scenes from American history among biblical ones. There are regular organ recitals and highlight tours (Mon 11am & 2pm, Tues–Sat 11am & 1pm, Sun 1pm; $14), plus "vertical" tours to the roof (Wed & Fri noon, Sat noon & 2pm; $20).

Columbia University

MAP P.140, POCKET MAP B1
Between Broadway and Morningside Drive from 114th to 120th sts. Subway #1 to 116th St.

Columbia University's campus (1754) is the oldest university in the city. Alumni include Barack Obama, Isaac Asimov, Ruth Bader Ginsburg and Kathryn Bigelow.

McKim, Mead, and White led the way in designing its new Italian Renaissance-style campus after it moved from Midtown in 1897, with the domed and colonnaded **Low Memorial Library** as the focal point. Hour-long tours (☎ 212 854 4900; free) of the campus leave Mon–Fri noon, 2pm & 4pm from the visitors' center on the second floor of the library.

Shops

Absolute Bagels

MAP P.140, POCKET MAP B2

2788 Broadway, between 107th and 108th sts. Subway #1 to 110th St-Cathedral Parkway. Daily 6am–9pm.

This tiny shop bakes hot, fresh, chewy bagels that some claim as the best in the city. After tasting one – whether loaded with egg salad, smeared with lox spread or just au naturel – you'll find it hard to disagree.

Barney Greengrass

MAP P.140, POCKET MAP C4

541 Amsterdam Ave, between W 86th and W 87th sts. Subway #1 to 86th St. ☎ 212 724 4707. Tues–Fri 8.30am–4pm, Sat & Sun 8.30am–5pm, takeout counter until 6pm.

Around the dawn of time, or at least a hundred years ago, the self-styled Sturgeon King began providing Upper West Siders with a beautiful array of smoked fish, cheese blintzes and the like. Be thankful that this deli-restaurant shows no sign of letting up.

Book Culture

MAP P.140, POCKET MAP B2

2915 Broadway, at 114th St. Subway #1 to 110th St. Mon–Fri 9am–10pm, Sat & Sun 10am–8pm.

One of the top independent bookstores left in the city, *Book Culture* offers an airy space conducive to browsing and a downstairs kids' room; the original branch at 536 112th St carries mainly academic titles (on its second floor); another Upper West Side location is at 450 Columbus Ave.

Westsider Rare & Used Books

MAP P.140, POCKET MAP B5

2246 Broadway, between 80th and 81st sts. Subway #1 to 79th St. Daily 10am–10pm.

All manner of titles (especially strong on art books) are crammed floor to ceiling and into every nook and cranny of this eclectic bookshop, which is ripe for browsing; pretty much all of them are in good shape and sold at reasonable prices. There's a related record store down on 72nd St.

Zabar's

Zabar's

MAP P.140, POCKET MAP B5
2245 Broadway, at W 80th St. Subway
#1 to 79th St. Mon–Fri 8am–7.30pm, Sat
8am–8pm, Sun 9am–6pm, café opens an
hour earlier.

A veritable Upper West Side
institution, this beloved family
store offers a quintessential taste
of New York: bagels, lox and all
manner of *schmears*, not to mention
a dizzying selection of gourmet
food. An attached café means you
can sample the goods right away if
you wish.

Cafés and snacks

Gray's Papaya

MAP P.140, POCKET MAP C6
2090 Broadway, at W 72nd St. Subway
#1, #2, #3 to 72nd St. ⓘ 212 799 0243.
Daily 24hr.

This popular hot-dog joint is an
NYC institution, famous for its
long-running "Recession Special":
two dogs and a drink for $6.50.

Hungarian Pastry Shop

MAP P.140, POCKET MAP B2
1030 Amsterdam Ave, between W 110th
and 111th sts. Subway B, C, #1 to 110th
St. Mon–Fri 7.30am–11.30pm, Sat
8.30am–11.30pm, Sun 8.30am–10.30pm.

If you're looking for a place to stop
and relax near St John the Divine
or Columbia, you won't do better
than this simple coffee house. Sip
your espresso and read all day if
you like – the only problem is
choosing among the home-made
pastries, cookies and cakes.

Peacefood Cafe

MAP P.140, POCKET MAP B5
460 Amsterdam Ave, at 82nd St, another
location at 41 E 11th St. Subway #1 to 79th
St, B, C to 81st St. ⓘ 212 362 2266. Daily
10am–10pm.

A friendly stop to pick up some
tasty vegan baked goods, or to
linger and make a full meal of
it: go for an array of roasted veg
($7.95–13.95), fried seitan on

focaccia ($14.95) or cheeseless
pizza ($12.95), perhaps washed
down with a gingerade ($4).

Restaurants

Bar Boulud

MAP P.140, POCKET MAP C6
1900 Broadway, between 63rd and 64th sts.
Subway A, B, C, D, #1 to 59th St–Columbus
Circle, #1 to 66th St–Lincoln Center. ⓘ 212
595 0303. Mon–Thurs 11.30am–2.30pm
& 5pm–midnight, Fri 11.30am–2.30pm &
5pm–1am, Sat 11am–3.30pm & 5pm–1am,
Sun 11am–4pm & 5–10pm.

Treat this Daniel Boulud restaurant
like a pre- or post-theatre wine bar,
and zoom in on the home-made
pâtés, terrines and charcuterie,
accompanied by a glass – or bottle
– from the Rhône. Full dinners
(entrées $25–35) are fairly priced
for the quality.

Café Luxembourg

MAP P.140, POCKET MAP B6
200 W 70th St between Amsterdam and
West End aves. Subway #1, #2, #3 to
72nd St. ⓘ 212 873 7411. Mon & Tues
8am–11pm, Wed–Fri 8am–midnight, Sat
9am–midnight, Sun 9am–11pm.

Popular Lincoln Center area bistro
that packs in a slightly sniffy crowd
to enjoy first-rate, contemporary
French food. Entrées $25–40; the
brasserie menu is a bit cheaper.

Calle Ocho

MAP P.140, POCKET MAP C5
45 W 81st St, between Columbus Ave and
Central Park West in the Excelsior Hotel.
Subway B, C to 81st St. ⓘ 212 873 5025.
Mon–Thurs 3.30–10pm, Fri 3.30–11pm, Sat
noon–3pm & 5–11.30pm, Sun noon–3pm
& 5–10pm.

Very tasty Latino fare, such as
ceviches ($16–19) and *chimichurri*
steak ($30), is served in a
colourfully decked-out restaurant
with a hopping bar. The mojitos are
as potent as any in the city.

Gennaro

MAP P.140, POCKET MAP C4

665 Amsterdam Ave, between W 92nd and W 93rd sts. Subway #1, #2, #3 to 96th St. ☎ 212 665 5348. Daily 5–11pm.

A rare outpost of good Italian food around these parts, though you'll have a wait for a table. Reasonably priced standouts include a warm potato, mushroom and goat cheese tart ($14.50).

Good Enough to Eat

MAP P.140, POCKET MAP C4

520 Columbus Ave, at 85th St. Subway #1 to 86th St. ☎ 212 496 0163. Mon–Fri 8am–10.30pm, Sat & Sun 9am–10.30pm.

Cutesy Upper West Side restaurant known for its cinnamon-swirl French toast ($13), meatloaf ($19) and weekend brunch specials.

Miss Mamie's Spoonbread Too

MAP P.140, POCKET MAP C2

366 W 110th St, between Columbus and Manhattan aves. Subway B, C to Cathedral Parkway (110th St). ☎ 212 865 6744. Mon–Thurs 11.30am–10pm, Fri & Sat 11.30am–11pm, Sun 11.30am–9.30pm.

Excellent soul-food restaurant with a 1950s-themed interior, addictive North Carolina ribs ($18.95) and some of the best fried chicken ($17.95) in the city.

Salumeria Rosi Parmacotto

MAP P.140, POCKET MAP C5

283 Amsterdam Ave, between 73rd and 74th sts. Subway #1, #2, #3 to 72nd St. ☎ 212 877 4800. Mon–Thurs noon–10pm, Fri noon–11pm, Sat & Sun 11am–11pm.

On your left as you enter is a deli counter with a dizzying array of gorgeous cured meats. Order lots of small plates: a selection of salumi and some cheeses (each choice $8–11, platters $20–29); anchovy with roast peppers ($14); pasta ($16–17); meatballs (if available).

Bars

Caledonia Bar

MAP P.140, POCKET MAP C5

424 Amsterdam Ave, between W 80th and W 81st Sts. Subway #1 to 81st St. ☎ 917 388 2342, ⊕ caledoniabar.com. Mon–Thurs 5pm–2am, Fri & Sat 4pm–4am, Sun 4pm–1am.

Sidle up to the bar in this dimly lit nook and choose from an extensive list of whiskeys—mostly Scotch ($12–34 a pour). And yes, they have Scotch eggs ($9) to accompany your drink.

Dead Poet

MAP P.140, POCKET MAP B5

450 Amsterdam Ave, between W 81st and W 82nd sts. Subway #1 to 79th St. Daily noon–4am.

You'll be waxing poetic if you stay for the duration of this sweet little bar's daily specials – usually involving $4 or $5 can or pints of beer. The backroom has armchairs, books and a pool table.

Dublin House Tap Room

MAP P.140, POCKET MAP B5

225 W 79th St, between Broadway and Amsterdam Ave. Subway #1 to 79th St. Mon–Sat 9am–4am, Sun 11am–4am.

Beneath the cool neon sign, this lively Irish pub is the place to go before or after a gig at the Beacon Theatre.

Prohibition

MAP P.140, POCKET MAP C4

503 Columbus Ave, at W 84 St. Subway B, C to 86th St. Mon & Tues 4.30pm–1am, Wed 4.30pm–1.30am, Thurs 4.30pm–2am, Fri & Sat 4.30pm–3am.

Stylish bar and lounge with funky, retro decor (check out the lamps in suspended wine bottles), a decent array of draught beers and diabolical Martinis. Free live music nightly (usually from 9.30pm or 10.30pm).

Clubs and music venues

Alice Tully Hall

MAP P.140, POCKET MAP C6

1941 Broadway at 65th St, Lincoln Center.

Subway A, B, C, D, #1 to 59th St-Columbus Circle, #1 to 66th St-Lincoln Center. ☎ 212 721 6500, ⓦ www.lincolncenter.org. Tickets $25–100.

A small performance hall for top chamber orchestras, string quartets and instrumentalists.

Beacon Theatre

MAP P.140, POCKET MAP B5

2124 Broadway, at W 74th St. Subway #1, #2, #3 to 72nd St. ☎ 212 465 6500, tickets ☎ 1-866 858 0008, ⓦ www.beacontheatre. com. Tickets $25–100.

This beautifully restored theatre caters to a mature rock crowd. One of the more established music venues in town, plenty of big names play here.

Metropolitan Opera House

MAP P.140, POCKET MAP C6

Lincoln Center, Columbus Ave, at 64th St. Subway A, B, C, D, #1 to 59th St-Columbus Circle, #1 to 66th St-Lincoln Center. ☎ 212 362 6000, ⓦ www.metopera.org. Tickets $20–495.

Home to the world-renowned Metropolitan Opera Company from September to May. Seats are expensive and sometimes hard to get, though $25 day-of rush tickets and $25–30 standing-room tickets are available in the mornings of the day of a performance (call for info).

Smoke

MAP P.140, POCKET MAP B2

2751 Broadway, at W 106th St. Subway #1 to 103rd St. ☎ 212 864 6662, ⓦ www. smokejazz.com. Mon–Sat 5pm–3am, Sun 4pm–3am; evening sets typically 7pm, 9pm & 10.30pm, frequent late night sets (free) as well. Cover free to $40.

This Upper West Side jazz joint is a real neighbourhood treat – nice bar, intimate seating, smooth sounds – and does creditable bistro-style dinners.

Symphony Space

MAP P.140, POCKET MAP B3

2537 Broadway, at W 95th St. Subway #1, #2, #3 to 96th St. ☎ 212 864 5400, ⓦ www.symphonyspace.org. Tickets free to $50.

Performing arts centre, with regular short-story readings, as well as music performances. Known for its uninterrupted reading of James Joyce's *Ulysses* every Bloomsday (June 16).

Beacon Theatre

Harlem and north Manhattan

The most famous black community in America, Harlem has been the bedrock of African-American culture since the 1920s, when poets, activists and jazz blended in the Harlem Renaissance. Though it acquired a notoriety for street crime in the 1970s, it is now a neighbourhood on the rise. Indeed, Harlem's streets are as safe as any other in New York. Though most tourists still visit Harlem solely to see its wonderful Gospel choirs on Sundays, you'll also find some fabulous West African and soul-food restaurants, a vibrant local jazz scene, plenty of historic sights and some of the prettiest streets in the city. Explore African-American history at the Schomburg Center, or visit contemporary temples of black culture: the Apollo Theater and Abyssinian Baptist Church. North of Harlem lies Washington Heights and Inwood, home to the largest Dominican population in the United States.

116th Street

MAP P.148, POCKET MAP C1–D1
Subway B, C, #2, #3, #6 to 116th St.

Harlem lies north of 110th Street, but the first area of interest lies along **116th Street**; it's here that the spirit of the late Malcolm

X is perhaps the most palpable. Look for the green onion dome of the **Masjid Malcolm Shabazz**, 102 West 116th Street, at Lenox Avenue; the mosque was renovated in the 1960s and named after him. Between Lenox and

Masjid Malcolm Shabazz

Fifth avenues, at no. 52, you'll pass the bazaar-like **Malcolm Shabazz Harlem Market** (daily 10am–8pm), its entrance marked by colourful fake minarets. The market's offerings include textiles, jewellery and clothing, all with a distinctly Afro-centric flavour. The stretch of 116th Street between Lenox and Manhattan avenues has become a hub for West African immigrants and is unofficially known as **Little Senegal**; it's lined with shops, beauty parlours and African restaurants. There are also some African-influenced buildings nearby, including the fanciful blue-and-white Moorish-style First Corinthian Baptist Church, 1912 Powell Boulevard, at 116th Street.

The National Jazz Museum in Harlem

Mount Morris Park Historic District

MAP P.148, POCKET MAP D1
Subway #2, #3 to 116th St or 125th St.
Centred on Malcolm X Boulevard (aka Lenox Avenue) between W 118th and 124th streets, this 16-block area, which is full of magnificent, four- to five-storey late nineteenth-century brownstones and quiet streets, was one of the first to attract residential development after the elevated railroads were constructed – it remains a relatively exclusive neighbourhood, with the likes of basketball legend Kareem Abdul-Jabbar living here (and Maya Angelou before she died).

125th Street

MAP P.148
Subway A, B, C, D, #2, #3 to 125th St.
125th Street between Broadway and Fifth Avenue is the working centre of Harlem and its main commercial drag. It's here that recent investment in the area is most obvious – note the presence of numerous chain stores and fashion retailers – spurred by the establishment of former president Bill Clinton's offices at 55 W 125th Street in 2001. Looming over the whole strip is the Brutalist **Adam Clayton Powell, Jr State Office Building**, commissioned in 1972 and built on the corner of Powell Boulevard. The building was named in honour of Harlem's first black congressman, and his 12ft-high bronze **statue** was unveiled here in 2005. The **National Jazz Museum in Harlem** (ⓦ jazzmuseuminharlem. org; Mon–Fri 11am–5pm; free), at 58 W 129th Street between Malcolm X Blvd and Fifth Avenue, organizes live jazz, and has a small exhibit of old jazz memorabilia and rare recordings.

The Studio Museum in Harlem

MAP P.148
144 W 125th St, between Lenox and Seventh aves. Subway #2, #3 to 125th St.
ⓣ 212 864 4500, ⓦ studiomuseum.org.
Thurs–Fri noon–9pm, Sat 10am–6pm, Sun noon–6pm. $7, free Sun.
The **Studio Museum in Harlem** is dedicated to showcasing contemporary African-American painting, photography and sculpture. The superb permanent collection includes works

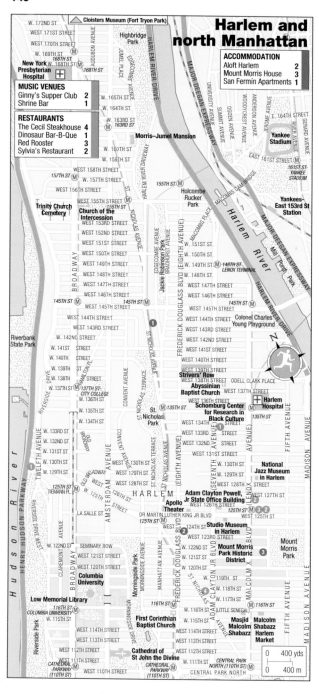

Harlem and north Manhattan

ACCOMMODATION
Aloft Harlem	2
Mount Morris House	3
San Fermin Apartments	1

MUSIC VENUES
Ginny's Supper Club	2
Shrine Bar	1

RESTAURANTS
The Cecil Steakhouse	4
Dinosaur Bar-B-Que	1
Red Rooster	3
Sylvia's Restaurant	2

by Harlem Renaissance-era photographer James Van Der Zee. A new purpose-built building designed by architect David Adjaye – with five storeys and 82,000-square-feet of gallery space – should be complete by 2020, but check the website for details on temporary exhibition spaces until then.

The Apollo Theater

MAP P.148
253 W 125th St. Subway A, B, C, D, #2, #3 to 125th St. ☎ 212 531 5300, Ⓦ apollotheater.org. Tours (min 20 people; by advance reservation only) Mon, Tues, Thurs & Fri 11am, 1pm, 3pm, Wed 11am, Sat & Sun 11am & 1pm. $17 Mon–Fri, $19 Sat & Sun.

From the 1930s to the 1970s, the **Apollo Theater** was the centre of black entertainment in northeastern America. Almost all the great figures of jazz and blues played here along with singers, comedians and dancers. Past winners of its famous Amateur Night (still running on Wed at 7.30pm; from $22) have included Ella Fitzgerald, Billie Holiday, the Jackson Five, Sarah Vaughan, Marvin Gaye and James Brown. Hip-hop diva Lauren Hill was actually booed at her debut as a young teen. Yet the Apollo has also become the spiritual heart of black America; James Brown's casket lay in state in the theatre, and when Michael Jackson died in 2009, an official exhibit was arranged inside a few days later.

Schomburg Center for Research in Black Culture

MAP P.148
515 Malcolm X Blvd, at W 135th St. Subway B, C, #2, #3 to 135th St. ☎ 212 491 2200, Ⓦ nypl.org/locations/schomburg. Exhibitions Mon & Thurs–Sat 10am–6pm, Tues & Wed 10am–8pm. Free.

Primarily a research library, the **Schomburg Center** also holds enlightening temporary exhibitions held in three galleries on site –

recent topics have included the struggle to end segregation in US schools. The library itself was created in 1925 by Arthur Schomburg, a black Puerto Rican obsessed with documenting black culture. Further enriching the site are the ashes of poet Langston Hughes, perhaps most famous for publishing *The Negro Speaks of Rivers* in 1921. The poem inspired the terrazzo and brass "cosmogram" in the atrium beyond the main entrance. Seven lines radiate out from a circle, and the last, "My soul has grown deep like the rivers", located in the centre, marks where he is interred.

Abyssinian Baptist Church

MAP P.148
132 Odell Clark Place (W 138th St), off Adam Clayton Powell Jr Blvd. Subway #2, #3 to 135th St. ☎ 212 862 7474, Ⓦ abyssinian.org. Tourists are welcome to the Sun 11.30am service only (2hr 30min). Free.

With its roots going back to 1808, the **Abyssinian Baptist Church** houses one of the oldest (and biggest) Protestant congregations in the country. In

Apollo Theater

the 1930s, its pastor, Reverend Adam Clayton Powell Jr, was instrumental in forcing the mostly white-owned, white-workforce stores of Harlem to employ the blacks whose patronage ensured the stores' economic survival. It's worth a trip here for its revival-style Sunday-morning services and gut-busting choir. Dress formally and remember that this is a religious service and not a show.

Strivers' Row

MAP P.148

Subway B, C, #2, #3 to 135th St.

On W 138th and 139th streets (between Adam Clayton Powell Jr and Frederick Douglass boulevards), **Strivers' Row** comprises three of the finest blocks of Renaissance-influenced row houses in Manhattan. Commissioned in 1891 during a housing boom, this dignified development within the burgeoning black community came to be the most desirable place for ambitious professionals to reside at the turn of the twentieth century – hence its

Strivers' Row

name. Today it remains an extremely posh residence for professionals of all backgrounds.

Morris–Jumel Mansion

MAP P.148

65 Jumel Terrace, at W 160th St between St Nicholas and Edgecombe aves. Subway C to 163rd St. ☏ 212 923 8008, ⓦ morrisjumel. org. Tues–Fri 10am–4pm, Sat & Sun 10am–5pm. $10.

This 1765 mansion, the oldest house in Manhattan, features proud Georgian outlines and a Federal portico, and served briefly as George Washington's headquarters before it fell to the British in 1776. Later, wine merchant Stephen Jumel bought the mansion and refurbished it for his wife Eliza, formerly a prostitute and his mistress. On the top floor, you'll find a magnificently fictionalized account of her "scandalous" life.

Cloisters Museum

MAP P.148

99 Margaret Corbin Drive, Fort Tryon Park. Subway A to 190th St. ☏ 212 923 3700, ⓦ metmuseum.org/cloisters. Daily 10am–5.15pm; closes 4.45pm Nov–Feb. $25, free with same-day Met Museum entry.

This reconstructed monastic complex houses the pick of the Metropolitan Museum's medieval collection. Most prized are the mystery-shrouded **Unicorn Tapestries**, seven elaborate panels thought to have been created in the late thirteenth century in France or Belgium. Among the Cloisters Museum's larger artefacts are a monumental Romanesque hall made up of French remnants and a frescoed Spanish Fuentiduena chapel, both thirteenth century. At the centre of the museum is the **Cuxa Cloister** from a twelfth-century Benedictine monastery in the French Pyrenees; its capitals are brilliant works of art, carved with weird, self-devouring grotesque creatures.

Restaurants

The Cecil Steakhouse

MAP P.148, POCKET MAP C1
210 W 118th St, between St Nicholas Ave and Powell Blvd. Subway B, C to 116th St. ☎ 212 866 1262. Mon–Thurs 5pm–midnight, Fri 5pm–1am, Sat noon–1am, Sun noon–11pm.

Stylish Afro-American steakhouse, featuring a wide range of pastas ($19–24) and superb steaks ($28–44), as well as burgers and seafood. Next door to Minton's Playhouse.

Dinosaur Bar-B-Que

MAP P.148
700 W 125th St. Subway #1 to 125th St. ☎ 212 694 1777. Mon–Thurs 11.30am–11pm, Fri & Sat 11.30am–midnight, Sun noon–10pm.

Get some of the best slow pit-smoked ribs here, smothered in a home-made sauce you'll delightfully taste for days after your meal. Or sample the "Big Ass Pork Plate" for $18.50.

Red Rooster

MAP P.148
310 Malcolm X Blvd, between W 125th and W 126th sts. Subway #2, #3 to 125th St. ☎ 212 792 9001. Mon–Thurs 11.30am–3pm & 4.30–10.30pm, Fri 11.30am–3pm & 4.30–11.30pm, Sat 10am–3pm & 4.30–11.30pm, Sun 10am–3pm & 4.30–10pm.

Marcus Samuelsson's restaurant brings a touch of class to Harlem with a sophisticated take on Southern comfort food. Sandwiches $18–24, with mains such as firepit BBQ chicken $22–38. Leave room for the "sundae kinda love" ($10).

Sylvia's Restaurant

MAP P.148
328 Malcolm X Blvd, between W 126th and W 127th sts. Subway #2, #3 to 125th St. ☎ 212 996 0660. Mon–Sat 8am–10.30pm, Sun 11am–8pm.

So famous that the late Sylvia has her own package food line, this

Dinosaur Bar-B-Que

is Harlem's premier soul-food landmark. While the BBQ ribs ($21.95) are exceptional and the candied yams are justly celebrated, *Sylvia's* is a bit of a tourist trap – avoid Sundays when tour groups arrive for the Gospel brunch.

Music venues

Ginny's Supper Club

MAP P.148
310 Malcolm X Blvd, between W 125th and W 126th sts. Subway #2, #3 to 125th St. ☎ 212 421 3821, Ⓦ www.ginnyssupperclub.com. Thurs 6pm–midnight, Fri & Sat 6pm–3am, Sun 10.30pm–12.30pm.

Stylish bar and jazz venue (under *Red Rooster*), with live sets accompanied by punchy house cocktails ($13–15) and excellent soul-food plates (from $27).

Shrine Bar

MAP P.148
2271 Powell Blvd, between 133rd and 134th sts. Subway B, #2, #3 to 135th St. ☎ 212 690 7807, Ⓦ www.shrinenyc.com. Daily 4pm–4am.

Funky bar, restaurant and live music venue (mostly jazz and world music), which also hosts comedy and poetry nights; shows start at 6pm most nights, and at 1pm on Sundays.

The outer boroughs

New York City doesn't end with Manhattan. There are four other boroughs to explore: Brooklyn, Queens, The Bronx and Staten Island. They cover an enormous area and you'll naturally want to pick your attractions carefully, although you could make Brooklyn the entire focus of a visit, and some of the more alluring parts of Queens, like Long Island City, are just a subway stop away from Midtown. Staten Island is the only borough that lacks an essential must-see sight or dynamic neighbourhoods for great ethnic food – the free ferry ride back and forth, with its views of Downtown and the Statue of Liberty, is excitement enough. Otherwise, between the New York Botanic Garden, Coney Island, Greek Astoria and more, you'll be torn in which direction to head.

Brooklyn Heights

MAP P.156, POCKET MAP G15

From Manhattan, simply walk over the Brooklyn Bridge, take the left fork near the pedestrian path's end and emerge in one of New York City's most beautiful, historic and coveted neighbourhoods. This peaceful, tree-lined area was settled by financiers from Wall Street, and has been home to literary figures such as Truman Capote and Tennessee Williams. Make sure you take in the **Promenade**, a terrace with terrific views of lower Manhattan.

DUMBO

MAP P.156, POCKET MAP G15

An acronym for Down Under Manhattan Bridge Overpass, **DUMBO** is a walk downhill from Brooklyn Heights Promenade and fronts the East River. It was a busy hub for ferries and trade in the nineteenth century, but the opening of the Brooklyn Bridge (see page 34) in 1883 led to the area's demise. In the past two decades luxury condo conversions and art galleries have made it lively again. Check out the shops on Water, Main, Washington and Front streets before drinking in the views from the water's edge.

Brooklyn Bridge Park

MAP P.156, POCKET MAP F15
Subway #2, #3 to Clark St, A, C to High St.
Ⓦ www.brooklynbridgepark.org.

The waterfront **Brooklyn Bridge Park** begins around Fulton Ferry Landing and runs alongside Brooklyn Heights down to Atlantic Avenue. Highlights include Jane's Carousel (May–Sept Mon & Wed–Sat 11am–7pm; Oct–April Thurs–Sun 11am–6pm; $2), the recreational areas of Pier 2, the child-friendly water park, sandpit and slides of Pier 6 and the picnicking lawns and brilliant views of the bridges and lower Manhattan throughout. You can also catch a ferry to Governors Island (see page 32), go kayaking, see outdoor movies and attend a theatrical event at St Ann's Warehouse (see page 165), which occupies a historic building.

BLDG 92

MAP P.156, POCKET MAP H14
Flushing Ave, at Carlton Ave, in the Brooklyn Navy Yard. ☎ 718 907 5992,
Ⓦ www.bldg92.org. Wed–Sun noon–6pm.
Free, Navy Yard tours (2hr) $30.

Another waterfront redevelopment success, the industrial park of once-derelict Brooklyn Navy Yard has become an attraction in its own right. Visit **BLDG 92** to get acquainted with the yard's history; the centre, a modular, energy-efficient glass structure attached to an 1857 brick house, holds a museum with three floors of exhibitions (an 11-tonne anchor hangs down to greet you as you enter).

New York Transit Museum

MAP P.156, POCKET MAP G16
Intersection of Boerum Place and Schermerhorn St, downtown Brooklyn. Subway #2, #3, #4, #5 to Borough Hall, A, C, F, R to Jay Street-MetroTech. ☎ 718 694 1600, ⓦ www.mta.info/mta/museum. Tues–Fri 10am–4pm, Sat & Sun 11am–5pm. $10, children 2–17 $5.

Housed in an abandoned 1930s subway station, the **Transit Museum** offers more than one hundred years' worth of transportation history and memorabilia, including antique turnstiles, and more than twenty restored subway cars and buses that you can hop on and off of. It's an excellent place for kids.

Brooklyn Heights

Red Hook

MAP P.156
This waterfront district, a former shipping centre, was once one of the more rough-and-tumble in the city, but now holds artists' galleries, unique restaurants, converted warehouses and, to some folks' chagrin, twin retail giants in IKEA and Fairway. Cut off from the subway system, **Red Hook** can be reached by water taxi or bus, a worthwhile venture to hit the **Red Hook Ball Fields** on summer weekends, where you can sample Latin American street food and watch soccer, or to take in fabulous views of the Statue of Liberty and lower Manhattan from the piers, while snacking on a key lime pie from Steve's Authentic Key Lime Pies (185 Van Dyke St).

The Brooklyn Museum

MAP P.154
200 Eastern Parkway, Prospect Heights, Brooklyn. Subway #2, #3 to Eastern Parkway. ☎ 718 638 5000, ⓦ www.brooklynmuseum.org. Wed & Fri–Sun 11am–6pm, Thurs 11am–10pm, first Sat of every month 11am–11pm. Suggested donation $16, aged 19 and under free.

One of the largest museums in the country, the **Brooklyn Museum** boasts 1.5 million objects and five floors of exhibits in its McKim, Mead, and White-designed Neoclassical home. A changing selection of Rodin sculptures greets you inside the door, while another exhibition showcases some detailed African carvings. The third floor holds arguably the museum's crown jewel in its delicately carved "Brooklyn Brown Head", one of 1200 pieces in the Ancient Egyptian Art section. A flight up, Judy Chicago's Dinner Party installation marks an important moment in feminist art, while the fifth floor tops things off with its American section – its uneven, but big names like Georgia O'Keeffe are represented. The Visible Storage Study Center on the same level is packed with Tiffany lamps, antique furniture and paintings that the museum doesn't have room to display elsewhere.

Brooklyn Botanic Garden

MAP P.154
Entrance on Eastern Parkway, next to Brookyn Museum. Subway #2, #3 to Eastern Parkway, B, Q, S to Prospect Park.
☏ **718 623 7200,** Ⓦ **www.bbg.org. Mid-March to Oct Tues–Fri 8am–6pm, Sat & Sun 10am–6pm; Nov to mid-March Tues–Fri 8am–4.30pm, Sat & Sun 10am–4.30pm. $15 (free winter weekends), children under 12 free.**

The **Brooklyn Botanic Garden** is one of the most enticing park spaces in the city and a relaxing place to unwind after a couple of hours in the museum next door. Though smaller, it is more immediately likeable than its more celebrated cousin in the Bronx (see page 159). Some 12,000 plants from around the world occupy 52 acres of manicured terrain. Highlights are mostly seasonal, but include the Rose Garden, Japanese Garden, Cherry Esplanade (April is a great time for this) and Celebrity

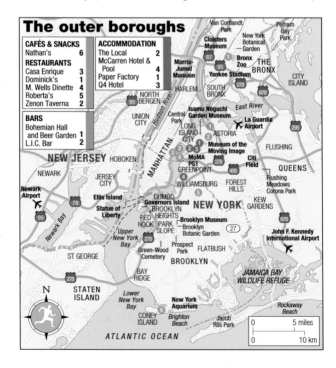

Prospect Park

Prospect Park

MAP P.156
Flatbush Ave and Prospect Park West,
Brooklyn. Subway #2, #3 to Grand Army
Plaza, F to 7th Ave or 15th St, B, Q to
Prospect Park. ☏ 718 965 8951, Ⓦ www.
prospectpark.org.

Energized by their success with
Central Park, architects Olmsted
and Vaux landscaped 526-acre
Prospect Park in the early 1860s,
completing it just as the finishing
touches were being put to Grand
Army Plaza outside (home to an
excellent farmers' market Sat 8am–
4pm). Focal points include the
Lefferts Homestead, an eighteenth-
century colonial farmhouse that is
open free of charge at weekends;
the Prospect Park Zoo (April–Oct
Mon–Fri 10am–5pm, Sat and Sun
10am–5.30pm; Nov–March daily
10am–4.30pm; $9.95); the lakeside
development, with enclosed and
open-air skating rinks; the carousel
(late March to mid-Nov Thurs–Sun
noon–5pm; $2.50); and the ninety-
acre Long Meadow, which cuts
through the centre.

Path, honouring Brooklyn's famous
sons and daughters.

Coney Island

MAP P.154
Subway D, F, N, Q to Coney Island-Stillwell
Ave or F, Q to W 8th St-NY Aquarium.
Ⓦ www.coneyisland.com. Boardwalk open
year-round, rides are seasonal (roughly
April–Sept).

Generations of working-class
New Yorkers came to relax at
one of Brooklyn's farthest points:
Coney Island, which at its
height accommodated 100,000
people daily. It has been through
some down-and-out times, but
the boardwalk makes for a fun
sunny-day stroll, and the rides
of **Luna Park** (late March to
Oct, days and hours vary),which
include the 90-year-old Cyclone
wooden roller coaster and the
newish Thunderbolt steel roller
coaster, are a thrill – as is the nearly
century-old Wonder Wheel. Other
summertime highlights include
the Fourth of July Hot Dog Eating
Contest at *Nathan's* (see page 160)
and the annual Mermaid Parade
(3rd or 4th Sat in June).

New York Aquarium

MAP P.154
Surf Ave and West 8th St. Subway F, Q to

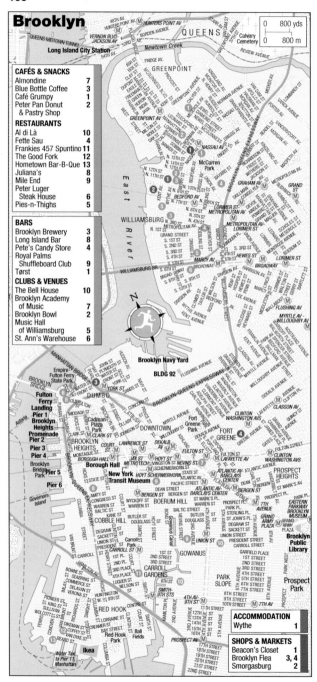

Brooklyn

CAFÉS & SNACKS

Almondine	7
Blue Bottle Coffee	3
Café Grumpy	1
Peter Pan Donut & Pastry Shop	2

RESTAURANTS

Al di Là	10
Fette Sau	4
Frankies 457 Spuntino	11
The Good Fork	12
Hometown Bar-B-Que	13
Juliana's	8
Mile End	9
Peter Luger Steak House	6
Pies-n-Thighs	5

BARS

Brooklyn Brewery	3
Long Island Bar	8
Pete's Candy Store	4
Royal Palms Shuffleboard Club	9
Tørst	1

CLUBS & VENUES

The Bell House	10
Brooklyn Academy of Music	7
Brooklyn Bowl	2
Music Hall of Williamsburg	5
St. Ann's Warehouse	6

ACCOMMODATION

Wythe	1

SHOPS & MARKETS

Beacon's Closet	1
Brooklyn Flea	3, 4
Smorgasburg	2

West 8th St–NY Aquarium. ☎718 265 3474, ⓦwww.nyaquarium.com. June–Oct Mon–Fri 10am–5pm, Sat & Sun 10am–5.30pm; Nov–May daily 10am–4.30pm. $24.95, children 3–12 $19.95.

The seashell-shaped New York Aquarium sits on Coney Island's boardwalk. The highlight is undoubtedly the "Ocean Wonders: Sharks" exhibit, which finds sharks and rays swimming above your head in a glass corridor; there are also regular seal feedings and sea lion shows.

Williamsburg

MAP P.156, POCKET MAP J11

With easy access to Manhattan and excellent waterfront views, it's not hard to see why **Williamsburg**, Brooklyn, has become one of the city's most happening spots, especially for live music and late-night carousing. The L train to Bedford Avenue will land you on the main stretch (though note that repairs to the line on nights and weekends may impact travel time; check the MTA's website for updates; use the ferry or G train to Metropolitan Ave as an alternative); vintage shops, plenty of galleries and artisanal-food purveyors can be found on surrounding blocks.

McCarren Park separates northern Williamsburg from the fashionable Polish enclave of **Greenpoint**, and the park serves as a big hangout, with summer concerts. Its historic pool, restored in 2012, briefly becomes an ice rink in winter. Further out, Bushwick also has its share of restaurants, street murals, art shows and rock clubs.

Astoria

MAP P.154, POCKET MAP J3

Developed in 1839 and named after John Jacob Astor, **Astoria**, Queens is known for two things: film-making (Paramount had a studio here between 1920 and 1928), and its vibrant Greek population.

Greek Astoria stretches from Ditmars Boulevard to Broadway, and from 31st Street across to Steinway Street, though plenty of Moroccans, Egyptians, Brazilians and others have moved in; it makes for a foodie haven, evidenced in the patisseries, fresh seafood restaurants and kebab stands.

The Museum of the Moving Image

MAP P.154, POCKET MAP J5

35th Ave, at 37th St, Astoria, Queens. Subway N, W to 36th St, M, R to Steinway St. ☎718 784 0077, ⓦwww.movingimage. us. Wed–Thurs 10.30am–5pm, Fri 10.30am–8pm, Sat & Sun 11.30am–7pm. $15, children 3–17 $9, Fri 4–8pm free.

Part of the old Paramount complex, the **Museum of the Moving Image** tells the fascinating story of cinema through state-of-the-art theatres, hands-on exhibits and vintage props. The museum's core collection, "Behind the Screen", holds old movie cameras and special-effects equipment; sketches and set models from *The Silence of the Lambs*; and enough *Star Wars* action figures to make an obsessed fan drool with envy. The film series and temporary exhibitions are an equal lure.

Kaufman Astoria Studios

Bronx Zoo

Isamu Noguchi Garden Museum

MAP P.154, POCKET MAP G5
9–01 33rd Rd, at Vernon Blvd, Long Island City, Queens. Subway N, W to Broadway, F to Queensbridge–21st St. ☎ 718 204 7088, ⓦ www.noguchi.org. Wed–Fri 10am–5pm, Sat & Sun 11am–6pm. $10, free first Fridays May–Sept.

While hard to reach, the **Isamu Noguchi Garden Museum** easily repays curiosity. The museum is devoted to the "organic" sculptures, drawings, modern dance costumes and Akari light sculptures of the prolific Japanese-American abstract sculptor Isamu Noguchi (1904–88), whose studio was here. His pieces, in stone, bronze and wood, exhibit a sublime simplicity.

MoMA PS1

MAP P.154, POCKET MAP H8
22–25 Jackson Ave, at 46th Ave, Long Island City, Queens. Subway #7 to 45 Rd–Courthouse Square; E, M to Court Square–23rd St, #7 to Court Sqaure, G to 21st St. ☎ 718 784 2084, ⓦ www.momaps1.org. Thurs–Mon noon–6pm. Suggested admission $10 (free with same-day MoMA ticket).

MoMA PS1 is one of the oldest and biggest organizations in the United States devoted exclusively to contemporary art and to showing leading emerging artists. Since its founding in 1971, this public school-turned-exhibition space has hosted some of the city's most exciting art displays and has some ongoing gems like James Turrell's *Meeting*. Summertime's Warm Up series (Sat afternoon) is a DJ-led dance-and-art party.

Flushing Meadows Corona Park

MAP P.154
Between the Van Wyck Expressway and Grand Central Parkway, east of 111th St, Queens. Subway #7 to 111th St or Mets-Willets Point. ⓦ www.nycgoparks.org.

Sprawling **Flushing Meadows Corona Park** contains a multitude of Queens cultural institutions and sports venues. Baseball's Mets play at **Citi Field**; the US Open Tennis Championships are held at the **Billie Jean King National Tennis Center**; the **Queens Museum** holds the awe-inspiring city scale model *Panorama of the City of New York*; and the **New York Hall of Science** holds good fun for kids. Elsewhere in the park are holdovers from the 1964–65 World's Fair.

Rockaway Beach

MAP P.154

Subway A (rush hour) to Rockaway Park-Beach 116th St or the A to Broad Channel, transfer to the S (Rockaway Shuttle – all times of day), which also takes you to Rockaway Park-Beach 116th St; there are numerous other stops the length of the peninsula and NY Ferries from Pier 11 (Wall Street) in Manhattan and along the Brooklyn waterfront.

The spit of **Rockaway** stretches for ten miles southwest of Brooklyn (though it's actually in Queens); its namesake beach, celebrated by the Ramones in song, runs along the shore from Beach 9th Street to Beach 149th Street. Hotspots like the hip Tacoway Beach and the Rockaway Beach Surf Club have recently popped up; there are places to rent boards and take surf lessons (the surfing sections are at 67th–69th sts and 87th–92nd sts); and excellent coffee and meals can be enjoyed from Cuisine by Claudette. Thing get lively for the **Riis Park Beach Bazaar**, 157 Rockaway Beach Boulevard (Ⓦ riisparkbeachbazaar. com; daily from 11am): free music programming, food vendors and beachy sports.

Yankee Stadium

MAP P.154
161 St and River Ave, Bronx Subway B, D, #4 to Yankee Stadium. ☎ 212 926 5337, Ⓦ newyork.yankees.mlb.com. Tickets $20–300.

Yankee Stadium is home to the New York Yankees, 27-time World Series champs and the most famous franchise in sports. Babe Ruth, Lou Gehrig, Joe DiMaggio and dozens more have formed a continuous line of superstars to the present day, though longtime franchise face Derek Jeter just retired. A brand-new stadium, inaugurated for the 2009 season, replaced the "House That Ruth Built"; the team's heroes are enshrined with plaques and monuments, and tours (☎ 646 977 8687; daily except home game days 11am–1.40pm, every 20min;

$20) take in these, the dugout, the clubhouse and batting cages. The venue doubles as the home ground to NYC's lone city-based soccer club, **New York City FC** (Ⓦ nycfc. com; home games March–Oct).

Bronx Zoo

MAP P.154
Main gate on Fordham Rd. Subway #2, #5 to East Tremont Ave/West Farms Square. ☎ 718 220 5100, Ⓦ www.bronxzoo. com. April–Oct Mon–Fri 10am–5pm, Sat & Sun 10am–5.30pm; Nov–March daily 10am–4.30pm. $22.95, children 3–12 $14.95; special rides and attractions extra, though discount for Total Experience tickets; Wed "pay what you wish".

The largest urban zoo in the United States, which first opened its gates in 1899, houses over six thousand animals and was one of the first institutions of its kind to realize its inhabitants both looked and felt better out in the open. The "Wild Asia" exhibit is an almost forty-acre wilderness through which tigers, elephants and deer roam relatively free, visible from a monorail (May–Oct; $6). The lemurs of Madagascar and the Congo Gorilla Forest are also highlights.

New York Botanical Garden

MAP P.154
Entrance across the road from the zoo's main gate. Subway B, D, #4 to Bedford Park Blvd, though Metro–North from Grand Central to Botanical Garden Station is easier. ☎ 718 817 8700, Ⓦ www.nybg. org. Tues–Sun 10am–6pm. All garden $28, children 2–12 $12 (less on weekends); grounds only $15, children 2–12 $4.

The late nineteenth-century **New York Botanical Garden** is a brilliant companion piece to the zoo opposite. Near the main entrance, the Enid A. Haupt Conservatory, a landmark crystal palace, showcases jungle and desert ecosystems, a palm court and a fern forest, among other seasonal displays. Close by are herb and perennial gardens.

Shops and markets

Beacon's Closet

MAP P.156, POCKET MAP H10

74 Guernsey St, between Nassau and Norman aves, Greenpoint, Brooklyn; other locations in Park Slope, Bushwick and the Village. Subway L to Bedford Ave. Ⓦ www. beaconscloset.com. Daily 11am–8pm.

This huge clothing exchange is great for finding excellent deals on vintage designer duds or making a bit of cash if you've got used stuff in good condition to spare.

Brooklyn Flea

MAP P.156, POCKET MAP J15 & G15

Industry City, 24 37th St, Sunset Park, Brooklyn (Sat 10am–5pm); Manhattan Bridge Archway Plaza, DUMBO (Sun 10am–5pm),. Subway D to 36th St- Fourth Avenue, F to York St. Ⓦ brooklynflea.com.

At both you'll find all manner of knick-knacks and vintage clothes, housewares and jewellery, as well as superb artisan food. The flea also runs Smorgasburg (see page 160). These have moved a few times over the years; check the website for any changes in times and locations.

Smorgasburg

MAP P.156, POCKET MAP H11

East River State Park, Williamsburg (Sat 11am–6pm); Prospect Park (Sun 11am–6pm). Subway L to Bedford Ave and B, Q to Prospect Park. Ⓦ www. smorgasburg.com.

From April to November, these two scenic parks brim with gourmet food vendors; come wintertime, they move indoors (in Industry City, in Brooklyn's Sunset Park). Come armed with cash and be prepared to join the queues for favourites like the salteñas (similar to empanadas) from Bolivian Llama Party. As with Brooklyn Flea, check the website for any changes in times and locations.

Cafés and snacks

Almondine

MAP P.156, POCKET MAP F15

85 Water St, Dumbo, Brooklyn. Subway A, C to High St, F to York St. Mon–Sat 7.30am–6.30pm, Sun 9am–6pm.

It just might be the best bakery in the city, with its exquisite chocolate cakes and fruit tarts, buttery croissants and tasty salami sandwiches. Eat in or, better yet, take it to the nearby park between the bridges.

Blue Bottle Coffee

MAP P.156, POCKET MAP H12

160 Berry St, between Fourth and Fifth sts, Brooklyn; seven other locations in the city. Subway L to Bedford Ave. Mon–Fri 6.30am–7pm, Sat & Sun 7am–7.30pm.

The first of a dozen or so city outposts of a well-regarded San Francisco coffee roaster. A cross between a café and a lab, the java used for iced coffee drips in giant bulbous tubes. Filters are lined up to make coffee to order and a working roastery fills the back.

Café Grumpy

MAP P.156, POCKET MAP J10.

193 Meserole Ave, at Diamond St, Greenpoint, Brooklyn. Subway G to Nassau Ave. Mon–Fri 7am–7.30pm, Sat & Sun 7.30am–7.30pm.

As celebrated in the TV show Girls, this is the original location in a minichain of ultracool coffee culture. A half dozen others are scattered around town.

Nathan's

MAP P.154

1310 Surf Ave, at Schweiker's Walk, Coney Island, Brooklyn. Subway D, F, N, Q to Coney Island-Stillwell Ave. ☎718 333 2202. Mon–Thurs & Sun 10am–11pm, Fri & Sat 10am–2am.

Home of the "famous Coney Island hot dog", served since 1916, Nathan's is a bona fide New York experience. It holds an annual Hot Dog Eating Contest on July 4.

Peter Pan Donut & Pastry Shop

MAP P.156, POCKET MAP H10
727 Manhattan Ave, between Norman and Meserole aves, Greenpoint, Brooklyn. Subway G to Nassau Ave. Mon–Fri 4.30am–8pm, Sat 5am–8pm, Sun 5.30am–7pm (donuts at 8am).

Old-school counter with formica and swivel stools. Perch on one and order delectable crullers, chocolate cake donuts… or any other variety.

Restaurants

Al Di Là

MAP P.156
248 Fifth Ave, at Carroll St, Park Slope, Brooklyn. Subway R to Union St. ☏718 783 4565. Mon–Thurs noon–3pm & 6–10.30pm, Fri noon–3pm & 6–11pm, Sat 11am–3.30pm & 5.30–11pm, Sun 11am–3.30pm & 5–10pm.

Venetian country cooking at its finest at this husband-and-wife-run restaurant. Standouts include beet ravioli ($13), Swiss chard gnocchi ($16) and braised rabbit ($29). Expect an hour-long wait (no reservations).

Casa Enrique

MAP P.154, POCKET MAP G8
5-48 49th Ave, between 5th St and Vernon Blvd, Queens. ☏347 448 6040. Mon–Fri 5–11pm, Sat & Sun 11am–3.30pm & 5–11pm.

A Michelin-starred Mexican restaurant – a rarity in NYC – can be found near Long Island City's main stretch. Made-to-order guacamole, tongue tacos and roast pork ribs highlight a menu of homespun regional dishes.

Dominick's

MAP P.154
2335 Arthur Ave, at 187th St, the Bronx. Subway B, D to Fordham Rd. ☏718 733 2807. Mon & Wed–Sat noon–9.30pm, Sun 1–8pm.

All you could hope for in a Belmont neighbourhood Italian: great, rowdy

Fette Sau

atmosphere, communal seating, wonderful food and low(ish) prices. Stuffed baby squid, veal *parmigiana* and chicken *scarpariello* are standouts. Cash only.

Fette Sau

MAP P.156, POCKET MAP J12
354 Metropolitan Ave, at Havemeyer St, Williamsburg, Brooklyn. Subway L to Bedford Ave, G to Metropolitan Ave. ☏718 963 3404. Mon 5–11pm, Tues–Thurs & Sun noon–11pm, Fri & Sat noon–midnight.

The industrial-chic vibe (it's in an old auto repair shop) of this barbecue specialist fits the neighbourhood. Order your meat by the pound (beef brisket, pork shoulder or pork belly $25), tack on a couple of sides (burnt end baked beans $65) and wash it down with a local microbrew ($7 pints).

Frankies 457 Spuntino

MAP P.156
457 Court St, between 3rd and 4th Pl. Subway F to Carroll St, Brooklyn. ☏718 403 0033. Mon–Thurs & Sun 11am–11pm, Fri & Sat 11am–midnight.

Though it's only been around 15 years, Frankie's feels like a

M. Wells

longtime classic, having helped usher in—then outlast most of—the new wave of the Carroll Gardens restaurant scene. You'll find rustic homemade pastas, Italian wines and, since an expansion, an attached pizza slice shop.

The Good Fork

MAP P.156
391 Van Brunt St, Red Hook, Brooklyn. Subway F, G to Smith–9th sts. ☏ 718 643 6636. Tues–Fri 5.30–10.30pm, Sat 10am–3pm & 5.30–10.30pm, Sun 10am–3pm & 5.30–10pm.

Though it's a neighbourhood restaurant at heart (in an out-of-the-way spot), it's worth making the effort for the inventive cocktails, delectable dumplings ($10) and Korean-inspired take on steak and eggs ($30).

Hometown Bar-B-Que

MAP P.156
454 Van Brunt St, at Reed St, Red Hook. Subway F, G to Smith–9th St, then bus #61. Tues–Thurs & Sun noon–10pm, Fri & Sat noon–11pm.

Reckoned by some as the best purveyor of 'cue in the city, *Hometown* does justice to pulled pork ($24/lb) and brisket ($28/lb). Lively roadhouse atmosphere; expect a longish line (no reservations).

Juliana's

MAP P.156, POCKET MAP F22
19 Old Fulton St, between Front and Water Sts, Dumbo, Brooklyn. Subway F to York St, A, C to High St. ☏ 718 596 6700. Daily 11.30am–10pm.

Patsy Grimaldi sold the naming rights to his famous *Grimaldi's* (right next door), and has come out of retirement to open this coal-oven pizzeria. He's still got the touch. Pies only ($20–32).

M. Wells Dinette

MAP P.154, POCKET MAP H8
22–25 Jackson Ave, between 46th Rd and 46th Ave, Long Island City, Queens. Subway G, #7 to Court Square, E, M to Court Square–Ely. ☏ 718 786 1800. Mon & Thurs–Sun noon–6pm.

In a faux-schoolroom in MoMA PS1 (see page 158), this

adventurous café serves up a
revolving menu of dishes like foie
gras and oats, beef tartare and a
spaghetti sandwich.

Mile End

MAP P.156, POCKET MAP H16
97A Hoyt St, between Pacific and
Atlantic, Boerum Hill, Brooklyn. ☎ 718
852 7510. Subway F, G to Bergen, A, C, G
to Hoyt–Schermerhorn. Mon 8am–4pm,
Tues–Thurs 8am–10pm, Fri 8am–11pm, Sat
10am–11pm, Sun 10am–10pm.

This cosy Montréal-style Jewish
deli serves tasty breakfast all day
and smoked meat sandwiches
that rival any in town, along
with takes on Old World home
cooking – for example, chicken
and latkes (potato pancakes). A
real treat.

Peter Luger Steak House

MAP P.156, POCKET MAP J13
178 Broadway, at Driggs Ave, Williamsburg,
Brooklyn. Subway J, M, Z to Marcy Ave.
☎ 718 387 7400. Mon–Thurs 11.45am–
9.45pm, Fri & Sat 11.45am–10.45pm, Sun
12.45–9.45pm.

Catering to carnivores since 1873,
Peter Luger's may just be the city's
finest steakhouse. The service is
surly and the decor plain, but the
porterhouse steak – essentially the
only cut served – is divine. Make
sure to order the bacon starter, too.
It's expensive; tabs can easily run to
$100 or so per person.

Pies-n-Thighs

MAP P.156, POCKET MAP J12
166 S 4th St, at Driggs Ave. Subway J, M,
Z to Marcy Ave, Williamsburg, Brooklyn.
☎ 347 529 6090. Mon–Fri 9am–4am &
5pm–midnight, Sat & Sun 10am–4pm &
5pm–midnight.

Tucked in a bright corner location,
P-n-T do exemplary Southern-
style food: great chicken biscuits (a
scone with a fried chicken filling;
$7.50), expertly fried chicken
($13.50 with waffles, $15 with a
side) and a changing rotation of
pies (key lime is a favourite; slices
$4.50–5.50).

Roberta's

MAP P.154
261 Moore St, at Bogart St. Subway L to
Morgan Ave, Bushwick, Brooklyn. ☎ 718
417 1118. Mon–Fri 11am–midnight, Sat &
Sun 10am–midnight.

Slightly in the middle of nowhere
(ever-burgeoning Bushwick),
this acclaimed spot serves up
some of the city's best pies in an
unassuming building – though the
courtyard is nice, and the place
hides a super-upscale restaurant
within a restaurant, Bianca (☎ 347
799 2807, blancanyc.com; book a
month ahead).

Zenon Taverna

MAP P.154, POCKET MAP J4
34-10 31st Ave, Astoria, Queens. Subway N,
W to 30th Ave, R, M to Steinway St. ☎ 718
956 0133. Daily noon–11pm.

Charred octopus ($19), grilled
meatballs ($11) and taramasalata
dip will get your meal off on the
right foot at the super-friendly
Greek-Cypriot tavern; whole fish or
one of the lamb specials ($28) keep
it headed in the right direction.

Bars

Bohemian Hall and Beer Garden

MAP P.154, POCKET MAP J3
29-19 24th Ave between 29th and 30th
sts, Astoria, Queens. Subway N, W to
Astoria Blvd. ☎ 718 274 4925. Mon–Thurs
5pm–1am, Fri 3pm–3am, Sat noon–3am,
Sun noon–midnight.

This Czech bar is the real deal,
catering to old-timers and serving a
good selection of pilsners as well as
hard-to-find brews. Out the back,
there's a very large beer garden,
complete with picnic tables,
trees, burgers and sausages, and a
bandshell for polka groups. Great
fun in good weather and worth
the trip.

Brooklyn Brewery

MAP P.156, POCKET MAP H11
79 N 11th St, Williamsburg,

THE OUTER BOROUGHS

Brooklyn. Subway L to Bedford Ave. Ⓦ brooklynbrewery.com. Mon–Thurs 5–11pm, Fri 5pm–2am, Sat noon–midnight, Sun noon–8pm.

Check out this stellar Williamsburg microbrewery, which hosts events year-round; hang out in their tasting room at weekends or take a free tour (Mon–Thurs 5–6.30pm, $18; Sat & Sun 1–6pm, free).

L.I.C. Bar

MAP P.154, POCKET MAP G8
45–58 Vernon Blvd, at 46th Ave, Long Island City, Queens. Subway #7 to Vernon Blvd-Jackson Ave or 45th Rd-Courthouse Square, G to 21st St. ☎ 718 786 5400. Mon–Fri 4pm–2am, Sat & Sun 1pm–2am.
A friendly, atmospheric place for a beer, burger and free live music (Mon, Wed, Sat & Sun); hunker down at the old wooden bar or in the pleasant garden.

Long Island Bar

MAP P.156, POCKET MAP G16
110 Atlantic Ave, at Henry St, Cobble Hill, Brooklyn. Subway #2, #3, #4, #5 to Borough Hall. Mon–Thurs & Sun 5.30pm–midnight, Fri & Sat 5.30pm–2am.
A recently revived relic whose vintage sign leads the way to a room with meticulously made cocktails and, in the fried cheese curds ($12), one of the best bar snacks going.

Pete's Candy Store

MAP P.156, POCKET MAP J11
709 Lorimer St, between Frost and Richardson sts, Williamsburg, Brooklyn. Subway L to Lorimer St, G to Metropolitan Ave. Mon–Thurs 5pm–2am, Fri & Sat 4pm–4am, Sun 3pm–2am.
This terrific little spot to tipple was once a real candy store. There's free live music every night, a reading series, Scrabble and Bingo nights, pub quizzes and some well-poured cocktails.

Royal Palms Shuffleboard Club

MAP P.156
514 Union St, between Third Ave and

Nevins St, Gowanus. Subway R to Union St. Tues–Wed 6pm–midnight, Thurs & Fri 6pm–2am, Sat noon–2am, Sun noon–midnight.
Perhaps it was inevitable for such a place to pop up, considering every other trend to hit (or be spawned by) Brooklyn, but this cheerful multipurpose spot does offer tropical cocktails, food trucks, DJs and, of course, courts for the eponymous sport ($40/hr).

Tørst

MAP P.156, POCKET MAP J10
615 Manhattan Ave, between Nassau and Driggs aves, Greenpoint, Brooklyn. Subway G to Nassau Ave. Mon–Thurs & Sun noon–midnight, Fri & Sat noon–2am.
A shiny new temple for beer drinkers, Tørst boasts reclaimed wood and a sleek metal bar, behind which some twenty draughts sit hooked up to the "flux capacitor", which allows bartenders to monitor and adjust the gas and carbonation. The results: flawless 5oz, 8oz or 14oz pours. A food menu with sharable plates and a very dressy hot dog is available too.

Clubs and venues

The Bell House

MAP P.156
149 7th St, between Second and Third aves, Gowanus, Brooklyn. Subway F, G, R to Fourth Ave-9th St. ☎ 718 643 6510, Ⓦ www.thebellhouseny.com.
A converted printing house in up-and-coming Gowanus provides the setting for indie band performances and wacky events – cookoffs, Burt Reynolds' film celebrations and so on. The front-room bar (daily 5pm–4am) is a pleasantly spacious place to drink.

Brooklyn Academy of Music

MAP P.156, POCKET MAP J16
30 Lafayette St between Ashland Place and St Felix St, Brooklyn. Subway #2, #3, #4,

#5, B, Q to Barclays-Atlantic Ave, D, M, N, R to Pacific St. ☏ 718 636 4100, Ⓦ www.bam.org.

America's oldest performing arts academy (1859) and one of the most daring producers in New York is worth crossing the river for, especially to catch African dance, European theatre troupes and rare movie screenings.

Brooklyn Bowl

MAP P.156, POCKET MAP H11
61 Wythe Ave, between 11th and 12th sts, Williamsburg. Subway L to Bedford Ave. Ⓦ www.brooklynbowl.com. Mon–Thurs 6pm–2am, Fri 6pm–4am, Sat 11am–4am, Sun 11am–2am. Shows $5–20 or more.

A converted warehouse with live concerts, DJ sets, a restaurant, oh yeah, and bowling. Roots drummer Questlove spins somewhat regularly here.

House of Yes

2 Wyckoff Ave, East Williamsburg. Subway L to Jefferson St. Ⓦ houseofyes.org. Wed–Sat 10pm–6am. Cover free–$30 (buy in advance).

This former warehouse now hosts lavish dance parties plus live theater and cabaret in East Williamsburg. Check the website to see if the weekly Blunderland Variety Show is on (Sat 6.30pm), a surreal combo of burlesque, circus and cabaret. You are expected to dress up for theme parties.

Music Hall of Williamsburg

MAP P.156, POCKET MAP H11
66 N 6th St, at Kent, Williamsburg, Brooklyn. Subway L to Bedford Ave. ☏ 718 486 5400, Ⓦ www.musichallofwilliamsburg.com. Tickets $15–30.

A large performance space with excellent acoustics. Set in an old factory this is one of the city's best spots for live music and indie-rock.

St. Ann's Warehouse

MAP P.156, POCKET MAP F22
45 Water St, at Dock St, Dumbo. Subway A, C to High St, F to York St. ☏ 718 254 8779, Ⓦ stannswarehouse.com.

This waterfront theatre, recently transplanted to what was once the crumbling Tobacco Warehouse, puts on avant-garde performances – plays, puppetry, concerts and the like.

Pete's Candy Store

ACCOMMODATION

Hotel Chelsea

Accommodation

Accommodation prices in New York City are extremely high: many hotels charge more than $250 a night for a double room; $400–500 in high season can be common. The traditional centre of hotel life is midtown Manhattan, but more and more new places are being built below 34th Street as well as out in the boroughs, especially Williamsburg (Brooklyn) and Long Island City (Queens). Booking ahead is near essential, and at certain times of the year – early to mid-autumn or the weeks leading up to Christmas – the city can seem sold out. There's hardly such a thing as a fixed room price. Rates in this chapter refer to the cost of the cheapest double room at peak times; be aware that prices can change on a daily basis, depending on a hotel's occupancy and other factors subject to the whims of the booking computer. For some places, rates might be up to half as much as what's listed here, depending on when you check; booking online – whether directly with the hotel or through a third-party travel site – can save lots of money, too. Taxes add 14.75 percent to your bill, plus $3.50 per night in "occupancy tax" and room fees.

Financial District

THE WAGNER AT THE BATTERY MAP P.26, POCKET MAP C24. 2 West St, Battery Park. Subway #1 to Rector St, #4, #5 to Bowling Green. ☎ 212 344 0800, ⓦ www.thewagnerhotel.com. The views of New York Harbor and the Statue of Liberty don't get much better than from this elegant high-rise hotel. It features a lounge for continental breakfast and evening drinks and 425-square-foot rooms with soothing muted tones. Weekend discounts. **$399.**

Soho and Tribeca

AKA SMYTH TRIBECA MAP P.38, POCKET MAP C21. 85 W Broadway, between Warren and Chambers sts. Subway A, C, #1, #2, #3 to Chambers St. ☎ 212 587 7000, ⓦ www.stayaka.com. One of the trendier boutiques in this part of town, with plush, contemporary design and furnishings with classical and Art Deco touches; 24-7 fitness

station, hip bar and restaurant, and large bathrooms amount the selling points. **$599.**

CROSBY STREET HOTEL MAP P.38, POCKET MAP D19. 79 Crosby St, between Spring and Prince sts. Subway R, W to Prince St, #6 to Spring St. ☎ 212 226 6400, ⓦ www.firmdale.com. It's expensive, but you get bright and spacious rooms set around a courtyard on the edge of trendy Soho, with luxurious bathrooms, floor-to-ceiling windows and contemporary art throughout. Rooms on the higher floors have spectacular views. Afternoon tea ($48) is served all day in the drawing room. **$700.**

FREDERICK MAP P.38, POCKET MAP C21. 95 W Broadway, at Chambers St. Subway A, C, #1, #2, #3 to Chambers St. ☎ 1–888 895 9400 or 212 566 1900, ⓦ www.frederickhotelnyc.com. Great Tribeca location, with smart, well-maintained rooms at reasonable prices, this is one of the best of the conventional hotels downtown. **$288**.

TRIBECA GRAND HOTEL MAP P.38, POCKET MAP C20. 2 Sixth Ave, between White and Walker sts. Subway #1 to Franklin St. ☎ 1-877 519 6600 or 212 519 6600, Ⓦ www.tribecagrand.com. Craving anonymity, the Tribeca Grand is unlabelled and tucked behind a brick facade. The lounge is perfect for drinks and the rooms are stylish, yet understated, though each bathroom boasts a phone and built-in TV. **$479**.

The Lower East Side

BLUE MOON MAP P.56, POCKET MAP E19. 100 Orchard St, between Delancey and Broome sts. Subway F to Delancey St, J, M, Z to Essex St. ☎ 212 533 9080, Ⓦ www.bluemoon-nyc.com. Five-storey Lower East Side tenement transformed into a hotel, with rooms named after 1930s and 1940s celebrities and decked out with period iron-frame beds and the odd antique – rooms on the 6th, 7th and 8th floors also come with fabulous views across the city. Continental breakfast and wi-fi included; dorm rooms available too. **$299**.

HOTEL 91 MAP P.56, POCKET MAP E21. 91 E Broadway. Subway F to E Broadway. ☎ 212 266 6800, Ⓦ www.thehotel91.com. Funky Lower East Side boutique, with a slight Asian theme – orchids grace every room, and a statue of Buddha sits in the lobby. Rooms are compact but well equipped, with LCD TVs and marble bathrooms. Free wi-fi. **$245**.

The East Village

BOWERY HOTEL MAP P.64, POCKET MAP D18. 335 Bowery, at E 3rd St. Subway #6 to Bleecker St. ☎ 212 505 9100, Ⓦ www.theboweryhotel.com. This fabulous, but pricey, boutique property oozes sophistication and tempts guests with iPod docks, floor-to-ceiling windows, marble tubs with a view and a hip lounge bar. **$575**.

The West Village

WASHINGTON SQUARE MAP P.76, POCKET MAP C18. 103 Waverly Place, at Washington Square Park. Subway A, B, C, D, E, F, M to W 4th St. ☎ 212 777 9515, Ⓦ washingtonsquarehotel.com. Located in the heart of Greenwich Village on the edge of the park since 1902. Don't be deceived by the posh-looking lobby – the rooms are surprisingly plain for the price (though rates are significantly cut in August). The Art Deco "Deluxe" rooms have a bit more character and continental breakfast is included. **$325**.

Chelsea and the Meatpacking District

CHELSEA PINES INN MAP P.86, POCKET MAP A17. 317 W 14th St, between Eighth and Ninth aves. Subway A, C, E to 14th St. ☎ 1-888 546 2700 or 212 929 1023, Ⓦ www.chelseapinesinn.com. Housed in an old brownstone, this super-friendly hotel offers clean, comfortable, shabby-chic rooms, all complete with a movie motif.

Favourite places to stay

There's something for every taste in the city, though even if you find the perfect accommodation for you, you'll probably still register some surprise at the (small) size of the room. Here are just a few of our favourites:

Best place for downtown chic: The Jane, see page 170
Best place to blow the expense account: Crosby Street Hotel, see page 168
Best place for a romantic getaway: Gramercy Park, see page 170
Best place to be in the heart of it all: The Mansfield, see page 171
Best place for a modest budget: The Frederick, see page 168
Best place for a room with a view: Ink48, see page 172
Best place for mixing function with form: Nomad, see page 170

Long popular with a gay and lesbian clientele. Best to book in advance. **$287.**

DREAM DOWNTOWN MAP P.86, POCKET MAP C12. 355 W 16th St, between Eighth and Ninth aves. Subway A, C, E, L to 14th St. ☎ 212 229 2559, Ⓦ dreamhotels.com. Visually stunning, this Miami-esque hotel has a lobby with cut-out "skylights" – the base of its swimming pool is lined with glass, so while you're checking in, you'll see guests gliding in the water overhead. Stylish all-white guest rooms have porthole windows and pops of pink, and there's exceptional concierge service plus a rooftop bar with magnificent views. **$550.**

HÔTEL AMERICANO MAP P.86, POCKET MAP B10. 518 W 27th St, between Tenth and Eleventh aves. Subway #1 to 28th St. ☎ 212 216 0000, Ⓦ www.hotel-americano. com. The first venture outside of Mexico by boutique developers Grupo Habita, the eye-catching *Americano* sits right on the High Line, with a sleek, modern style all of its own. Some evidence: Japanese-style platform beds, showers looking out onto the skyline and separate elevators for guest and public use. **$500.**

THE JANE MAP P.86, POCKET MAP A17. 113 Jane St, at West St. Subway A, C, E, to 14th St, L to Eighth Ave. ☎ 212 924 6700, Ⓦ www.thejanenyc.com. Equipped with a hip bar-club, this chic place has small rooms inspired by ship's cabins. Bunk-bed rooms (shared bathroom) are a good deal, but there are also pricier captain's cabins (en suite). **Bunks $135, Captain's $325.**

MARITIME MAP P.86, POCKET MAP C11. 88 Ninth Ave, between W 16th and 17th sts. Subway A, C, E, L to 14th St-Eighth Ave. ☎ 212 242 4300, Ⓦ www. themaritimehotel.com. The nautical theme runs through this contemporary hotel, and rooms come with porthole windows – as well as complimentary bike use and gym access. **$436.**

STEWART HOTEL MAP P.86, POCKET MAP D9. 371 Seventh Ave, at W 31st St. Subway #1, #2, #3 to 34th St-Penn Station. ☎ 212 563 1800, Ⓦstewarthotelnyc.com. This large hotel

is housed in a 1929 building; a redesign brought some artistic flair to the place and added petite queens to its stable of suites with kitchenettes. Though it's a bustling address, the elegant lobby, in-room spa service and a menu of pillow options all help foster relaxation. **$380.**

Union Square, Gramercy Park and the Flatiron District

ACE MAP P.94, POCKET MAP D10. 20 W 29th St, at Broadway. Subway R, W to 28th St. ☎ 212 679 2222, Ⓦ www.acehotel. com/newyork. Capturing the spirit of old New York, yet fully modern, the *Ace Hotel* symbolizes bohemian chic. A whole host of different room styles are on offer (including cheaper bunks), with retro-style fridges, guitars, muted tones and cool artwork. **$399.**

GIRAFFE MAP P.94, POCKET MAP E10. 365 Park Ave, at 26th St. Subway #6 to 28th St. ☎ 212 685 7700, Ⓦ www. hotelgiraffe.com. A small, boutique hotel with a personal touch, the *Giraffe* offers deluxe rooms with tiny terraces and all the amenities; there's a wine and cheese hour (daily 5–8pm) in the lobby with live music accompaniment (save for weekends). **$440.**

GRAMERCY PARK MAP P.94, POCKET MAP E10. 2 Lexington Ave, at E 21st St. Subway #6 to 23rd St. ☎ 212 920 3300, Ⓦ www.gramercyparkhotel.com. An Ian Schrager overhaul gave new life to this once bohemian hotel, located in a prime Gramercy spot with access to the private park. The rooms are bold and luxurious. **$599.**

NOMAD MAP P.94, POCKET MAP D10. 1170 Broadway, at W 28th St. Subway R, W to 28th St. ☎ 212 796 1500 or 1 855 796 1505, Ⓦ www.thenomadhotel. com. A competitor for the same crowd as the nearby *Ace* (see page 170), with a celebrated on-site restaurant, the welcoming *NoMad* offers stylish, spacious rooms with damask patterns, Iranian rugs, clawfoot tubs, king-size beds and a mishmash of tasteful art on the walls – different in each space. A definite cut above. **$535.**

THE ROGER MAP P.94, POCKET MAP D9. 131 Madison Ave, at 31st St. Subway #6 to 33rd St. ☎ 1 888 448 7788 or 212 448 7000, ⊛ www.therogernewyork.com. Full of cleanliness and sharp contrasts, *The Roger* has a comfortable lobby and well-appointed rooms. Some come with small terraces with views of the Empire State Building. **$420.**

Midtown

AFFINIA SHELBURNE MAP P.102, POCKET MAP E9. 303 Lexington Ave, between E 37th and E 38th sts. Subway #4, #5, #6, #7 to 42nd St–Grand Central. ☎ 212 689 5200, ⊛ www.affinia.com. Luxurious hotel in the most elegant part of Murray Hill. Many rooms have kitchenettes ($30 extra), its restaurant *Rare* specializes in gourmet burgers, and there's a rooftop bar. **$410.**

ALGONQUIN MAP P.102, POCKET MAP D8. 59 W 44th St, between Fifth and Sixth aves. Subway B, D, F, M to 42nd St. ☎ 212 840 6800, ⊛ www.algonquinhotel.com. At New York's classic literary hangout, you'll find a resident cat named Hamlet, suites with silly names and a whole lot of style and tradition. The bedrooms have been refurbished to good effect. **$479.**

CHAMBERS MAP P.102, POCKET MAP D7. 15 W 56th St, between Fifth and Sixth aves. Subway F to 57th St. ☎ 1 866 204 5656 or 212 974 5656, ⊛ www. chambershotel.com. Designed by architect David Rockwell, *Chambers* is well placed for Central Park and MoMA, though you can just sit and admire the 500 original works of art in the hallways. Modern, tasteful rooms approximate a New York apartment, as do the mezzanine lounge spaces. **$445.**

IBEROSTAR 70 PARK AVENUE HOTEL MAP P.102, POCKET MAP E9. 70 Park Ave, at 38th St. Subway S, #4, #5, #6, #7 to 42nd St–Grand Central. ☎ 1-877 707 2752 or 212 973 2400 ⊛ www.70parkave.com. This classy boutique hotel is adorned with re-

creations of classical friezes and frescoes, and original lighting and furnishing design featuring rich woods and muted earth tones. Extras include a 24hr fitness centre, flat-screen TVs, wi-fi and a nightly wine reception. Pet-friendly. **$425.**

IROQUOIS MAP P.102, POCKET MAP D8. 49 W 44th St, between Fifth and Sixth aves. Subway B, D, F, M to 42nd St. ☎ 1 800 332 7220 or 212 840 3080, ⊛ www. iroquoisny.com. A former haven for rock bands, this reinvented "boutique" hotel has comfortable, tasteful rooms with Italian marble baths and a health centre, library and an upscale French restaurant. One of the hotel's noted visitors is immortalized in the suite named after him: James Dean lived here 1951–53 (room #803). **$449.**

LIBRARY MAP P.102, POCKET MAP D8. 299 Madison Ave, at E 41st St. Subway #4, #5, #6, #7 to 42nd St–Grand Central. ☎ 212 983 4500, ⊛ www.libraryhotel.com. The *Library's* unusual concept has each floor devoted to one of the ten major categories of the Dewey Decimal System. Coloured in shades of brown and cream, the rooms are average-sized but nicely appointed, with big bathrooms and bookish throw-ins. The hotel throws wine and cheese get-togethers weekday evenings. **$423.**

THE MANSFIELD MAP P.102, POCKET MAP D8. 12 W 44th St, between Fifth and Sixth aves. Subway B, D, F, M to 42nd St. ☎ 1 844 591 5565 or 212 277 8700, ⊛ www. mansfieldhotel.com. One of the loveliest, friendliest hotels in the city, the *Mansfield* is both grand and intimate. With its recessed floor spotlighting, copper-domed salon, clubby library and Thursday night jazz in the bar, there's a charming, quirky feel about the place. **$359.**

THE METRO MAP P.102, POCKET MAP D9. 45 W 35th St, between Fifth and Sixth aves. Subway B, D, F, M, N, Q, R, W to 34th St. ☎ 1 800 356 3870 or 212 947 2500, ⊛ www.hotelmetronyc.com. A very stylish hotel, with minimal Hollywood theming, a delightful seasonal rooftop terrace, clean rooms, wi-fi and free continental breakfast. **$379.**

POD 51 MAP P.102, POCKET MAP E8. 230 E 51st St, between Second and Third aves. Subway #6 to 51st St. ☎ 212 355 0300, Ⓦ the pod hotel.com. This pleasant budget hotel is one of the best deals in Midtown. All 370 "pods" (solo, double, bunk, queen or "odd" reminiscent of a ship's quarters) come with a/c, iPod docks, free wi-fi and flat-screen TVs, though some share baths. The open-air roof deck is a bonus, with stunning views. There are multiple other Pod hotels in the city: E. 39th St, Times Square and Williamsburg, Brooklyn. **$229. (bunk with shared bath $195).**

ROGER SMITH MAP P.102, POCKET MAP E8. 501 Lexington Ave, at E 47th St. Subway #6 to 51st St. ☎ 1 800 445 0277 or 212 755 1400, Ⓦ www.rogersmith.com. Lots of style and personality: individually decorated rooms and bold artwork on display in the common areas. A very light breakfast is included. **$369.**

Times Square and the Theater District

414 MAP P.116, POCKET MAP C8. 414 W 46th St, between Ninth and Tenth aves. Subway C, E to 50th St. ☎ 212 399 0006 or 1-866/414-HOTEL, Ⓦ www.414hotel.com. Popular with Europeans but welcoming to all, this guesthouse, which has larger-than-ordinary rooms in two townhouses, makes a nice camp a bit removed from Times Square's bustle. The backyard garden is a wonderful place to enjoy your morning coffee. **$429.**

AMERITANIA AT TIMES SQUARE MAP P.116, POCKET MAP C7. 54 230 W 54th St, at Broadway. Subway B, D, E to Seventh Ave. ☎ 855 767 5050 or 212 247 5000, Ⓦ www.ameritanianyc.com. One of the coolest-looking hotels in the city, with well-furnished rooms including marble bathrooms; there's a bar/restaurant off the high-tech, funky lobby. **$404.**

CASABLANCA MAP P.116, POCKET MAP D8. 147 W 43rd St, between Sixth Ave and Broadway. Subway B, D, F, M, #1, #2, #3 to 42nd St. ☎ 1 888 922 7225 or 212 869 1212, Ⓦ www.casablancahotel.

com. Moorish tiles, ceiling fans and *Rick's Café* are all here in this unusual and understated theme hotel. While the feeling is 1940s Morocco, the rooms are all up to date. **$388.**

CITIZENM NEW YORK TIMES SQUARE MAP P.116, POCKET MAP C8. 218 W 50th St, between Broadway and Eighth Ave. Subway #1 to 50th St. ☎ 212 461 3638, Ⓦ citizenm.com. The first US outpost of this trendy Dutch chain (there's now another on the Lower East Side), this stylish, limited-service hotel offers compact, minimalist rooms with Samsung tablet, plus a guests-only rooftop lounge and use of Apple computers in the library. Breakfast is $19 extra (booked online). **$370.**

DISTRIKT MAP P.116, POCKET MAP C9. 342 W 40th St, between Eighth and Ninth aves. Subway A, C, E to 42nd St-Port Authority. ☎ 212 706 6100, Ⓦ www.distrikthotel.com. With a city neighbourhood theme, the welcoming *Distrikt* has nice-sized rooms done in classy muted browns and beiges; choose one of the upper floors for the best views. The street outside is on the unsalubrious side. **$368.**

THE FRENCH QUARTERS MAP P. 116, POCKET MAP C8. 346 W 46th St, between Eighth and Ninth aves. Subway C, E to 50th St. ☎ 212 359 6652, Ⓦ frenchquartersny. com. These New Orleans-themed serviced apartments are a great deal and subsequently very popular – book months ahead. The elegant rooms feature kitchenettes, DVD players and separate sitting areas. Continental breakfast included. **$280.**

INK48 MAP P.116, POCKET MAP B8. 653 Eleventh Ave, between 47th and 48th sts. Subway C, E to 50th St. ☎ 877 843 8869 or 212 757 0088 Ⓦ www.ink48.com. Located on an industrial strip, this old printing press has been re-made into a dashing hotel; all rooms face outwards – many to the Hudson – for splendid views (best from upper-floor corner rooms), and have modern decor and lofty ceilings. The rooftop bar, *Press Lounge*, is a plus, as is the spa. Dog-friendly. **$389.**

KNICKERBOCKER MAP P.116, POCKET MAP D8. 6 Times Square, Broadway, at 42nd St. Subway #1, #2, #3, N, Q, R, S, W to Times Sq–42nd St. ☎ 1 855 865 6425, Ⓦ www.theknickerbocker.com. This century-old Beaux Arts landmark, once a high-society hotel built by John Jacob Astor, was reopened in 2015. The largish rooms are elegantly appointed but not overdone. $600.

PARKER NEW YORK MAP P.116, POCKET MAP D7. 119 W 56th St, between Sixth and Seventh aves. Subway F to 57th St. ☎ 212 245 5000 or 800 543 4300, Ⓦ www.parkermeridien.com. This hotel maintains a shiny, clean veneer, with spacious, modern rooms, a huge fitness centre, rooftop swimming pool and 24hr room service. The tucked-away, ground-floor *Burger Joint* (see page 120) is a fun place for a bite to eat. $500.

ROOM MATE GRACE MAP P.116, POCKET MAP D8. 125 W 45th St, between Sixth and Seventh aves. Subway B, D, F, M, #1, #2, #3 to 42nd St. ☎ 212 354 2323, Ⓦ www.room-matehotels.com. You won't find many hotels like this one, with a lobby that more closely resembles a concession stand; a tiny glassed-in pool overlooked by a louche loungey bar; different, funky retro wallpaper on each floor, and ultra-modern rooms with platform beds. $409.

SALISBURY MAP P.116, POCKET MAP D7. 123 W 57th St, between Sixth and Seventh aves. Subway F, N, Q, R, W to 57th St. ☎ 212 246 1300, Ⓦ www.nycsalisbury.com. Good service, large rooms with kitchenettes and proximity to Central Park are the attractions here – along with rates that can run very inexpensive, especially on Sundays and Mondays. $332.

The Upper East Side

WALES MAP P.130, POCKET MAP D4. 1295 Madison Ave, between E 92nd and E 93rd sts. Subway #6 to 96th St. ☎ 866 925 3746 or 212 876 6000, Ⓦ www.hotelwalesnyc.com. Just steps from "Museum Mile", this Carnegie Hill hotel

has hosted guests for over a century. Rooms are attractive with antique details, thoughtful in-room amenities and some views of Central Park. There's also a rooftop terrace and free continental breakfast. $375.

The Upper West Side

LUCERNE MAP P.140, POCKET MAP B5. 201 W 79th St, at Amsterdam Ave. Subway B, C to 81st St, #1 to 79th St. ☎ 1 800 492 8122 or 212 875 1000, Ⓦ www.thelucernehotel.com. This beautifully restored 1904 brownstone, with its extravagantly Baroque red terracotta entrance, charming rooms and friendly staff, is just a block from the American Museum of Natural History and close to the liveliest stretch of Columbus Avenue. $370.

NYLO MAP P.140, POCKET MAP B5. 2178 Broadway, at 77th St. Subway #1 to 79th St. ☎ 1 800 509 7598 or 212 362 1100, Ⓦ www.nylohotelnyc.com. Sizeable rooms, community balconies and no-nonsense design make this updated hotel a good option. $340.

Harlem

ALOFT HARLEM MAP P.148. 2296 Frederick Douglass Blvd, at W 124th St. Subway A, B, C, D to 125th St. ☎ 212 749 4000, Ⓦ www.aloftharlem.com. The first hotel to open in the neighbourhood since the 1960s has a bright, stylish interior and airy, loft-inspired rooms with platform beds. $305.

Williamsburg

MCCARREN HOTEL & POOL MAP P.154, POCKET MAP H11. 160 N 12th St, between Bedford Ave and Berry St, Williamsburg. ☎ 718 218 7500, Ⓦ mccarrenhotel.com. Subway L to Bedford Ave. Just off the main Williamsburg strip and overlooking McCarren Park, this chic option features a seasonal outdoor pool (also the location for summer concerts and movies), compact but comfy rooms and a rooftop lounge with the requisite Manhattan views. $315.

WYTHE MAP P.156, POCKET MAP H11. 80 Wythe Ave, at N 11th St. Subway L to Bedford St. ☎ 718 460 8000, ⓦ www. wythehotel.com. This old factory has been smartly converted into a chic boutique hotel; various industrial touches have been preserved and emphasized, whether exposed brick or floor-to-ceiling warehouse-style windows. "Baby queens" and bunks offer a good deal, though you may want to pay extra for more space and the Brooklyn or Manhattan-side views from higher floors. **$355.**

Long Island City

PAPER FACTORY MAP P.154, POCKET MAP J6. 37-06 36th St, at 37th Ave, Long Island City, Queens. Subway R, M to 36th St, N, Q to 36th Ave. ☎ 718 392 7200, ⓦ www.paperfactoryhotel.com. A stylish hotel in an increasingly popular part of town, the *Paper Factory* was, indeed, once an exemplar of its name. Rooms have a certain rough-hewn chic, and many rooms come with views of the neighbourhood or Manhattan skyline. **$259.**

Hostels

Hostels can offer savings as well as a sociable vibe, but there are, relatively speaking, limited options in the city – at least that fit the bill in terms of quality and prime location. Wherever the case, book ahead: reservations are usually essential.

AMERICAN DREAM MAP P.94, POCKET MAP E10. 168 E 24th St, between Third and Lexington aves. Subway #6 to 23rd St. ☎ 212 260 9779, ⓦ www. americandreamhostel.com. A great location helps this clean, hospitable hostel be a good option for a short-term budget stay; complimentary wi-fi and continental breakfast included. Prices increase at weekends. **Shared rooms $55–85/person (depending on 2- or 3-person room), singles $95–110.**

CHELSEA INTERNATIONAL HOSTEL MAP P.86, POCKET MAP C10. 251 W 20th St, between Seventh and Eighth aves. Subway C, E, #1 to 23rd St. ☎ 212 647 0010, ⓦ www.chelseahostel.com. In the heart of Chelsea, this is a smart downtown choice.

Guests must leave a $10 key deposit. No curfew; passport required and advance reservations near essential. **Shared rooms $60–80/person, private doubles $135–175.**

THE LOCAL MAP P.154, POCKET MAP G7. 1302 44th Ave, Long Island City, Queens. Subway E, M to Court Sq-23rd St. ☎ 347 738 5251, ⓦ www.thelocalny.com. This newish hostel has basic but bright rooms and a café-bar; the surrounding neighbourhood is a nice change of pace. **Dorms $50–65, private double $130–180.**

Q4 HOTEL MAP P.154 POCKET MAP H7. 29-09 Queens Plaza N, at 29th St, Long Island City, Queens. Subway E, M, R to Queens Plaza. ☎ 718 706 7700, ⓦ q4hotel.com. Hip hostel in up-and-coming Long Island City, with some of the cheapest rates in New York. Neat, clean dorms, small but stylish doubles and spotless bathrooms, plus you get access to shared kitchen, TV lounge and pool and ping-pong tables. **Dorms from $35, doubles $140.**

B&Bs and apartments

Bed-and-breakfast accommodation can be a good way of staying right in the centre of Manhattan at an affordable price. But don't expect to socialize with your temporary landlord/lady – chances are you'll have a self-contained room and hardly see them. Reservations are normally arranged through an agency

such as those listed below; book well in advance. Try Craigslist (ⓦ newyork. craigslist.org) for everything from apartment swaps to short-term rentals; more holiday apartment listings can be found on HomeAway (ⓦ homeaway.com), Vacation Rentals by Owner (ⓦ www.vrbo. com) and Airbnb (ⓦ www.airbnb.com).

COLONIAL HOUSE INN MAP P.86, POCKET MAP C10. 318 W 22nd St, between Eighth and Ninth aves. Subway C, E to 23rd St. ☎ 212 243 9669 or 800 689 3779, Ⓦ www.colonialhouseinn.com. You won't mind that this B&B is a little worn around the edges (though it has recently been updated) – its attractive design and association with Gay Men's Health Crisis make for a feel-good accommodation experience. Only deluxe rooms include en-suite bathrooms, while some rooms even have refrigerators and fireplaces, and sleep four. Continental breakfast included. **Doubles $195, suites (which can sleep up to five) can run to $425.**

JONES STREET GUESTHOUSE MAP P.76, POCKET MAP B18. 31 Jones St, between Bleecker and W 4th sts. Subway A, B, C, D, E, F, M to W 4th St, #1 to Christopher St, contact via email only. Ⓦ www. jonesstreetguesthouse.com. Rare B&B in the heart of the West Village, just off Bleecker; two nicely renovated en-suite rooms, spotlessly clean, with friendly owners in the apartments above (their duplex can also be rented) – closest you'll get to "living like a local". Breakfast is courtesy of a $5 per person voucher at nearby *Doma*. Free wi-fi. **Single $240–260, double $260–280.**

MOUNT MORRIS HOUSE MAP P.148. 12 Mt Morris Park W, between W 121st and W 122nd st. Subway #2, #3 to 125th St. ☎ 917 478 6214, Ⓦ mountmorrishousebandb.com. This guesthouse is an elegant brownstone built in 1888, just across the street from Marcus Garvey Park in Harlem. The five sumptuous suites are loaded with period antiques and feature parquet floors, fireplaces and high ceilings. No breakfast, but shared kitchen comes with tea and coffee (and freshly baked cakes every day). **$225.**

SAN FERMÍN APARTMENTS MAP P.148. 195 Edgecombe Ave, between 142nd and 145th sts. Subway A, B, C, D to 145th St. ☎ 917 940 2682, Ⓦ sanferminapartmentsny.com. Set in a lovely 1910 brownstone in Sugar Hill (Harlem), this guesthouse features three comfortable en-suite doubles, and three doubles with shared bath, all dressed in a cool contemporary style. Small kitchen included. **$150.**

ESSENTIALS

Taxis on Columbus Circle

Arrival

By air

New York City is served by three major airports: most international flights use John F. Kennedy, or **JFK** (☎ 718 244 4444, ⊚ jfkairport.com), in Queens, and **Newark Liberty** (☎ 973 961 6000, ⊚ newarkairport.com), in New Jersey, which has easier access to Lower Manhattan. Most domestic arrivals touch down at **LaGuardia** (☎ 718 533 3400, ⊚ laguardiaairport.com), also in Queens, or at Newark.

Getting into the city

From JFK, the NYC Airporter (☎ 212 875 8200, ⊚ nycairporter.com) runs **buses** to Grand Central Terminal (every 20–30min 11am–7pm; 1hr; $19 one-way, $35 round-trip). The **AirTrain** (24hr daily; ☎ 1-877 535 2478, ⊚ panynj.gov; $5) runs between JFK and the Jamaica and Howard Beach subway stations in Queens; at Jamaica you can connect to the E, J or Z subway lines, and at Howard Beach to the A line, into Manhattan (from both stations: 1hr; $2.75). Alternatively, the **Long Island Railroad** (LIRR) runs faster trains from the Jamaica station to Penn Station (35min; $16 peak).

From LaGuardia, NYC Airporter (see above) takes up to one hour to get to Grand Central and Port Authority (every 20–30min 11am–7pm; $16 one-way, $30 round-trip). Alternatively, for $2.75 (with **MetroCard**), take the #M60 bus to 106th St in Manhattan, where you can transfer to downtown-bound subway lines.

From Newark, **Newark Airport Express Bus** (☎ 877 863 9275, ⊚ newarkairportexpress.com) runs buses to Grand Central Station, Port Authority Bus Terminal and Penn Station (every 30min–1hr, 24hr; $17 one-way, $30 round-trip). For train services, take the short **AirTrain** (every 3–15min; 24hr) ride to Newark Airport Train Station and connect with frequent NJ Transit or Amtrak trains heading into the city (every 20–30min 4.30am–2.30am; $13). The AirTrain costs $5.50, but if you buy a NJ Transit or Amtrak ticket before leaving the system, the AirTrain ticket is included.

Taxis are available at all airports: reckon on paying $30–40 from LaGuardia to Manhattan, a flat rate of $52 from JFK and $50–70 from Newark; you'll also be responsible for the turnpike and tunnel tolls – an extra $8 or so – as well as a fifteen- to twenty-percent tip for the driver. Note that bridges between Brooklyn/Queens and Manhattan are free, but the Queens Midtown Tunnel has a toll of $8.50 ($5.76 if your taxi has an electronic E-ZPass). You should only use official yellow taxis that wait at designated ranks – just follow the signs out of the terminal.

By bus or train

Greyhound and most other long-distance **bus** lines (with the exception of the Chinatown buses, which arrive in Chinatown, and Mega Bus/Bolt Bus which drop off on the streets of Midtown) terminate at the Port Authority Bus Terminal, W 42nd St and Eighth Ave.

Amtrak trains come in to Penn Station, at Seventh Avenue and W 33rd St. From either Port Authority or Penn Station, multiple subway lines will take you where you want to go.

Emergency numbers

For Police, Fire or Ambulance dial ☎ 911.

Getting around

Buses

Bus and subway information ☎ 718 330 1234 (daily 6am–10pm). New York's **bus system** is clean and usually efficient. It is often extremely slow in peak hours, but it can be your best bet for travelling crosstown. Pay on entry with a **MetroCard** ($2.75, express $6.50) or exact fare in coins; you can transfer for free from subway to bus, bus to subway, or from bus to bus, in one direction within two hours.

City tours

Big Onion Walking Tours ☎ 212 439 1090, ⒲ bigonion.com. Excellent walking tours by guides with advanced degrees in American history ($25).
Circle Line Pier 83, at the end of W 42nd St at the West Side Highway, ☎ 212 563 3200, ⒲ circleline.com. Boat cruises around Manhattan ($37 1hr 30min, $43 2hr30min).
Gray Line ☎ 1 800 669 0051, ⒲ newyorksightseeing.com. Double-decker hop-on, hop-off buses touring the main sights (around $49 for 24hr).
Big Apple Jazz Tours ☎ 212 439 1090, ⒲ bigapplejazz.com. Fabulous introduction to the Harlem jazz scene, minibus tours take in clubs and jazz history (from $99).
Hush Hip Hop Tours ☎ 212 391 0900, ⒲ hushtours.com. Bus tours of hip-hop haunts, given by legends such as Grandmaster Caz and Rahiem ($35–75).
Liberty Helicopter Tours Pier 6 on South St, between Broad St and Coenties Slip ☎ 212 967 6464 or ☎ 1 800 542 9933, ⒲ libertyhelicopter.com. Helicopter tours ($224 for 12–15min to $309 for 16–20min/person).

Cycling

New York's bike share scheme is dubbed **Citi Bike** (⒲ citibikenyc. com; 24hr Pass is $12, the 3-Day Pass is $24). Pay at any bike station kiosk with a credit card. Trips of less than thirty minutes are free with your pass.

The subway

The fastest way to get around is the user-friendly **subway**, open 24hr. A number or letter identifies each train and route, and most routes in Manhattan run uptown (north) or downtown (south), rather than crosstown. Every trip, whether on express or local lines, costs $2.75 if you pay by **MetroCard**, available at station booths or debit/credit card-capable vending machines (you'll pay $3 for a single ticket without a MetroCard). MetroCards can be purchased in any amount from $5.50 to $80; a $20 purchase gives you $21 on your card. Unlimited-ride cards – the best deal if you intend to be on the go – allow unlimited travel for a certain period of time: a 7-day pass costs $32 and a 30-day pass is $121 (there is no one-day pass).

Taxis

Taxis are reasonably priced – $3 upon entry and $0.50 for every 1/5 mile, with a $0.50 surcharge 8pm–6am, and a $1 surcharge Mon–Fri 4–8pm. Most drivers take up to four passengers, refuse bills larger than $20, and ask for the nearest cross street to your destination. It's customary to tip ten to twenty percent. **Boro Taxis** are painted light green and serve areas not commonly covered by yellow cabs (northern Manhattan and the outer boroughs). They follow the same rates and rules as yellow cabs.

Directory A-Z

Cinema

For first-run movies and blockbusters, head to megaplexes such as AMC Empire 25 at 234 W 42nd St, between Seventh and Eighth aves (☎ 1 888 262 4386), or Regal Union Square at 850 Broadway and 13th St (☎ 212 253 6266). Good places for indie flicks, old classics and documentaries are IFC Center, 323 6th Ave, at W 3rd St (☎ 212 924 7771, ⊛ ifccenter.com), Film Forum at 209 W Houston St and 6th Ave (☎ 212 727 8110, ⊛ filmforum. org), the Paris Theater at 4 W 58th St (☎ 212 688 3800, ⊛ citycinemas. com) and the Walter Reade Theater at the Lincoln Center, 165 W 65th St, at Broadway (☎ 212 875 5601, ⊛ filmlinc.org). Tickets at most cinemas are around $15 (buy online at ⊛ movietickets.com).

Consulates

Australia, 34/F, 150 E 42nd St, (☎ 212 351 6500, ⊛ usa.embassy.gov.au/ new-york).
Canada, 1251 6th Ave, at 50th St (☎ 212 596 1628).
Ireland, 17/F, 345 Park Ave, between 51st and 52nd sts (☎ 212 319 2555, ⊛ dfa.ie/irish-consulate/newyork).
New Zealand, 295 Madison Ave, at 41st St (☎ 212 832 4038).
South Africa, 333 E 38th St, between First and Second aves (☎ 212 213 4880, ⊛ southafrica-newyork.net/ consulate).
UK, 845 3rd Ave, between 51st and 52nd sts (☎ 212 745 0200, ⊛ gov.uk).

Crime

In two words: don't worry. New York has come a long way in recent years. While the city can sometimes feel dangerous, the reality is somewhat different. New York is America's safest city with a population over one million. Take the normal precautions and you should be fine; carry bags closed and across your body, don't let cameras dangle, keep wallets in front – not back – pockets, and don't flash money around. You should also keep a firm grip on your tablet or phone on the subway (these are occasionally snatched just as the doors close). Mugging can and does happen, but rarely during the day. Avoid wandering empty streets or the subway late at night (especially alone). If you are unlucky enough to be mugged, try to stay calm and hand over the money.

Electricity

110V AC with two-pronged plugs. Unless they're dual voltage (most mobile phones, cameras, tablets and laptops are), all Australian, British, European, Irish, New Zealand and South African appliances will need a voltage transformer as well as a plug adaptor (hair-dryers are the most common problem for travellers).

Health

Drugstores can be found every few blocks – CVS and Duane Reade are the city's major chains, and many open 24hr (such as the Duane Reade at 1470 Broadway, near Times Square).

If you do get sick or have an accident, medical costs can be incredibly expensive; organize insurance before your trip, just in case. It will cost upwards of $125 simply to see a doctor or dentist (plus extra for any treatment you receive), and prescription drugs can be very pricey – if you don't have US medical insurance, you'll have to cough up the money and make a claim when you get home.

Should you find yourself requiring a doctor or dentist, ask if your hotel has links to a local practice. Doctors in Manhattan often have long waiting lists, however, and will be reluctant to see a new patient at short notice – if you have a minor ailment or injury a good option is to visit one of a growing number of **walk-in clinics** (no appointment required); CityMD (ⓦcitymd.com) has several branches in the city including 216 East 14th St, 345 W 42nd St and 315 West 57th St. Most are open daily 8am–10pm (with shorter hours Sat & Sun) and charge a basic fee of $125.

If you have an accident or need urgent attention head to the 24-hour emergency rooms at these and other Manhattan hospitals: New York Presbyterian (Cornell), East 70th Street at York Avenue (ⓣ212 746 5050, ⓦnyp.org); and Mount Sinai, 1468 Madison Avenue at East 100th Street (ⓣ212 241 6500, ⓦmountsinaihealth.org). Should you be in a serious accident don't worry, a medical service (ambulance) will pick you up and charge later (at least $1500).

Treatment is generally excellent, but note that even basic care at a hospital emergency room can rise from $300 to $15,000 incredibly fast (fees for drugs, appliances, supplies and the attendant physician are all charged separately) – only go if you are very sick. Treatment for a simple leg break, for example, will total around $3000 – but if it requires surgery your final bill could range $20,000–35,000.

Internet

Wireless is king in New York. Most hotels offer it for free, and it's also available at wi-fi hotspots like Times Square, Bryant Park, most subway stations and complimentary at cafés like Starbucks. The new Link NYC scheme (ⓦlink.nyc) is gradually replacing over 7,500 pay phones on New York streets with new structures called "Links",

each providing superfast free wi-fi, phone calls (free to anywhere in the US), device charging and access to city services, maps and directions. If you're travelling without your own device, a free alternative is to stop by a branch of the New York City Public Library, where wi-fi and computer internet access and printing are available. You first need to get a guest pass at the Stephen A. Schwarzman Building (the main library building; Mon and Thurs–Sat 10am–6pm, Tues and Wed 10am–8pm, Sun 1–5pm), at 42nd St and Fifth Ave. With the pass, you can reserve time slots at computers in person or via ⓦnypl.org.

Left luggage

The best place to leave luggage is your hotel, but you can also use Schwartz Luggage Storage ($10/day per item; ⓣ212 290 2626, ⓦschwartztravel.com) at 357 West 37th St, near Penn Station (daily 8am–11pm).

LGBTQ New York

There are few places in America where gay culture thrives as it does in New York. Chelsea, Hell's Kitchen, the Villages, the Lower East Side and Park Slope are the biggest hubs of gay life. If you're looking for local resources, check out *Gay City News* (ⓦgaycitynews.nyc), *GO* magazine (ⓦgomag.com) or the listings in the free weekly *Time Out*.

Lost property

If you lose something on a bus or on the subway, contact NYC Transit Authority, at the W 34th St/Eighth Ave Station on the lower-level subway mezzanine (Mon, Tues & Fri 8am–3.30pm, Wed & Thurs 11am–6.30pm; ⓦlostfound.mtanyct.info). For items lost in a taxi call ⓣ311 or file a report online (ⓦnyc.gov); try to get the taxi's medallion number (printed on your receipt).

Money

On a moderate budget, expect to spend at least $250 per night on accommodation in a low-to mid-range, centrally located hotel in high season, plus $40–50/person for a moderate sit-down dinner each night and about $20 more per person per day for takeout and grocery meals. Getting around will cost $32/person per week for unlimited public transportation, plus $7–10 for the occasional taxi ride. Sightseeing, drinking, clubbing, eating haute cuisine and going to the theatre will add exponentially to these costs.

With an ATM card you'll have access to cash from machines all over New York, though, as anywhere, you will usually be charged a fee for using a different bank's ATM network (usually $3). Most banks are open Monday–Friday 8.30am–5pm, and a few have limited Saturday hours (major Citibank branches tend to open Sat 9am–3pm). Major banks – such as Citibank and Chase – will exchange currency at a standard rate. For banking services – particularly currency exchange – outside normal business hours and at weekends, try major hotels, though the rate won't be as good.

Opening hours

The opening hours of specific attractions are given throughout the Guide. As a general rule, most museums are open Tuesday to Sunday, 10am–5 or 6pm, though most have one night per week where they stay open at least a few hours later. Government offices, including post offices, are open during regular business hours, usually 9am–5pm. Store hours vary widely, though you can generally count on them being open Monday–Saturday from around 10am–6pm, with limited Sunday hours. Many of the larger chain or department stores will stay open to 9pm or later, and you generally don't have to walk more than a few blocks anywhere to find a 24-hour deli. On national public holidays, banks and offices are likely to be closed all day, and some shops have reduced hours.

Phones

In the US, AT&T and T-Mobile use the GSM standard for mobile phones, and most foreign companies partner with them to provide service to travelling customers. Note that unless you have a tri-band phone, it is unlikely that a mobile bought for use outside the US or Canada will work inside the States. If you have a smartphone this should work in the US, but roaming charges, especially for data, can be extortionate; even checking voicemail can result in hefty charges. Check with your phone company before you travel. If you have a compatible (and unlocked) GSM phone and intend to use it a lot, it can be much cheaper to buy a US SIM card ($10 or less) to use during your stay (you can also buy a micro-SIM or a nano-SIM). AT&T (ⓦ att.com) is your best bet. Some US

Public holidays

January 1: New Year's Day; **3rd Monday:** Dr Martin Luther King Jr's Birthday; **February 3rd Monday:** Presidents' Day; **May Last Monday:** Memorial Day; **July 4:** Independence Day; **September 1st Monday:** Labor Day; **October 2nd Monday:** Columbus Day; **November 11:** Veterans' Day; **4th Thursday:** Thanksgiving Day; **December 25:** Christmas Day

networks also sell basic flip phones (with minutes and a local number) for as little as $25 (no paperwork or ID required).

Public telephones are becoming harder to find due to the popularity of mobile phones; the new Link NYC scheme (see page 181) is gradually replacing pay phones in the city with internet stations, though these will also offer free phone calls to anywhere within the USA. The cost of a local call on a public payphone is 25¢ for three or four minutes, depending on the carrier (each phone company runs its own booths). Calls elsewhere within the US are usually 25–50¢ for one minute; overseas rates are much pricier, so buy a prepaid calling card ($5, $10 or $20), from a grocery store or newsstand.

To call home internationally: dial 011 + country code + number, minus the initial 0 (to call Canada, just start with the area code). Country codes are as follows: Australia (61), New Zealand (64), UK & Northern Ireland (44) and Ireland (353).

Post
International letters and postcards usually take about a week to reach their destination; rates are currently $1.15 for all international letters and postcards. To find a post office or check up-to-date rates, see ⓦusps. com or call ☎1 800 275 8777.

Smoking
Smoking has been banned in virtually all indoor public areas (including malls, bars, restaurants and most work places) in New York, plus all city parks, beaches and pedestrian plazas – fines start at around $100 for breaking this law.

Time
New York City is on Eastern Standard Time (EST), which is five hours behind

Greenwich Mean Time (GMT), three hours ahead of Pacific Standard Time, fourteen to sixteen hours behind East Coast Australia (variations for Daylight Savings) and sixteen to eighteen hours behind New Zealand (variations for Daylight Savings).

Tipping
Tipping in a restaurant, bar, taxi, or hotel lobby, on a guided tour, and even in some posh washrooms, is a part of life in New York. In restaurants in particular, it's unthinkable not to leave the minimum (fifteen percent of the bill or double the tax) – even if you disliked the service.

Tourist information
For general enquiries, call ☎311. The best place for information is the Official NYC Information Center, between 44th and 45th streets at Times Square (daily 8am–7pm; ☎212 484 1222, ⓦnycgo. com). They have bus and subway maps, information on hotels and accommodations (including discounts), and up-to-date leaflets on what's going on in the arts and elsewhere. You'll find other small tourist information centres and kiosks all over the city; inside Macy's, Herald Square (Mon–Sat 10am–10pm, Sun 10am–9pm); City Hall Park, on Broadway opposite the Woolworth Building (daily 9am–6pm); and Pier 15, Seaport District NYC (daily: May–Aug 9am–7pm; Sept–April 9am–5pm).

Leading weeklies include glossy *New York magazine* ($6.99; ⓦnymag. com), which has reasonably comprehensive listings, the venerable *New Yorker* magazine (ⓦnewyorker. com; $8.99) and *Time Out New York* (ⓦtimeout.com/newyork; free every Wednesday) – a clone of its London original, combining the city's most comprehensive what's-on listings with

New York-slanted news stories and entertainment features.

The *New York Times* ($2.50; ⓦnytimes.com) is an American institution and prides itself on being the "paper of record". It has solid, sometimes stolid, international coverage, and places much emphasis on its news analysis.

Travelling with children

Perhaps contrary to belief, New York is a child-friendly city: there's tons to keep their attention, including many sights specifically geared towards kids, and lots of public spaces in which to blow off steam.

Though some parents might have fears of taking small children on the subway, it's perfectly safe; indeed, the kids will probably get a kick out of it, crowds, noise and all. Your main problem will be getting your stroller (if you're using one) up and down the stairs – though you'll often find people willing to lend a hand. Most restaurants, save perhaps the fanciest and trendiest, easily accommodate children.

If you're in need of a babysitter, consider contacting the Babysitters' Guild (ⓣ212 682 0227, ⓦbabysittersguild.com), a fully licensed organization with a carefully selected and experienced staff.

For listings of what's going on when you're in town, check out ⓦnymetroparents.com or ⓦnewyorkfamily.com, or magazines like *Time Out* and its specialized edition for kids (ⓦtimeout.com/new-york-kids), *TONY Kids*.

Travellers with disabilities

New York City has had disabled access regulations imposed on an aggressively disabled-unfriendly system. There are wide variations in accessibility, making navigation a tricky business.

At the same time, you'll find New Yorkers surprisingly willing to go out of their way to help you. For wheelchair users, getting around on the subway is next to impossible without someone to help you, and even then is extremely difficult at most stations. Several, but not all, lines are equipped with elevators, but this doesn't make much of a difference. The Transit Authority is working to make stations accessible, but at the rate they're going it won't happen soon.

Buses are another story, and are the first choice of many disabled New Yorkers. All MTA buses are equipped with wheelchair lifts and locks. To get on a bus, wait at the bus stop to signal the driver you need to board; when he or she has seen you, move to the back door, where he or she will assist you. For travellers with other mobility difficulties, the driver will "kneel" the bus to allow you easier access. For more travel information for people with disabilities call ⓣ718 596 8585 (daily 6am–10pm).

Taxis are a viable option for visitors with visual and hearing impairments and minor mobility difficulties. For wheelchair users, taxis are less of a possibility unless you have a collapsible chair, in which case drivers are required to store it and assist you; the unfortunate reality is that most drivers won't stop if they see you waiting. If you're refused, try to get the taxi's medallion number and report the driver at ⓣ311. Most of the major hotels in New York have wheelchair-accessible rooms, including roll-in showers.

Traveler's Aid (ⓦtravelersaid. org), a nonprofit organization, has professional and volunteer staff who provide emergency assistance to disabled or elderly travellers at

JFK Airport: you can find volunteers at the Ground Transportation Counters in each terminal or via their main office in the arrivals area of Terminal 4 (daily 10am–6pm). They also operate at Newark Airport.

The Mayor's Office for People with Disabilities, 100 Gold St, 2nd floor (℡ 212 788 2830, ⓦ nyc.gov/mopd), offers valuable general information and resources for travellers with disabilities.

Festivals and events

Chinese New Year

The first full moon between Jan 21 and Feb 19
Chinatown bursts open to watch a giant red, green and gold dragon made of wood, cloth and papier-mâché run down Mott Street.

St Patrick's Day Parade

March 17 ⓦ nycstpatricksparade.org
Irish bands and organizations celebrate an impromptu 1762 march by Irish militiamen on St Patrick's Day. A parade heads up Fifth Avenue between 44th and 86th streets.

Celebrate Brooklyn/ Summerstage

June–Aug
These two summer-long music festivals, featuring many free events, take place in Prospect Park's Bandshell and Rumsey Playfield in Central Park.

Gay Pride

Third or fourth week of June
ⓦ nycpride.org
The world's biggest Pride event kicks off with a rally and ends with a parade, street fair and dance. Activities centre on the West Village.

US Open

First two weeks of September
ⓦ usopen.org
Try to catch a day session for this Grand Slam tennis tournament, held in Flushing, Queens.

West Indian American Day Carnival

Labor Day ⓦ wiadcacarnival.org
Held on Eastern Parkway, Brooklyn's largest parade is modelled after the carnivals of Trinidad and Tobago and features music, food, dance and colourful floats with sound systems.

Village Halloween Parade

Oct 31 ⓦ halloween-nyc.com
New Yorkers get their freak on at America's largest Halloween celebration. Spectacular puppets, sexy cross-dressers and scary monsters parade up Sixth Avenue from Spring to W 23rd sts.

New York City Marathon

First Sunday in November ⓦ www. tcsnycmarathon.org
Some 50,000 international runners assemble for this 26.2-mile run through the five boroughs. One of the best places to watch is Central Park South, near the finish line.

Macy's Thanksgiving Day Parade

Thanksgiving Day ⓦ macys.com/ social/parade
New York's most televised parade, with big corporate floats, marching bands from around the country and Santa Claus's first appearance of the season. It winds its way from W 77th Street down Central Park West to Columbus Circle, then down Broadway to Herald Square.

Chronology

Early days New York and the surrounding area is occupied by Native Americans, most notably the Lenape tribe.

1609 English explorer Henry Hudson, working for the Dutch, sails past Manhattan upriver as far as Albany.

1624 Dutch colony established on Governors Island.

1626 Peter Minuit arrives as governor. He moves the Dutch settlement to Manhattan, which is named New Amsterdam, and numbers some 300 inhabitants.

1647 New Amsterdam's most famous governor, Peter Stuyvesant, is appointed.

1664 Revolt against Stuyvesant's dictatorial rule coincides with surrender to British naval troops, who rename the colony New York.

1754 Ivy League Columbia University founded as King's College.

1772 Alexander Hamilton arrives in New York from the Caribbean.

1776 British naval vessels arrive to capture New York after the Declaration of Independence; fire destroys much of the city, which is occupied by British troops until 1783.

1780 Hamilton marries Elizabeth Schuyler.

1789 George Washington takes the oath as America's first president on Wall Street. New York is capital of the new nation for one year.

1792 Buttonwood Agreement, signed by 24 stockbrokers on Wall Street, signals beginning of New York Stock Exchange. It is formally organized in 1817.

1804 Hamilton is killed after a duel with Aaron Burr in Weehawken, New Jersey.

1825 Opening of the Erie Canal makes New York a major shipping port. Fulton Street dock and market area built.

1831 Founding of New York University (NYU).

1835 Great Fire of New York destroys most of the buildings on the southern tip of Manhattan around Wall Street.

1856–71 The city is ruled by a corrupt group of politicians known as Tammany Hall. Their leader is deputy commissioner William "Boss" Tweed, who is finally indicted for corruption in 1873.

1861–65 Though not a theatre of the Civil War, class and racial tensions lead to the Draft Riots of 1863, in which 1000 people are killed.

1876 Central Park opens to a design by Fredrick Law Olmsted and Calvert Vaux.

1880s Millions of immigrants (southern Italians and eastern European Jews) settle in the Lower East Side.

1883 The Brooklyn Bridge links Manhattan with Brooklyn.

1885 Emergence of Tin Pan Alley on 28th St in Manhattan, where music publishers and popular songwriters like George Gershwin ply their trade.

1886 The Statue of Liberty, a gift from the French people to America, is unveiled.

1891 Carnegie Hall completed, funded by Scottish-born steel magnate and philanthropist Andrew Carnegie.

1898 The outer boroughs of Brooklyn, Queens, the Bronx and Staten Island are formally incorporated into New York City. The population swells to three million.

Early 20th century The first skyscrapers are built, most notably the Flatiron Building (1902) and the Woolworth Building (1913).

1902 Macy's opens at Herald Square.

1913 The New York Highlanders baseball team (established here in 1903) becomes known as the New York Yankees.

1915 The Equitable Building fills every square inch of its site on Broadway, propelling zoning ordinances in 1916 that demand a degree of setback to allow light to reach the streets.

1920 Prohibition forbids the sale of alcohol. Economic confidence of the 1920s brings the Jazz Age and Harlem Renaissance.

1925 New York Giants football team established.

1927 Duke Ellington's band begins famous residency at the Cotton Club in Harlem.

1929 Wall Street Crash. America enters the Great Depression. Many of the lavish buildings commissioned and begun in the 1920s reach completion. Skyscrapers combine the monumental with the decorative in a new and distinctive Art Deco style: Chrysler Building (1930) and Empire State Building (1931). Rockefeller Center, the first exponent of the idea of a city-within-a-city, is built throughout the decade.

1932 Lucky Luciano takes control of the Five Families of the New York mafia; he is imprisoned in 1936.

1934 Fiorello LaGuardia elected Mayor (which he would remain until 1945). To rebuild New York after the Depression, he increases taxation, curbs corruption and improves the city's infrastructure with new bridges, roads and parks (with much federal funding).

1939 Blue Note Records founded. Jazz legend Charlie Parker moves to New York, where he helps create bebop; he dies in the city in 1955.

1949–50 Miles Davis records his seminal album *Birth of the Cool* in New York for Capitol Records, heralding a new era in jazz.

Late 1940s to 1950s The East Village becomes home to the Beat poets – Jack Kerouac, Allen Ginsberg and William Burroughs.

1950 United Nations established in New York. The UN secretariat building introduces the glass curtain wall to Manhattan.

1958 The plaza of the newly built Seagram Building causes zoning regulations to be changed again – this time to encourage similar public spaces.

1959 Frank Lloyd Wright's Guggenheim Museum opens.

1961 Bob Dylan moves to Greenwich Village and becomes a leading figure in the folk music movement.

1964 Race riots in Harlem and Brooklyn. Jimmy Hendrix moves to Harlem and becomes a regular performer at *Cafe Wha*? in Greenwich Village. The minimalist Verrazano Narrows Bridge links Brooklyn to Staten Island.

1965 Malcolm X is assassinated at Washington Height's Audubon Ballroom.

1968 New Madison Square Garden is built on the site of the old Penn Station.

1969 The Stonewall riots in Greenwich Village inaugurate the gay-rights movement.

Early 1970s A low point for New York as the city struggles to attract investment; Harlem drug lords Frank Lucas and Nicky Barnes flood the city with heroin. However, The World Trade Center Towers are built in 1972, dramatically altering the New York skyline; hip-hop emerges on the streets of the South Bronx.

1973 CBGB opens on the Lower East Side; becomes epicentre of punk music; Blondie and the Ramones perform in 1974.

1975 Mayor Abraham Beame presides over New York's decline as city financing reaches crisis point and businesses leave Manhattan. New York comes close to financial collapse, as its lack of essential services and collapsing infrastructure drive people away.

1977 New York City Blackout (25hr): city suffers looting and civil unrest. *Discothèque Studio 54* opens – remains home of cool until 1986.

Late 1970s Vociferous Ed Koch elected mayor (1978). Virtually no new corporate development until the Citicorp Center (1977) adds a new profile to the city's skyline; its popular atrium is adopted by later buildings.

1979 The first hip-hop record, *Rapper's Delight*, released by The Sugarhill Gang (actually from New Jersey); Frank Sinatra records "Theme from New York, New York" – it becomes the city anthem.

1980 John Lennon is murdered outside his apartment on the Upper West Side.

1980s Corporate wealth returns to Manhattan. The mixed-use Battery Park City opens to wide acclaim. Donald Trump emerges as a major real-estate developer.

1984 Rick Rubin and Russell Simmons create Def Jam Records. Beastie Boys become their first major success.

1987 Black Monday: the stock exchange crashes and the Dow Jones index plunges 508 points in one day.

1988 The Tompkins Square Park Police Riot, which inspires a scene in the musical *Rent*.

1989 David Dinkins becomes first black mayor of New York City, defeating Ed Koch and Rudolph Giuliani.

Early 1990s NYC's budget deficit again reaches record proportions. East Coast hip-hop renaissance led by Nas, Notorious B.I.G. and later Mos Def and Jay-Z.

1993 Puerto Rican salsa superstar Héctor Lavoe, "El Cantante", dies in New York.

1994 Rudolph Giuliani is elected mayor – the city's first Republican mayor in 28 years, signalling a desire for change.

2001 World Trade Center's Twin Towers destroyed on September 11 by two planes hijacked by terrorists; Downtown Manhattan essentially shut down for several weeks. Mayor Rudy Giuliani cuts a highly composed and reassuring figure as New Yorkers struggle to come to terms with the assault on their city. Michael Bloomberg succeeds Giuliani as mayor a few months later.

2002 Tribeca Film Festival established with the backing of Robert De Niro.

2005 Michael Bloomberg is re-elected mayor.

2006 Legendary punk club CBGB closes.

2007 New York Giants win Superbowl XLII.

2008 US mortgage crisis finally hits Wall Street in a big way: the Dow Jones slumps 500 points and, after more than 150 years, Lehman Brothers goes bankrupt; several other merchant banks are sold.

2009 Michael Bloomberg is re-elected mayor for a third time, after backing

a controversial extension of term limits. Yankees win World Series for 27th time. Miracle on the Hudson: Captain "Sully" Sullenberger lands his Airbus on the Hudson River after a bird strike takes out the engines at LaGuardia Airport.

2012 NY Giants and Eli Manning win Superbowl XLVI. The city is hammered by Hurricane Sandy, with several neighbourhoods in Downtown Manhattan and Brooklyn flooded: the damage takes many months to clear up.

2013 Bill de Blasio becomes the first Democratic mayor since 1993, winning the election by a landslide.

2014 The new One World Trade Center opens, 13 years after 9/11.

2015 New York City FC becomes first Major League Soccer (MLS) team based in the city (Yankee Stadium).

2016 New York tycoon Donald Trump elected the 45th President of the United States (as a Republican).

2017 Bill de Blasio wins second term as mayor, in another landslide.

2018 The New York Stock Exchange reaches new highs when the Dow Jones index hits 25,000 for the first time.

SMALL PRINT

Publishing Information
Fifth edition 2019

Distribution
UK, Ireland and Europe
Apa Publications (UK) Ltd; sales@roughguides.com
United States and Canada
Ingram Publisher Services; ips@ingramcontent.com
Australia and New Zealand
Woodslane; info@woodslane.com.au
Southeast Asia
Apa Publications (SN) Pte; sales@roughguides.com
Worldwide
Apa Publications (UK) Ltd; sales@roughguides.com
Special Sales, Content Licensing and CoPublishing
Rough Guides can be purchased in bulk quantities at discounted prices. We can create special editions, personalised jackets and corporate imprints tailored to your needs. sales@roughguides.com.
roughguides.com
Printed in China by RR Donnelley Asia Printing Solutions Limited
A catalogue record for this book is available from the British Library
The publishers and authors have done their best to ensure the accuracy and currency of all the information in **Pocket Rough Guide New York**, however, they can accept no responsibility for any loss, injury, or inconvenience sustained by any traveller as a result of information or advice contained in the guide.

Rough Guide Credits

Editor: Sian Marsh
Cartography: Katie Bennett
Managing editor: Rachel Lawrence
Picture editor: Aude Vauconsant
Cover photo research: Michelle Bhatia

Original design: Richard Czapnik
Senior DTP coordinator: Dan May
Head of DTP and Pre-Press: Rebeka Davies

Author biographies
Stephen Keeling has been calling New York City home since 2006. He worked as a financial journalist for seven years before writing his first travel guide and has written several titles for Rough Guides, including books on Puerto Rico, New England, Florida and Canada.
Andrew Rosenberg is a copy editor and sometimes writer. He lives in Brooklyn with his wife, Melanie; son, Jules; and cats Octavius and Louise.

Help us update

We've gone to a lot of effort to ensure that the Fifth edition 2019 edition of the **Pocket Rough Guide New York** is accurate and up-to-date. However, things change – places get "discovered", opening hours are notoriously fickle, restaurants and rooms raise prices or lower standards. If you feel we've got it wrong or left something out, we'd like to know, and if you can remember the address, the price, the hours, the phone number, so much the better.

Please send your comments with the subject line "**Pocket Rough Guide New York Update**" to mail@uk.roughguides.com. We'll credit all contributions and send a copy of the next edition (or any other Rough Guide if you prefer) for the very best emails.

Photo Credits

(Key: T-top; C-centre; B-bottom; L-left; R-right)

Aaron Wax/Matthew Marks Gallery 20C
Alamy 2CR, 4, 12B, 15T, 18C, 19T, 21T, 30, 32, 35, 36, 37, 50, 57, 64, 67, 68, 73, 77, 88, 99, 100, 113, 134, 135, 153, 161
Angus Oborn/Rough Guides 2T, 33, 52, 79, 80, 90, 96, 114/115, 122, 129, 136, 142, 150, 155
Apexart 41
Curtis Hamilton/Rough Guides 176/177
David Paler Photography/Jewish Heritage Museum 29
Dreamstime.com 11T, 14T, 19C
EdLLederman/Whitney Museum of American Art 16T
Ellen Silverman/Maialino 98
Frank Oudeman/Asia Society 134
Gabriele Stabile/Momofuku Noodle Bar 6
Getty Images 111, 121, 123, 147
Gordon Polatnick 17T
Greg Roden/Rough Guides 2BL, 5, 11B, 19B, 24, 42, 47, 49, 70, 83, 110, 125, 145, 151, 165

iStock 10, 12/13T, 15B, 18C, 20T, 21C, 34, 46, 63, 74, 85, 92, 93, 95, 105, 107, 109, 117, 124, 128, 132, 133, 141, 149, 157, 166/167
Jesse Winter/M. Wells Dinette 162
Justin Foulkes/4Corners Images 2BR
Laura J Clowes/John's Pizzeria 17B
Massimo Borchi/4Corners Images 1
New York Public Library 104
Poul Ober Photography 45
Shutterstock 12/13B, 22/23, 28, 39, 54, 66, 78, 87, 91, 103, 108, 118, 127, 131, 139, 146
Susannah Sayler/Rough Guides 14B, 16B, 18T, 20B, 59, 69, 158
The Delancey 60
Timothy Schenck/Grand Central Oyster Bar & Restaurant 112
Zenon Taverna 21B

Cover: Statue of Liberty **Michele Falzone/AWL Images**

Index

NOTES

ROUGH
GUIDES

ESCAPE THE EVERYDAY

ADVENTURE BECKONS
YOU JUST NEED TO KNOW WHERE TO LOOK

roughguides.com